ᴇ❧ Other Books by Cathleen Rountree

On Women Turning 60: Embracing the Age of Fulfillment

On Women Turning 50: Celebrating Midlife Discoveries

On Women Turning 40: Coming into Our Fullness

The Heart of Marriage: Discovering the Secrets of Enduring Love

50 Ways to Meet Your Lover: Following Cupid's Arrow

On Women Turning 70

On Women Turning 70

Honoring the Voices of Wisdom

Interviews and Photography by
Cathleen Rountree

Jossey-Bass Publishers
San Francisco

Jossey-Bass books and products are available through most bookstores.
To contact Jossey-Bass directly, call (888) 378-2537, fax to (800) 605-2665, or visit our website at www.josseybass.com.

Substantial discounts on bulk quantities of Jossey-Bass books are available to corporations, professional associations, and other organizations. For details and discount information, contact the special sales department at Jossey-Bass.

Manufactured in the United States of America.

Credits are on p. 242.

Interior design by Paula Goldstein.

Library of Congress Cataloging-in-Publication Data

Rountree, Cathleen.
    On women turning 70: honoring the voices of wisdom /
interviews and photography by Cathleen Rountree. — 1st ed.
      p. cm.
    ISBN: 0-7879-4512-9
    1. Aged women—Interviews. 2. Aged women—Psychology. I. Title.
II. Title: On women turning seventy.
    HQ1061.R594 1999
    305.26—ddc21
                                                98-40145

FIRST EDITION
HB Printing   10 9 8 7 6 5 4 3 2 1

Contents

With love and appreciation, this book is dedicated to

Pat Ward Zimmerman
Christiane Corbat Westlake
Carolyn Gold Heilbrun
Marilu A. Lindley

☙

# Acknowledgments

Having an editor who understands your work as a writer is a necessity (though one not always met); having an editor who truly appreciates your efforts is a rarity. Leslie Berriman at Jossey-Bass Publishers is such an editor. I want to ask her, "Where have you been all my writing life?" Thanks for believing in this project, Leslie, and for knowing that women in their seventies—far from being invisible—are absolutely voices of wisdom who deserve to be honored. Thanks to Alan Rinzler, also at Jossey-Bass, who knew instantly that this was a valuable project and who introduced me to Leslie.

My literary agent, Ellen Levine, is God's gift to the authors in her "stable." All writers should be so blessed to have someone like Ellen standing behind them, beside them, and in front of them when need be.

Several people were enormously helpful in suggesting participants for this book and in introducing me to those people; many thanks to Pat McAnaney for Madeleine L'Engle, Ann Richards for Liz Smith, Fay Weldon for Doris Lessing, Elena Featherstone for Betita Martinez, Rose Styron for Inge Morath, Claire Braz-Valentine for Marge Frantz, Vicki

Noble for Elinor Gadon, Allie Light and Irving Saraf for Mitsuye Yamada, Essie Mormen for Enola Maxwell, Terry Sendgraf for Anna Halprin, Linda Leonard for June Singer, and Sandy Miranda for Lee Robins. This book would have been very different without your assistance.

To my classmates at Pacifica Graduate Institute, I offer my warmest affection for your support, and I especially thank the cheerleading squad of Leah Friedman, Kwame Scruggs, Madeleine Waddell, Richard Stromer, Peter Plessas, Marie Elliot-Gartner, and the best roommate I could have had, Char Wolf.

My professors at Pacifica have been inspiring and encouraging. My sincere appreciation to Kathleen Jenks, Dennis Slattery, Ginette Paris, Dawn George, Hendrika De Vries, Patrick Mahaffey and Christine Downing. Also thanks to the numerous staff members on campus, especially those in the library (Mary Lou Kravetz and Mark Kelly), those in the bookstore (Sarah, Louise, and Bill), and those in the administration (Edie Barrett and Diane Huerta).

I wish to offer my deepest gratitude to each woman who participated in *On Women Turning 70* and who gave so generously of her time, her wisdom, and her inspiring presence.

For services rendered in times of need, much appreciation to Hope Rhode, Nick Fetterhoff, Connie Rogers, Dennis St. Peter, Carolyn Gallaghan, Doug Broyles (the computer god!), Alec Cast, Pat and Kate McAnaney, and Danuta Lake.

My friends continue to provide the love and nurturing that sustain me. My love and affection to Christiane Corbat (I missed you this year!), Deanne Burke, Alec Cast, Michael Park and Kevin Connelley, Dan and Kalen Delaney, Riane Eisler, Ronnie and Larry Purcell, Katherine Spilde, Lisa Leeman, Michael and Diane Wright, Karen St. Pierre and Peter Samuels, Linda Leonard, Maurine Doerken, Allie and Irving, Ruth Morgan, Pilar Montero, Deena Metzger, Channe and Penn Melnick, Vicki Noble, Deanne Newman, Jerry and Paula Prohaska, Char and Greg Wolf, Hal and Sidra Stone, Susanne and Ann Short, Heather Shea, Pat Zimmerman, Marie and Randy Kramer, and Manuel and Laura Gomes.

Finally, I want to express my love and appreciation for the most incredible son, Christian Wright, who just heals my heart. And Sienna, my Mr. Wonderful, I promise you more walks on the beach!

In each of my books, I have inevitably forgotten to mention someone hugely important to me in my life. Whoever you are, I thank you!

Aptos, California   CATHLEEN ROUNTREE
January 1999

Introduction

Old age is ten years beyond your own chronological age.

KAY SEIDELL, in Charlotte Painter and Pamela Valois, *Gifts of Age*

Time and trouble will tame an advanced young woman, but an advanced old woman is uncontrollable by any earthly force.

DOROTHY L. SAYERS

If Marilyn Monroe were alive as I finish writing this book, she would have been seventy-two years old. Actually, that's younger than most of the participants in *On Women Turning 70*. I thought often of Marilyn this year, just as I have carried her with me for more than forty-two years. She initially blazed into my consciousness in 1955 when I was seven. That year, I saw my first Marilyn Monroe film, *The Seven-Year Itch,* at a premiere at Grauman's Chinese Theater in Hollywood.

I have frequently asked myself, "If she had lived, who would Marilyn have been today?" As a woman who desperately wanted children but who couldn't have them because of gynecological problems, would she, like African American expatriate Josephine Baker, have adopted ten children and built her life around them? As a woman who loved animals, would she, like Brigitte Bardot (another sex symbol of the prefeminist era), have used her influence as an animal rights activist? Or, like Joanne Woodward today, would she have expressed her admiration for the craft of acting by becoming a consummate drama coach? "I'm looking forward to eventually becoming a marvelous—excuse the word *marvelous*—character actress," Marilyn, the talented comedienne, said optimistically in an interview for *Redbook* shortly before her death by suicide in 1962. That was one year before the publication of *The Feminine Mystique* by Betty Friedan, a woman I interviewed for this book who chose a very different life path from Marilyn's.

But, mirroring the social attitude of her times, Marilyn was terrified of aging. "Imagine being old," she remarked to a friend once. "Imagine when no one will turn to look at me. I'll be like that old woman there—an old, gray sheep in a hair net. It must be like being a ghost, moving among other people, and no one noticing you at all." Compare this with what Liz Smith—America's most popular gossip columnist—insisted about the benefits of age during my interview with her: "The best thing that happened to me in old age was that I got to be successful after I was about ready to retire. I got to be very successful. It's been really rewarding, a lot of fun, and I'm not conflicted about [my success] at all." Or what Leah Friedman—a woman who began work on a Ph.D. at age sixty-nine—triumphantly proclaimed when I interviewed her about what it means to be seventy: "I like being old. It's the best time of my life. The important thing about being seventy is that I define what seventy is by who I am and the way I live. I don't have to conform to what somebody else thinks seventy is or what society says seventy is. *We* define the age; the age does not define us." Or what Betty Friedan forcefully declared when we spoke about older women and invisibility: "You're operating from an obsolete concept! Women are *not* perceived as invisible in their seventies. Women that I know are not invisible in their seventies. They're more vigorous. They have established themselves in whatever field they're in. Today it depends on what a woman is doing."

I would like Betty's perspective to be accurate, but after having this book rejected by numerous publishers ("No one cares about women in their seventies," each one haughtily decreed to my agent), I'm afraid I cannot agree with her. Although I do gratefully acknowledge that the age of invisibility may have moved up from a woman's forties and fifties to her sixties and seventies, invisibility remains a fact of life for most older women. Doris Lessing concurred that a cultural prejudice does indeed exist: "The invisibility thing began to happen to me along about my fifties, when I suddenly became aware that men were no longer noticing me." She added, "I have to say, I don't mind being invisible. The young people don't see you at all. You are an *old* person. It's this Western culture's fear of old age that we're afflicted with."

In the documentary film, *Margaret Mead Observed,* the famed anthropologist named those words that have become synonymous with women in their fifties—*postmenopausal zest.* Margaret Mead assured us that this state awaits all women after they leave behind their childbearing years. She further promised that in our fifties, we will have "more energy than at forty." What I didn't know—until after I saw the documentary—is that when she uttered these words, she was not fifty, as I had assumed, but seventy! In this book, Elinor Gadon—who is in her mid-seventies—confirmed Margaret Mead's words by announcing, "I am most fortunate in having tremendous energy—far more than most people who are forty years younger than I."

I think of Beatrice Wood, a woman who died in the spring of 1998— less than a month before her 105th birthday. I had the great pleasure of meeting and interviewing this artist one year before her death. At seventy, Beatrice Wood was still in the prime of her life; she would live thirty-five years longer. I wonder how differently women would think about their own later life if they knew they would have continued good health and creative productivity for several more decades.

My own journey from forty to seventy (in the literary sense) has taken but a dozen years. My interest in the subject of women and aging began when I was thirty-eight years old and had just moved to Los Angeles from Berkeley, where I had lived for nearly twenty years. From the University of California at Berkeley, I received degrees in the history of art and the practice of fine art, with an emphasis in painting. In Berkeley, I raised my only child—my son, Christian. I also owned and operated the restaurant Rountree's there. When I moved away from my familiar lifestyle and from my friends, I had to reinvent myself.

I had never thought much about age before, but in the youth-obsessed culture of southern California, I suddenly felt obsolete and old. During that summer of 1986, I struggled to find people for whom I felt some affinity. This was long before the crush of books on women's health and age issues appeared, although luckily I had come across *Gifts of Age* by Charlotte Painter and Pamela Valois. That book delighted in the aging process as it presented intimate glimpses into the lives of thirty-two remarkable women. Looking back now, I find it easy to see *Gifts of Age* as the forerunner of my own work, which I would eventually come to call "the decade series."

In my quest for role models, I soon discovered that countless other women were also on the same search. We wanted to feel good about who we were and who we were becoming. Of all I have learned in the past twelve years, undoubtedly the most important piece is that as women age, they become more themselves. As May Sarton wrote in *At Seventy: The Journals of May Sarton* (New York: Norton, 1993), "This is the best time of my life. I love being old. I am more myself than I have ever been. I am happier, more balanced, and more powerful." It is that "selfness" that we all long for, the ability for the inner psyche and the outer expression to concur. This quality could also be called authenticity. When we are in our thirties, we sense that there is "more" to life. I now believe that the "more" for which we ceaselessly search outside ourselves is a level of comfort and acceptance with who we are inside. Unfortunately, it can take decades to reach that place—unless we have some powerful mentors.

That is what the decade series has been all about for me: finding role models, listening to them, learning from them, and then sharing their wisdom with my readers. I can recall, both imagistically and viscerally, the impression that each of the few hundred women I have interviewed over the past twelve years has left on me. It has been as if I received a direct transmission from every individual, a transmission that operated on an energetic level as well as on an aural one. I always knew when it happened, and I would alert myself, "This is it. Pay attention. Remember." But it wasn't about remembering words so much as it was about awakening a heretofore hidden bit of wisdom that lay dormant inside me, just as it does in everyone. I felt a sense of awe at witnessing someone else's inner life so intimately, and I felt closer to the female world with all its innate wisdom. It's as if we are born with knowledge within us, but it takes so many decades of gaining experience, of living, to begin to make sense out of it and to recognize it.

When you meet people who have lived long enough to develop "self-ness," authenticity, and power, you feel more powerful yourself in their presence. It is said about the Greek goddess Aphrodite that the mere human woman felt more beautiful in her presence. That is what these women have done for me—they have taught me to be "more myself," more forgiving of my mistakes and indiscretions. Of all the women I have interviewed, none would choose to go back and change anything about her past, because each woman knew that her entire life had caused her to be the woman she is now.

It took me five years to believe in myself enough and to develop the discipline to complete my first book, *On Women Turning 40: Coming into Our Fullness.* I received at least fifteen rejections from publishers, but I persisted because I knew that *On Women Turning 40* was a worthwhile project. Plus, it had become my lifeline to other women. I became a crusader, and this crusade made my life meaningful. During my early forties, while I wrote that first book, both my beloved maternal grandmother and my father died. The deaths of two immediate family members brought me a gift—a new awareness of mortality. Martin Amis has said so incisively that after forty, when we receive the information about the inevitability of our own death, it's as if we come to the end of a forty-year vacation. "It's an information that sort of thickens the face," he deftly remarked.

By the time the forties book was off and running, it seemed like the natural course of action was to continue with the next decade. "I've turned forty," I reasoned. "I want to discover what's ahead for me at fifty." Thus, *On Women Turning 50: Celebrating Midlife Discoveries* came to be. The decade series has brought extraordinary women into my life—Maxine Hong Kingston, Frances Moore Lappé, Judy Chicago, Barbara Boxer, Cokie Roberts, Natalie Goldberg, Linda Leonard, Gloria Steinem, Ellen Burstyn, Isabel Allende, Jean Bolen, Sylvia Earle, Allie Light, Dolores Huerta, Riane Eisler, Marion Woodman, Mary Travers, Jane Goodall, Ursula Le Guin, Fay Weldon, Rose Styron, Ann Richards, Maureen Stapleton, Betty Friedan, Liz Smith, Betye Saar, Ruth Asawa, Doris Lessing—to list a few of the more recognizable names. (Without question, however, the lesser-known but equally accomplished women have been commensurate in their ability to inspire.) Who wouldn't feel blessed by having had the opportunity to meet one or two of the women mentioned above, let alone all of them? And blessed I have been. Among women in their fifties, I found the insistent *cri de coeur* to be, "Life begins at fifty!" This only made me look forward to turning fifty, which I did on July 7, 1998. There wasn't a moment of regret or trepidation. After all, I already had been fifty (vicariously speaking) since my mid-forties.

With each decade, my interest in aging and women's developing wisdom expanded. I found, without exception, that women become more fascinating as they age. Or, as Rilke once wrote in describing the French sculptor Auguste Rodin, they acquire "the magnificent ripeness of age." I continued to pursue that mystery of "magnificent ripeness" in turning to the sixties. If writing *On Women Turning 60: Embracing the Age of Fulfillment* taught me anything, it was to appreciate each stage of life, the age I am right now, today. Women in their sixties have a profound cognizance of the limitations of time. They think in terms of "the time left" and of making it count, because they know that the time awaiting them is significantly shorter than what has already elapsed. Some of the women I interviewed were putting their mothers into nursing homes; others were burying them. Practically all had grandchildren, and these women loved being grandmothers and witnessing the continuing cycles of life.

That brings us to the present volume—*On Women Turning 70: Honoring the Voices of Wisdom*. As I mentioned earlier, my own journey from forty to seventy (in the literary sense) has taken just a dozen years. It felt significant that while I was writing about turning seventy, I turned fifty. In fact, that prompted one of my interview questions: "What advice would you have for a younger woman, say, in her late forties, who is about to turn fifty?" Betty Friedan responded, "What you can look forward to is liberation from the limitations. You don't have to prove anything to anybody, do you? And you've fulfilled whatever roles are prescribed for you. If you've gotten married, if you've had kids, the kids are raised. So the rest of your life is just where you want to take it." She suggested that women try something new every week in order to keep their spirit and curiosity active. And Leah Friedman offered me a fruitful scenario: "I've lived an entire life since I was fifty."

With each decade, I had intimations of what I could expect, but it's been the seventies book that has held the most surprises. I anticipated that the women I met would be warm, witty, and wise, but I was unprepared for the sheer vitality, sagacity, impertinence, and disarming honesty. "I am more myself than I have ever been. I am . . . more powerful," May Sarton wrote in *At Seventy*. And her sentiment was repeated over and over among the women in this book. Betye Saar, an artist who lives in Los Angeles and who has dyed a portion of her closely cropped, curly hair purple, had this to say about being in her seventies: "I feel really independent. It's my house, it's my garden, it's my body—I can do what I want with them. If I want my hair purple, it's purple."

I was also unprepared for the discursive attitude about the question of invisibility among older women and the battle of semantics over the use of the term *old*. Leah Friedman said, "I don't want to avoid the term, and I don't want people to avoid it with me. There's nothing wrong with being old and calling it old." On the other hand, seventy-eight-year-old Enola Maxwell proclaimed, "The truth of the matter is that I refuse to be old. I'll never get old. I can live to be a hundred, and I still won't get old. Old age is not good for you!" Or, as Liz Smith proposed, "I don't think people should act like they're old. I think they're just as old as they act." And then there is Lee Robins, the sociologist; as a seventy-five-year-old widow, she married a doctor she met at Washington University, where they both worked.

I may have made the journey from forty to seventy in only twelve years, but the words of wisdom I have heard along the way have been enormously nurturing as well as formative.

This year, several new women friends have graced my life. Katherine is thirty years old, Lisa and Leslie are forty, Paula is nearly sixty, Deanne and Mary are sixty, and Leah is seventy. So the lineage of wise women and their younger sisters continues. In *On Women Turning 60,* Mary Travers gave me advice on this matter when she spoke about making friends. "Pick up some young ones," she said with her characteristic humor, "because when you get closer to the finish line, it's very helpful to have people you have an emotional relationship with who are not dying or dead." Fortunately, Mary decided to "pick up" me.

When you think about women in their seventies, who comes to mind? Did you know that the eternal child, the Dimpled Darling Shirley Temple Black is seventy? What about Rosalyn Carter, Coretta Scott King, Rosemary Clooney, Grace Paley, Shirley Chisholm, Ruth Prawer Jhabvala, Shelley Winters, Celeste Holm, Maya Angelou, Dr. Joyce Brothers, Ann Landers, Abigail Van Buren, Dr. Ruth Westheimer, the late Bella Abzug, Jan Morris, Gerda Lerner, Ann Truitt, Joan Sutherland, Jeanne Moreau, Maria Tallchief (the ballerina), Lauren Bacall, Wislawa Szymborska (the Polish poet who, in 1996, at the age of seventy-three, won the Nobel Prize in Literature), or Angela Lansbury?

Speaking of Angela Lansbury, the controversial cancellation of her popular television program, *Murder, She Wrote,* allegedly occurred because of her age. Shortly after the cancellation, Lansbury made a public statement on the national news program *60 Minutes* to air her plight. She was not going to take it lying down. According to the demographic statistics, the fastest growing group in the population consists of Americans living into their eighties and nineties. So why is the "graying of America" met with such "a pervasive media blackout of images of older people active in work, play, sports, and love of everyday American life," as Betty Friedan points out in her well-researched book *The Fountain of Age?* Could it be that the American culture has it backward? That as the aging population strives to maintain or regain the "perfection" of youth, the truth is that we actually age to perfection, not away from it?

One archetype of youth, beauty, and resilience in Hollywood culture for many decades has been Elizabeth Taylor. Because of her status as a movie goddess, the public has watched Elizabeth's countless acts of seemingly self-willed survival and transformation since she was a twelve-year-old starlet in her first film, *National Velvet.* What has always struck me as terribly sad is that, rather than accepting the physical changes that time naturally bestows on us all, Elizabeth (along with her public, I might add) has fought either to preserve or to recapture an image of herself that was arrested in development—an image of the perfection of youth. In 1997, as she recovered from brain surgery, it was unnerving for us to see photos of the "real" sixty-something Elizabeth with a shock of white hair. We, the public, had never before seen her in this state. Many of us thought, "If Elizabeth Taylor is old, and if I have been watching her movies for nearly fifty years, that means I must be getting old, too." But it was also a relief, because Elizabeth was relinquishing her pretension. She finally allowed herself to say without apology, "This is who I am, and this is what I look like."

Betty Friedan said it best when she remarked, "It takes so much effort to hold onto the illusion of youth, to keep the fear of age at bay, that in doing so we could fail to recognize the new qualities and strengths that might emerge." Just as Elizabeth Taylor was a role model of affectation in the past, she now became an exemplar of authenticity. Perhaps this is what Rilke meant when he referred to the "magnificent ripeness of age." That ripeness is the selfness, the uniqueness, and the genuineness inherent in every human being who works hard to uncover it and to allow it to unfold. As Madeleine L'Engle sagely remarked, "The great thing about getting older is that you don't lose all the other ages you've been." Like the time rings on the interior of tree trunks, or the hollow Russian dolls that nestle inside one another, we carry all of our various selves from each age ensconced within us.

It is comforting to imagine that Marilyn in her seventies might have been at peace with "being old." That she might have seen her invisibility as a bonus. As Betye Saar put it, "Gray [hair] makes you invisible. I can do and say anything I want because I'm invisible. In a way, that's not negative. There is a sort of release to being invisible. Who cares what I do? Who cares what I say? Who cares how I look? I can just do whatever I want."

In *Two Old Women,* a beautifully told tale based on an Alaskan legend of betrayal, courage, and survival, two women elders, ages seventy-five and eighty, are abandoned by their migrating tribe. The tribe faces starvation brought on by unusually harsh Arctic weather and a shortage of fish and game. The women are left for the winter to die of exposure to the elements and of starvation. The two women surprise the tribe, however, by surviving. Ironically, it is the other tribe members who suffer the most and who die. The two old women have been quite self-sufficient, not merely surviving but also stockpiling fur pelts, garments, dried fish, and cured meats. Enough, in fact, to share with the rest of the tribe members when they return. The other members now feel gratitude toward and respect for the two women. The ones they thought to be the most helpless and useless have proven to be strong and autonomous. The story ends as the chief appoints the two women to honorary positions within the tribe. The people try to help the old ones in any way they can, but the women will not accept their assistance, because they have learned to appreciate their hard-earned independence. And the people show their respect for the two old women by listening to what they have to say. The tribe vows never again to abandon their elders, and they keep their promise. "They had learned a lesson taught by two whom they came to love and care for until each died a truly happy old woman." This is a fable about how to deal with ourselves and with each other as we age in a youth-oriented society. Appreciating and honoring "the voices of wisdom" are paramount to respecting life itself in all its stages of growth, ripeness, and decay.

Seven years ago, in my introduction to *On Women Turning 50,* I wrote these words: "Writing this book has been a way of cultivating my future, which includes my inevitable aging—tilling the soil, planting the seeds, feeding and watering early naked shoots in the private Giverny of my mind and heart. This interior garden has been fostered by the gift of elder wisdom from each woman [I have met] who, by developing her own intrinsic inner authority, speaks the truth of her own life, thus inspiring and empowering others to do the same. It is my vision that the seeds which I have planted in this metaphorical garden will, by the time I turn fifty, blossom into a prism of new treasures."

Now that I have turned fifty—without pain, disappointment, or a fear of the future (or those hideous black balloons!)—I am partaking of that garden of treasures planted seven years ago. And with each book I write in the decade series, I continue to plant new seeds. For each decade brings the promise of never-before-experienced opportunities for growth and personal development, for creative expression and contribution to our community. In *On Women Turning 70,* I invite you to encounter new role models for aging exuberantly, for becoming more faithful to yourself, for becoming more authentic. I invite you to honor the voices of wisdom within. As Betty Friedan said, "The rest of your life is just where you want to take it."

Basically, I don't think people should act like they're old. I think
they're just as old as they act. Old people aren't exempt from
having fun and dancing and having sexual desires and frittering
away their time and enjoying their leisure and playing. I don't
know why so many of them give up.

LIZ SMITH

Liz Smith

Profile

"If you want a good role model, I'm telling you I'm not," insisted Liz Smith, America's most popular gossip columnist, several times during our interview. "I don't do things that are good for me—like exercise. I do run around all day, but I don't exercise. I don't eat right. When I have an ache or a pain and finally go to the doctor, it always disappears as soon as I go, so I don't take illnesses too seriously."

She doesn't think people should accept their age. "That advice to 'act your age' is about the worst advice I ever heard," she asserted. Sounds about right coming from a woman whose looks place her anywhere between the ages of fifty and seventy. How can you act your age when you're not sure what that age is? She refers to herself as "the world's oldest adolescent, emotionally and practically."

I met Liz Smith through a letter of introduction from her close personal friend, former Texas governor Ann Richards. Ann had recommended Liz for my book *On Women Turning 60*. Even her best friends don't know her age! Seventy-four when we met, Liz told me, "I'm a lot older than Ann. She's just a youngster."

Born and raised in Texas, Liz Smith considers herself "southwestern to the bone." After receiving a bachelor's degree in journalism and nearly a master's degree in English at the University of Texas, she jumped on a train in 1949 at the age of twenty-four and headed straight for New York City. She had a marriage and divorce behind her and now admits that she knew a lot less than she thought she did. She arrived with fifty dollars in her pocket and was "dying to be a journalist." She worked obsessively, and at various times she was a staff writer, editor, or freelance contributor working for such magazines as *Cosmopolitan, Sports Illustrated, New York, Ladies Home Journal, Vogue,* and *Esquire.*

It wasn't until 1975 that Liz received her big break from the *New York Daily News* when, because of her "easy and comfortable style" and her sense of humor, she was chosen to be a new syndicated columnist. Although at the time she feared that gossip was "a washed-up genre," ultimately, she couldn't resist having such an important forum in America's largest newspaper and best tabloid. The first column appeared in February 1976, and Liz was elated when "people instantly responded well."

With her droll sense of humor, Liz described herself as a "chronicler of the ways and means and social mores of the celebrities of our time." "Celebrities of our time" is not an overstatement; Liz Smith broke the news of Donald Trump's divorce from his first wife, Ivana, and attended Elizabeth Taylor's wedding to Larry Fortensky. She is fondly referred to as gossip's "godmother," or "good ole gal," which shows that she is as well liked as she is well known. She also enjoys appearing four mornings a week on the Fox network.

The "surprise of her life" came in 1995 when *New York Newsday* offered Liz a reported one million dollars to move her byline to their publication. She was seventy-three years old. Elated by finally having a sense of financial remuneration, she was thrilled to accept. She doesn't think of herself as "rich," but she feels secure in the knowledge that she can take care of herself, whatever the future brings. "Having enough money is important for anyone," Liz told me, "but especially for single, older women."

The day of our meeting, Liz looked nothing like a clothes-conscious matron. She was comfortable yet stylish in a well-fitting pair of Levi's and a cool, crisp white oxford shirt. One could have called her trendy if one didn't know that she has always dressed like this, not just since it became chic. "I'm not a very formal person," Liz said, in regard to her attire. "I'm either all dressed up or I'm not dressed up at all. I have to dress up so much to go out at night to events that I'm happy when I don't have to."

After fifty years away from Texas, she still has a recognizable native accent and idiom. Her brilliant blue eyes, windswept blond hair, and dazzling smile give her a cheerleader's ebullience. We met at her office in a high-rise in the Murray Hill section of New York's midtown. St. Clair, her assistant (one of three), was gracious and obviously fond of Liz, for whom he has worked for the last thirty-five years. The *Newsday* deal has allowed Liz more privacy than she has had all these years; she now rents a second apartment for herself in the same building as her office. She indulged in a Mercedes. But she also has more money for charities, such as her favorite one, Literacy Partners.

Liz Smith is the first to acknowledge that her life is indeed privileged. For a woman who spent her teenage years lying on the floor of her family's living room reading Walter Winchell and dreaming of emulating the most powerful social and political commentator of the 1940s and 1950s, whose column appeared in more than two thousand newspapers, life hasn't turned out so bad.

A Lucky, Lucky Life

I'm trying to write a book now about my life. So that's quite a challenge. A memoir. That's a real challenge to me, and that's fun. I hope I can do it. I don't know if I can do it; I always think I can't do things. And then I surprise myself. Really, I'm surprised at my whole life! I'll tell you when I surprised myself is when *New York Newsday* wanted me to leave the *Daily News* and come write for them. Then they offered me so much money to come! That was very surprising. I didn't really expect that. So I was very pleased and proud of myself, even though, of course, you never get the money. You never see it; you aren't aware that you've made it. The government takes half of it before I see any of it. It was a contract over a number of years. Eventually, it worked out to be an awful lot of money, so that was surprising and thrilling. I thought, "Who is this person they are referring to? Are they crazy?"

The best thing that happened to me in old age was that I got to be successful after I was about ready to retire. I got to be very successful. It's been really rewarding, a lot of fun, and I'm not conflicted about [success] at all. Who knows how idiotic I might have been if I'd been successful right off the bat? I'd been "starving in the garret" for years. People in journalism don't make any money, or they used to not make any money. But I had a wonderful struggle in New York to get ahead. I was very ambitious. I've had a terrific time since the moment I got off the train at Penn Station in 1949. I was just out of the University of Texas, but I had been married and divorced, so I was older than most people at twenty-four.

Getting older, being on television, making some money—I found all those things very satisfying. I'm one of the lucky people who can go on working. Unless I get sick, I'll go on working until I drop. That's lucky! I don't think people should retire, as long as they like what they're doing.

If not, they can retire and do something they enjoy, like indulge in philanthropy or even travel or whatever they want. I'm not saying that everybody needs to work, but they can't just give up on their life. I think you go on acting like you've always acted. I love New York. I love my life. It's been fabulous. I enjoy doing a variety of activities.

I didn't make any money until about twenty years ago, when I started appearing on television. Then I began to make better money from the column and better money from freelancing and better money for television appearances. I think being a late bloomer is fine. I was always working and having a ball. I just never made any money for years in journalism. Then I worked in jobs in television where I didn't make any money either.

I have to say that success is loving your work. That's not my definition. It's Peggy Lee's. I think you need to love what you're doing. Then you're successful. I think money is important. You need a little security. But I sure never had any until I was almost ready to retire. I didn't make much money for a lot of years. I had to become an institution before they began to offer me really good deals. I've been here so long now that I'm sort of like an institution. Everybody knows me in New York. People on the street yell, "Hi, Liz," or they see me on television. So it's kind of like a small town. I think I'm perceived in an affectionate way. I'm a real cheerleader and booster; I'm not into attacking people.

I think I have the best of all possible worlds. I have a little bit of fame, but not enough to bother you where you can't have any privacy. It's nice when people recognize you. I went to the theater the other day unexpectedly. I was supposed to go see *Victor/Victoria,* and Julie Andrews wasn't in it, so I walked off. And then I thought I'd go in and see *The Gin Game.* At the box office, I gave them my credit card, and they gave me a free ticket. They wouldn't take my credit card. Those are the perks, and lots of nice things like that happen to me.

I'm very lucky, but I'm tellin' you, I worked hard for it, you know? I do know I'm privileged. I always say "I'm overfed, overentertained, overstimulated, overpaid." But I don't have any regrets about any of it.

I don't have any regrets about never having children either. There are so many children in the world, and all my friends have them, and my brothers have them. I have sixteen nieces and nephews. It hasn't been something I've ever wanted. I think I was too selfish. I was too busy having fun. I wanted to get ahead and finally came to care about my work late in life. I can't take any credit for caring so much about my work. I've enjoyed it. I *love* journalism. I *love* news. I *love* reporting. And I like books, plays, museums, dancing. I love all the stuff that you are exposed to in New York. If you want it, it's all here. But if you're poor, you're in bad shape. It's just not a good city to be poor in. No city is, but this one particularly.

New York is not a good place to retire to. It's too hard on most people, unless you have money. I think this city is very tough on a lot of old people who just can't get out of here. They'd be much better off in some nice little town somewhere.

Oh, yeah, I've had a facelift. It was a long time ago. I was only forty-six—almost thirty years ago. Sure, it was worth doing. I had a scar on my eye from an accident, and I wanted to get it fixed. It was pressing on my eye and impairing my sight. The plastic surgeon said, "I have to do both your eyes to make them match." I said, "Well, let's do a whole facelift." He said, "You're a little bit young." That was when forty-six was considered *very* young. I think it really helped me. It gave me a big boost. I would do it again now, but I don't have time. I have natural old age now.

All these women have their faces done and don't have a line in their faces; it's ridiculous. But I'm all for that, if you can afford it. I think it's great. It's a big morale booster. A lot of people are against facelifts only because they're frightened or they think it's vain or they feel they should deny themselves. I think that's ridiculous. You should do whatever makes you feel good about yourself. And you should do whatever you can to make yourself look as good as you can. I have certain friends I think should have their faces done. They'd look absolutely ravishing. If they were trying to work in television like I am, they would probably have to, because the camera doesn't do you any favors.

These procedures are so good now. They have all of these new techniques—things I don't even know about. I'm for anything that makes you feel good: makeup, having your hair done. That's one of the perks of old age and being on television—I have my hair done almost every day. That's great; I love it. That's another morale builder. I'm not too good at doing things like that for myself.

What is my schedule? Well, when I do television—four days a week—I get up about seven o'clock, rush up to Fox, and they do my makeup. And then I come back when that's done and work on the column until noon, and maybe sometimes I have a lunch, sometimes I don't. Yesterday, I had an interesting day. I did two things for television in the afternoon. I did the History Channel interview on what various people think about history. It was a philosophical interview. Then I did an interview about Truman Capote for A&E's *Biography.*

I never do the same thing twice, except to do the column. The column is a must, and we have to file it by about two in the afternoon, so I try to do it in the morning. Then in the afternoon, I usually have to write a script for the television program for the next day, and then I go have my hair done, because I'm going to be on television. And they don't have hair-dressers there that early.

I wouldn't care if I never traveled again. I've traveled a lot. I do like to get out of New York and go to the country. I go to my friends' houses, which is fun. I've got a lot of friends with wonderful houses. I'm not just stuck on being in the city. I'm going on a trip to Greece in June, but I'm just going because two rich married friends want to go. I've already been through the Greek islands. It's just that traveling is not what I like to do; I'd rather sit down somewhere and read history. You don't read when you travel. You're too tired.

Basically, I don't think people should act like they're old. I think they're just as old as they act. Old people aren't exempt from having fun and danc-ing and having sexual desires and frittering away their time and enjoying their leisure and playing. I don't know why so many of them give up.

I don't think about death much. I don't care. I'm not concerned with it. I don't see any point in worrying about it. There's nothing you can do about it. You can't get any final satisfaction about what is to happen and when it's going to come. So what's the point? I don't want to borrow trouble. I wouldn't want to die a painful death. I admit I'm a coward, but dying doesn't seem so awful to me. It's just part of the rest of it, and since we don't know what it is, we might as well find out. And then if we don't have any consciousness to know, what's the point of worrying about it? I don't believe in a vengeful God or anything like that. I don't believe in hell. If there's an afterlife, that's great. I believe there might be. I don't know. That's just wishful thinking, I guess. I just never worry about that; it's not one of my priorities.

You know, it's funny—I have never thought I was aging. I never thought of myself as aging. I've still got the same point of view I've always had. I think of myself as much younger than I am, I guess. I'm just surprised at how fast everything has gone by, but I think everybody feels that.

I'm like anybody. I hear all these horror stories about people getting so sick and everything. That's terrible. I'd like to avoid that. I'd love to avoid going to a nursing home. I have a little bit of money. I think I've got enough that I could get along, even if I couldn't work. That's a big advantage. I think that's rare for single women. I'm not taking a lot of credit for not having any fears. It's partly having lived expansively and having had a great time and finally making some money so I have a little bit of security. Maybe that makes me more sanguine about the future than some people can be. But I don't have anybody who's going to take care of me. That's for sure!

I didn't do anything special for my seventieth birthday. But on a recent birthday, I had a big party where I got up and announced that I was going back to being sixty, that I wasn't going to say anything about my real birthday anymore. But, of course, I've already broken my promise. I said I wasn't going to lie about my age—I was just going to change it. People change their lives, they change their faces, they change their names, they change their sex—they change all kinds of things. So I didn't see why I couldn't change my age if I wanted to. This got a big laugh. It was widely reported in the paper, and then the next Sunday the *Times* printed a picture of me with the caption, "Liz Smith on her sixtieth birthday," which I thought was so funny. They didn't put *sixtieth* in quotes, either. Maybe rolling back my age helped me. Next year, I'm going to give myself a sixty-first birthday, and we'll see how long I can get away with it before I crack up and fall into little crumbling pieces.

I just don't think you should accept your age. That advice to "act your age" is about the worst advice I ever heard. I'm always thinking, "What am I going to do when I grow up?" It's as if I haven't done anything yet! I would say to all women, "Don't give up your dreams and your desires.

Don't give up the ship. Don't give up. Just keep on." I would say, "Try to save some money, and invest it so you don't have to be dependent on outside means, because you can't really depend on this government, and you can't be dependent on others. When you think you can depend on people, you're usually surprised."

The greatest gift I got with age is that I'm finally able to allow myself to be friends with men, instead of being in some adversarial push-me/pull-me thing. Now I have lots of men friends who I'm really enjoying.

It would be nice to be going down the shady lane with a companion, but that doesn't seem to be in the cards again, so that's OK, too. There are a lot of other things in life. I used to ask my mother if she would be inclined to marry again if my father died, and she would say, "Why would I do that? Then I'd just have some other old man to take care of." She hated cooking, so when my father died, she had a ball. She loved him, and she felt he died too young, but she had a wonderful time after, because she never did anything she didn't want to anymore.

She died about six years ago. I was able to help her, and my brothers were very attentive to her, so she got good value out of her children. She lived a good life. She did her own housework at ninety-four and a half. One day, she had a massive stroke and died. Better that than to hang around suffering. No question. I certainly hope that happens to me.

I haven't really paid any attention to the different decades in my life. I still feel like I always did. Everyone was going on about being forty and how terrible it was to be forty. I didn't know what they were talking about! I didn't believe I was forty any more than I believe now that I'm seventy-four. I don't get it!

Recently, I quit ever saying anything about age, because I decided it's just a downer, a tendency to put yourself down. That's what it is. It isn't that you expect people not to know. Everybody knows my age, but I just don't want to give in to it.

What happens to old people is that they have an accident, and then they can't recover from it because they don't have the physical stamina to come back. That usually finishes them off or changes their life. Of course, something like that could happen to me. Maybe it will, but maybe it won't. I don't know. Why worry? That's just the way it is. I'm lucky I've never been really sick. I've been in a few accidents, but I've never had a serious illness.

And no matter how much luck I might have, if I had been sick or something, things would be different. I've got a young friend who I'm very fond of, and she has Crohn's disease. I just feel so sorry for her. I can't imagine how she struggles on against it. It's so difficult. People say you make your own luck but, nah, I think I've just been lucky. And so, since I have been, I thought I'd just go on trying to act like I was until the building falls down around me. I guess I'm a fatalist. What will be, will be. You can't control it. I could exercise and eat better, and maybe I'd stay healthy longer, but life is short. I'm always making these resolutions that I'm gonna do better, but so far I haven't stuck with them. And now I'm seventy-four, and I'm wondering if all this concern with health and exercise is worth it.

I've been lucky, really lucky. I had great parents, I had great brothers, I have fabulous friends. And one of the most satisfying things about the peculiarities of my career is I got to meet so many wonderful people that I admire. I love all these newspeople. I'm friends with Dan Rather and Peter Jennings and Barbara Walters and Diane Sawyer; they're all my friends. Lots of good, wonderful writers like Dominick Dunne and Norman Mailer. Life's been such a thrill. ✖

About this issue of aging, I want to make a terribly *important point. People decide to get old. I've seen them do it. Why they do this, I don't know. But I do think it's terribly important that people not make that inner decision. Because then they sit around and they're old. It's easy not to do it, in fact. It's not about staying young but about not getting old.*

DORIS LESSING

Doris Lessing

*[Her books] have traced an evolutionary progress of the soul,
which to some extent transforms the reader as [s]he reads.*

JOYCE CAROL OATES, *Southern Review*, Oct. 1973

Profile

"Myth never was, but always is," was the Zenlike conundrum that Joseph
Campbell, the teller of timeless myths, often articulated. Certainly, we live
in a mythic imagination, whether or not we are aware of it. Doris Lessing
speaks to a consciousness of the mythic in her work, as one can see
from the titles of her works: *Martha Quest, Briefing for a Descent into Hell,
Shikasta Re: Colonised Planet 5, The Sirian Experiments, The Wind Blows
Away Our Words,* and *Each His Own Wilderness.* That is only a partial list-
ing; she is the author of more than thirty books, including novels, short
stories, reportage, poems, plays, and two librettos.

It is all too easy for an adoring public to put a favorite writer on a
pedestal and to make that person into an icon. In my experience, great
writers attempt to remove themselves from such a formidable—and
isolating—height. "Read my books!" is their usual plea. Doris Lessing is
no different. "I have many writers as friends who are extremely agreeable
and attractive people, and I very much enjoy being with them. But if I
really want to know what these people are like, I read a book by them.

This is where you meet the real person. This is where you are hearing what he or she is really thinking."

Doris Lessing told me this quite amicably when I visited her home in the West Hampstead area of London in the spring of 1998. Of course, she is correct. However, after reading *The Grass Is Singing* or *The Summer Before the Dark* or *Particularly Cats . . . and Rufus,* would I have really known that she loves French literature and was keeping an English translation of Stendahl's *La Vie de Henri Brulard* open in the upstairs bathroom? ("I can read French badly. I prefer to read it in English.") How could I have guessed that the videos she was watching that week included such an eclectic array as a BBC documentary on birds and migration; French films from the 1930s, including Marcel Carné's *Le Jour Se Lève* and Marcel Pagnol's *Marius;* and the British movie *Scandal,* based on the Conservative Party in England that toppled in the early 1960s?

Perhaps most important, I would never have met Cat, Doris's enormous (much larger than a small dog) black-and-white companion of eighteen years. El Magnifico is Cat's real name. He's also called General Pink Nose III, and he seems to have a whole list of names, but she tends to call him Butchkin. "If you'd seen him in his prime," Doris exulted, "he looked wonderful." The moment I walked in, I could just see his magnificence. Absolutely. I didn't even notice that he was missing his entire right foreleg. Poor pussycat. He had cancer on his shoulder, and the vet decided to take the whole leg off three-and-a-half years ago. "You see his handsome fur," Doris crooned. And she seemed to suffer at Cat's suffering— and at the knowledge that it couldn't be very much longer. "It is not too good now. Poor cat. He's sad. A sad cat. And I'm sad."

There's a limit to our communication with animals, no matter how much we love them. "I would like to know how he feels about taking painkillers. I hate taking painkillers. But I can't ask him. I do not know what effect the painkillers at night are having on him, except they are making him very confused. If he doesn't have them, he's in terrible pain. I would love five minutes of talk just to ask him, "Cat, what would you like me to do, poor cat?" Her concern continued throughout the several hours I spent with them. Yes, it was sad.

Our conversation ranged from cultural topics to hearsay, from the personal to the political. Recently, her daughter, Jean, who lives in Cape Town, South Africa, and her granddaughter, who is studying law at Oxford, were visiting her for a month. "We have been to every theater. I can tell you what you should see and what you can miss," she offered, insisting that I see *Flight* by Bulgakov. I asked about her friend Salman Rushdie's current status after the 1989 *fatwa,* or death sentence, placed on him by Ayatollah Khomeini, the Iranian spiritual leader of the time. "He has his minders with arms, and he is in a safe house," she told me. "He comes out and has a very public life. But authorities have caught people trying to assassinate him. What he's in danger from now is not the government but madmen. They've been promised, don't forget, two million pounds (or is it dollars?) *and* paradise. You'd have to spend the dollars in paradise, I suppose, but for some lunatic, it's pretty persuasive, isn't it? So he's OK. Rushdie's working, which is the main thing, I think."

We talked about power and greed in a frightening world in which, just that week, nuclear devices had been detonated by both India and Pakistan. I mentioned Henry Kissinger's famous quote, "The ultimate aphrodisiac is power," and how Lily Tomlin had retorted, "I'd hate to see what gets him off!" Amused, Doris recalled the day Kissinger came to visit her in the early 1960s. "I admire him for this. He was wanting to meet the enemy. He was sure that I was representative of the New Left, which in fact I wasn't. He kept talking about kitten bombs: 'We have developed a kitten nuclear bomb, which would kill just a hundred thousand people.' Actually it was very funny. He was frightening, because he didn't see how terrifying it was, this language he was using. Perfectly normal for him to talk about taking out a hundred thousand people, and he used the same language as the Communists: 'The end justifies the means.' Now, of course, I would know better than to argue with him at all, because I don't argue with that kind of ideology any longer." I suggested that this could be material for an incredible play. "I 'spose so," Doris answered nonchalantly. "It could be called 'A Non-Meeting of Minds.'"

I found Doris direct but warm, totally defined and self-confident but gracious. Her intelligence is monumental; she is interested in everything.

We laughed a lot. Few people I've met have the advantage of knowing her true nature. Occasionally, a frighteningly deep sigh would heave her chest and shoulders up and down. It was usually because my California jargon of *consciousness* and *spirituality* had baffled her or because I'd asked a question that bored her or, in the case of Catholicism, reminded her of something she disliked. I steered away from routine biographical queries. I already knew that Doris Lessing had lived an unusual life.

She was born in 1919 in the exotic land of Persia (now Iran) to British parents. The family moved to a three-thousand-acre maize farm in Southern Rhodesia (now Zimbabwe) in the mid-1920s. In defiance of her mother's ambitions for her, Doris left school at fourteen. (She considers herself fortunate to have escaped the indoctrination of the university system.) Twice married and divorced, she bore three children. During the early 1940s, she joined a small Salisbury group in organizing a communist party, open to both black and white members. In time, she acquired a considerable understanding of marxist ideology. In 1949, Doris left Southern Rhodesia for England with her youngest child, Peter, whom she was to raise. In London, Doris was as low in morale as in money, but she had, nevertheless, brought along her own salvation—the manuscript of *The Grass Is Singing.* That story studied the psychic deterioration of the wife of a poor white farmer on the lonely South African veld and her obsessive relationship with a black houseboy who eventually murders her. It became her first published novel in 1950.

Perhaps Doris is best known in the United States for her novel *The Golden Notebook,* first published in 1962. In that book, Anna Wulf, suffering from writer's block, becomes immensely self-analytical and seeks to understand her disorderly life by keeping four notebooks, thereby attempting to come to terms with her life through her art. The fragmentation of her self is symbolized by the multiplicity of notebooks. Doris's intensely personal books, written largely out of her own impassioned experience, are nevertheless largely concerned with people caught in the social and political upheavals of the twentieth century. Her wide-ranging interests and concerns—the new theories of psychiatry; marxist theory; feminism; racism; Sufism, a form of mysticism; the sciences; the destruction of the environment—have all found their way into the writing of a most unconventional and original woman.

After I said my good-byes and thank-yous, I walked down Doris's street feeling like I was in an altered state, like I'd been in another, perhaps mythic, dimension. As I turned the corner, I noticed the street sign— Agamemnon Road. A block further was Achilles Road. The one after was Ulysses Road. What power hath the mythic imagination?

A Thing of Temperament

I had experiences that are useful for writers or artists. That is, I had a very stressed childhood. I'm not saying unhappy childhoods are necessary, but I think stressed ones are good, because it makes children very keen observers. And this is what you use all your life, of course, as a writer.

If you just observe women's lives, you'll see that they have to deal with the plumber and the roof and the cat and a vet, which I've just done. It's very difficult to have a schedule from eight to one, which I would like to have, because it's always being interrupted. I have a house, and there are usually people staying here. I'm sure I don't have to tell you that with a house, there is something that always has to be attended to. I've noticed that my male writing friends tend to be able to shut themselves up in a room and write, whereas I've never known a woman who can do that.

I'd *like* to have a routine for writing. I would like to be able to get up, do all the things one has to do, and get straight to my typewriter at about eight and be totally uninterrupted until one or two. This very seldom happens, I assure you. But that's what I would like. I have energy again in the early afternoon. But I know writers who are perfectly happy writing primarily in the afternoon, which actually amazes me.

I very much dislike words like *higher consciousness*. I think you write from different levels. Words like *higher* and *lower* are terribly misleading. I think that the difficulty, when you're writing, is to find what I call the tone of voice. That is, the appropriate way for this particular book or story. It might take a long time to get that right, and if you get it wrong, you might just as well throw it all away—it's got no life in it. I don't mean a literal voice. I mean some kind of label I use to try and describe the appropriate tone for a book, because you have to get that before a book will come to life. It's very easy to write from the top of your head, and it very often has no life in it at all. For example, *The Marriages Between Zones Three, Four, and Five*—I had that in my mind for about ten years, but I simply couldn't think of a way to do it. And when I thought of using that ancient device as story-teller, suddenly it came into place—the tone of the book, everything. Not just like that; it *did* take me a long time to do it, you know. That's what you have to do when you're writing a book—you have to find that way of do-ing it that works for that book.

I do think writers are cleverer when they're writing. You're thinking very hard. When you're writing, you're writing from the most intelligent part of yourself. You're not the same person as the one sitting in the kitchen gossiping. You are thinking in a better way. If you want to meet a writer, you read the books. That's where we are. If you know a lot of writers, you'll find that the ordinary person has very little to do with what you meet when you're reading a book—which is why I'm always astounded that people want to meet writers, because we're just boring, like everyone else.

I find the idea of love fascinating. I think that Byron said it, didn't he: "Man's love is of man's life a thing apart, / 'Tis woman's whole existence." It may not be true now, but how often do you see young women throwing everything over for a man? You see it often. There's still a certain threat in it. Falling in love isn't only about women. I think men also fall in love, after all. Falling in love is not a process; it's usually like a thunderclap. But it's very disruptive indeed, and it makes people temporarily crazy, in my view.

What interests me about that is, of course, what is it all about? We take it absolutely for granted.

Now, there are degrees of being in love, aren't there? What interests me is, to be pompous, what is its evolutionary function, this falling in love? It apparently has no purpose whatsoever. None. It's got nothing to do with procreation. I'm not talking about being attracted or deciding to get married. I'm talking about falling in love. I'm talking about eros. This is what fascinates me. I don't see the point of it. I don't see what the use of it is, and yet it is so strong, so destructive, so violent. This is what interested me in writing *Love, Again.*

Yes, I did fall in love at sixty-five. It's irrelevant whether I did or not. Everybody falls in love. I talk to older people, and when they're being truthful, they'll confess that they fall in love at the most inappropriate ages, often with people much younger than themselves. This is what is interesting. It's got nothing to do with reproduction or anything. But we never ask ourselves about it. We never say, "What is it for? What *is* it, in fact?" This astonishing need to submerge yourself in someone else. And it usually seems to be with the most inappropriate people. That is what's so absolutely interesting.

I've had some very interesting letters from readers since I wrote that book. Some were extremely funny, I have to say. Inappropriately falling in love. Absolutely amazing. Of course, a lot of them just keep quiet, because older people aren't supposed to fall in love. The most remarkable one I know is a woman who has a lover in South America. She's seventy, I should think. They meet once a year. He's about thirty. Neither family knows about it, of course. It's a passion. What is it about? I know about a lot of these that go on quietly.

You didn't mention the connection between real falling in love and serious depression, because I'm sure there's a connection, a gradation between the miseries of falling in love and grief. Whenever I meet a psychiatrist, I ask, "Would you say there's a connection between grief and depression?" And quite often they'll say, "Oh, no, they're quite different." Well, I don't think they are different. I think they're very similar, in fact. Not that I've ever had real depression, but my friends have had it. I know people who are serious depressives. One thing they have in common is a ghastly childhood, every one of them, which is not without interest.

I fell in love, and then I plunged into grief, which I never, ever had done in my life. Not even when people close to me died. I moved from one emotion to the other, and it was pulverizing, it was painful. I understand exactly why people commit suicide. What is interesting is that it is *physically* painful. Don't you think that's interesting? It's very interesting that an emotional pain should be so vividly physical, which I never even thought about before. When you wake up in the morning with your heart so painful you can hardly bear it, don't you think that's extraordinary?

I don't think it's necessarily an advantage to suffer. Western culture very much values suffering. I've become very skeptical about it all. We love it when people suffer. We just adore it. We identify. I just saw the most astonishing thing in one of our newspapers. A feminist said about Sylvia Plath, "We learned so much from her." I thought, "My God, what does that say about the women's movement? Admiring this pathetic suicide." Yes, I have read Ted Hughes's new book, *Birthday Letters,* about his relationship with Plath. I like it. I knew them all. To me, there's nothing surprising in what he wrote. I don't know why people found it surprising. He was living with a woman, in an obviously very deep relationship, and she commits suicide and becomes this angel on the monument, and he's so unfairly and wickedly blamed for everything. I think that he's done very well to come through that as well as he's done. Particularly with the kids to bring up. It's terrible. I've always liked his poetry very much. He's a very nice man, this Ted Hughes, this villain.

I'm very unhappy with that word *belief,* you know? Very. But I think about the topic of reincarnation as I do about many of these ideas. It seems to me to explain a lot of things. Like the instant affinities between people or the antipathies between two people. It's quite irrational. "Where's the proof?" I ask, as a child of the scientific age. But it's quite possible. Reincarnation is a surprisingly useful theory. I know someone, for example—the most rational person in the world, a very good and old friend of mine—who says that, from his very early childhood, he has known everything there is to know about the organization of the Roman army. He took it for granted when he was a child, and it occurred to him that this was a bit peculiar. He could never find anything to read or study about it that he didn't already know. He knew it all. Now this could be explained by the theory of reincarnation. But on the other hand, there are all kinds of ways of explaining it. This kind of thing is interesting.

I do think you can tap into information. When you're writing a book on a subject you've never written on before, it's amazing. First, you discover you know much more about it than you think you do, because all your life you've been hearing about it. Information comes into your mind, but then what really fascinates me is that from that moment, books on that subject appear as if by magic. People start talking about the subject. It's astonishing. It's as if you've plugged into some wavelength. All I know is that when I start writing a book, the pleasure comes from the thought that I'm now going to learn a lot about a subject that I never knew before. Because once you start writing, information on that topic suddenly comes in from anywhere—the radio or television or books. It's a very strange thing, actually. Then it makes one wonder, "What are we blind to? What haven't we yet seen?" There must be an awful lot that we're blind to, that we take for granted.

My son John died when he was over fifty. He was a coffee farmer in Zimbabwe. To put it mildly, he didn't look after himself. He drank too much, ate too much, and he lived very, very hard. He had a heart attack and was warned. Another heart attack. What killed him was a drought. You probably don't know, but they had the most terrible drought in Zimbabwe. Years of it. Have you ever seen a drought? You don't want to. I was on that farm just a couple of months before he died. The dam had a puddle of water in it. There were animals to feed, and the birds were dropping off of trees. The heat . . . the trees dying . . . And he was suffering because he adored animals and nature. He was a great stiff-upper-lipper, which is very bad. He wouldn't admit that he was miserable. Anyway, the really awful part of the story is he had a heart attack, and the rains came a day later. I know that if he had just managed to stay alive another day . . .

The Africans I was meeting at that time said, "Ah, yes, God is punishing us because the victims of such-and-such war were not properly buried." Wars are very bad for cultures that have elaborate burial prescriptions. Have you ever thought about that? Bodies have to be buried in a certain way. Otherwise, the ancestors are angry. In a war, well, they can't be buried; people have to go on. So then you have this burden of guilt on everyone, as well as everything else.

About this idea of free will versus predestination . . . What I think is that it is probable that we are put on this earth in order to learn. (Observe how I'm putting it; I will not say "I believe," because I don't like great pronouncements.) How otherwise do you explain this passion for learning that is so deep? I don't know if they have it in America, but here there is an astonishing phenomenon—everyone is off at night classes learning this and studying that. I think people who are inclined to it, who have aptitude for it (however you define that), are here to learn. That doesn't mean everyone. I don't see the whole of humanity as the same.

I don't like to use the word *God,* because it is so debased. I'm not happy with the word *God* at all. I think where life came from is some kind of gigantic experiment, in my view. Why should we assume that we're the only people in the universe? My ideas are much more like science fiction than they are like religion. I play with ideas—like saying, "*If* there are other people in our planetary system." What's going on on those planets right out there? We always assume that our present level of knowledge is the highest there can be. It's a very strange thing in any field you care to mention, for example in anthropology. They find a bone in an African gorge, and that becomes the last word in information. Then they find another bone somewhere in Java; then that is the truth. And this is how we are. We seem to have to think in terms of what we know now as if it's the highest. And as if *we* are the highest. First, I think probably our history is much older than we think it is. *Much.* One doesn't have to be a genius to think this thought, because every time the scientists come up with it, the date gets further and further back. Then, I think that there's no reason at all we shouldn't be a field of experiment for a higher intelligence.

The nearest to my ideas is in *The Sirian Experiments,* where I was playing with the idea that this world is in fact a place of experiment for higher, more evolved people. I'm not saying I believe it, you understand. But the whole point about us is that we have an extremely limited grasp. Our senses are adequate only for functioning in this world and reproducing ourselves. Just one little example—with a very slight difference in our eyes, we would see the sun differently. This would never have occurred to us until certain kinds of photography came into being, and we saw what the sun looks like—not through our eyes but with a different kind of camera. We assume that what we see and what we think are all there is.

All I know about living is that all the time I'm saying, "How is it I never saw that before? It's obvious." It must be happening to you, too. Things that you haven't seen. "Good God, you're blind that you haven't seen that before," I often think.

Back to free will and predestination, where do they fit into being put here to learn? If you look at us from even a short distance, we're always in a very narrow slot of possibilities, aren't we really? Now, of course, there are many more choices. Looking back over my life—forgive me for that pompous phrase—I think, "OK, what else could I have done?" If I'm looking at being intellectual, I see places where I could have done something different, but not if I'm looking at being emotionally driven. There's a point where I think you have to be quite old not to be emotionally driven, particularly for women. Mind you, I think men are also emotionally driven. I often think we make these distinctions wrongly. In fact, we have far more in common than we've got separating us now.

I was married very young, as you know, twice. Looking back, it was quite good, really. I mean, I behaved very well. In the way that females behave very well. When you think of how totally unsuited I was to these men and they to me, I think we did it very well. Particularly Godfrey Lessing. You cannot imagine two people more unsuited to each other. We behaved beautifully. He was a German refugee, you see. In those days, a lot of marriages took place to keep people out of internment camps or to get them nationalities. It was a whole industry going on, which people have now forgotten about. That went on for quite a long time. There were two things. In Southern Rhodesia, you couldn't just live in sin. You could now. Secondly, this was the middle of the war, and he was a German. In the middle of war, people don't necessarily say, "Well, he's an anti-Fascist." They don't bother to discriminate. He had the internment camp threat over him, so he married me. I'm making it sound dramatic; it wasn't. It was the obvious thing to do. I'm amazed now at the lightheartedness. I thought, "Well, since I'm stuck here, I might as well have a baby." With his agreement. I don't regret it, but it was a bit mad. We *thought* we were going to go into all kinds of dramatic futures. Of course, we weren't.

About free will, I can think about times in my life when I could have genuinely done something else. That presumably is free will of a kind. But I couldn't *not* have gotten married for the first time and the second time. Yet they were stupid things to do, both of them. There may be other things that could have led me to where I am today. I wouldn't necessarily have had to do exactly what I did. And anyway, is where one is today such a good situation? Not necessarily at all. I mean, anyone who's alive after so many decades has been bloody lucky, when you think of the number of ways I could have been killed or the diseases I could have had. We spend all our time in planes, trains, and cars. Have you ever thought about the amount of time in your life you've spent traveling? It is the most amazing thing. We take it for granted. We're always going somewhere. It's all extremely dangerous. In the old days, people just walked.

I've just finished an adventure story that has really brought this home to me, because you know you know things, and yet you don't really know them. I have set the story in the future (it doesn't really matter where it is—it could be in the past), but the thing is, civilization has broken down as we know it. In the story, I have this brother and sister who suddenly realize what we take for granted. They have to walk; there is no transport. In the past, if there was a major breakdown, the people had to use a river—you either walked, or you got onto a river. This is what things were like. It was extremely slow and very dangerous. It's quite new that people should whiz about the world. It is astonishing to go from California to London in ten hours. I do think we take far too much for granted.

This idea of the invisibility of older women . . . I have to say, I don't mind being invisible. The young people don't see you at all. You are an *old* person. It's this Western culture's fear of old age that we're afflicted with. It's not as bad as in America, where you're obsessed with it. In China, they're actually *interested* in old people. When I went there for two weeks, I discovered this. It's quite interesting, completely different. They think we might have something to say about things.

I do find in talking to people of my age, you know, the thing that we will often say is that we see young people making the same mistakes we made, and yet they're not interested in what we have to say. Now, having been that young person, I understand exactly why; young people define themselves against the older generation. But it's a very funny way to define yourself, when you come to think of it. They could define themselves in all kinds of other ways, not, "I am against everything the older lot have done." That must be quite new, I should think. I don't know enough about history to know when that became the norm, but it's recent, I suspect. There's an automatic contempt for the older generation.

I had a fascinating experience recently with a man on the street selling a magazine produced by homeless people. I always buy it, but one day there was a man with one copy left, and I said, "Aren't you selling that?" and he said, "I wouldn't expect you to buy it." I said, "Why not?" He said, "We don't think it's right for old people to buy it." I said, "How do you know if I can afford it?" He said, "I'd feel bad." I said, "You're depriving me of self-respect." He never saw it that way. We had a conversation about it. I think how deeply it goes, this thing.

The invisibility thing began to happen to me along about my fifties, when I suddenly became aware that men were no longer noticing me. Then, when we get really old, we can be invisible to anyone—apart from people who know us, of course. I'm not necessarily saying this is a bad thing. It's quite interesting not to be noticed, because you can listen very attentively. It's a public invisibility that is extraordinary. You walk down the street, and there's a flock of children, and you know that they literally haven't seen you. Their eyes are not adjusted to seeing. It's not a tragedy. What *is* a tragedy is that, as I say, in the past and in other countries, old people were found useful because of what they knew. But now they're not.

Something you don't know yet, at your age, is that one has very much less energy in one's seventies. I have lost energy badly in the last decade. I find myself saying, "No, you can't do that. You've only got so much time left. Don't waste time on that." Of course, I never used to think like that. A lot of choosing goes on about what I need to do; I simply don't have time. My message to you is, "Do it now, because you won't have as much energy later." I was recently reading my 1982 diary. In one year, I wrote *Shikasta, The Marriages,* and half of *The Sirian Experiments.* I could never do that now. Then, I just took it for granted. Now my writing comes out to about one book a year. It may seem prolific, but this is what I do. I don't do much else. I've never had a taste for luxury, I'm glad to say. I've never enjoyed it. I have friends, you see, who really enjoy living high. What I really enjoy and what is my great extravagance is very good theater and opera tickets.

About this issue of aging, I want to make a *terribly* important point. People decide to get old. I've seen them do it. It's as if they've said, "Right, that's it. Now I'm going to get old." Then they become old. Why they do this, I don't know. Maybe they like to be dependent. But I do think it's terribly important that people not make that inner decision. Because then they sit around and they're old. It's easy not to do it, in fact. It's not about staying young but about not getting old. Now, I'm not talking about illness or health but *attitudes.* People who decide to get old, do. That's quite different from the cultural prejudice we were discussing earlier. For example, when I was in Pakistan looking at the Afghan refugee problem, I met a lot of the Afghan refugees. Women fifty or younger were old, old women— much older than I was, and I was years older than they. That's because they'd had fifteen children, and half of them had died, and they haven't had enough to eat, and there are problems with malnutrition. But there's an attitude at work here; they're *expected* to be old women, so they're old women.

Staying young is not something that interests me. It's a bit of a lost cause, isn't it? Even for people who have cosmetic surgery, there's a point at which they are not young. So you've just had seven facelifts. Everyone knows you have. I suppose it's a way of passing the time, but surely there are more interesting things to do. It's hard work. I know, because I have a couple of friends who do it. It's a full-time job. That's what they do. That's what they spend their time at. There's not a question to me of having facelifts or spending a lot of time on being young, because it's boring. You can decide to have your hair dyed, for example, but then you think, "I just can't be bothered with it." I thought, "You're going to have to go once a week and have your roots done. Do you really want to do this?"

I think most older people are continually surprised when they look in the mirror, because nothing has changed inside; you accept that you're the same as you always were. Yet the outside changes all the time. It's what one has to accept.

What am I thinking about the world of politics and the women's movement these days? In a somewhat complicated way, we've come back to free will and predestination. The thing about politics is that I think we're all under the impression that we are in charge of events, and we are not. We're always running along after events like a puppy dog yapping. What actually happens again and again is that something completely unexpected happens, like India setting off nuclear bombs. No one expected them to do that. While I'm fascinated by politics, and I think it's the greatest theater in the world, I don't take it seriously.

The women's movement, to me, has been such a disappointment. It had so much energy in the sixties and, to my mind, most of it was wasted talking. Perhaps there will be another wave of energy, but I look back on it and feel ashamed, actually, that it was such a waste. It benefited white, middle-class, young women. It hasn't done much for others. If you go to

(I hate the phrase) a Third World country or see the women in a Muslim country fighting about the law or bringing up ten kids on forty pounds a month—now these are women I admire very much. But I think most of the women's movement has been hot air.

Feminism reflects a total fascination with suffering and failure and pain. Look at Diana. How is it that this woman has become such an icon? It says something terrible about women that this could happen. Why do we have to identify all the time with failure? That is what's so frightening. She was a failure. Whether she was nice or not, who cares? I'm sure she was delightful. But she failed desperately, and this woman has become a kind of international symbol. I find it terrifying that it could be so. Awful. And yet it doesn't seem to strike anyone. I could make a whole list of failed women that we admire. Diana was physically ill and obsessed with her appearance. This is how she defined herself, but surely we can do better than that. And her love life was a bloody tragedy with a succession of men. She ended up with this pathetic character who, in his own terms and culture, was a disaster and was killed, and she becomes an *icon*. Yes, we just love failure and tragedy. Why do we? It's still part of worshiping or idolizing the misery in life.

I forgot to mention Marilyn. One of the most bizarre things in my life was that shortly after Marilyn died, I was walking on the street, and I heard two old women, older than I, say to the other, "Oh, you're not going to do a Marilyn on us, I hope." Meaning (because at that time we still thought she'd killed herself), "You're not going to commit suicide, are you?" Two working-class women coming home identifying with Marilyn Monroe! Don't you think that's strange? What about glamorous stars who do *not* use drugs and alcohol. I mean, whoever says, "I want to be Meryl Streep"? You laugh, but it's true. Or Sophia Loren. Or the Queen of Jordan, an extraordinary woman. Or Princess Anne, who is just as much involved with the unfortunate as Princess Diana, but who doesn't make a song and dance about it. Or the brave women who stand up to Muslim bigots? Or Toni Morrison? Why don't we identify with the fighters and survivors. Success and happiness are boring. They're un-Marilyn. I can't think what is the matter with us. Something is deeply, deeply wrong with us.

What about my own mortality? You mean death? You're an American—you can't say *death*. It's not touchy to me; I'm not afraid of dying. I'm interested in the whole thing. I never have been afraid. I have always been interested in it. I've always thought about death; I'm not one of those people who doesn't think about it. Curiosity about what happens afterward, if anything. And if nothing happens, we won't know. Large numbers of greater intelligences than you and I have believed that something or other will continue, that some part of us will continue, because there's so much evidence for it from so many different places.

Everybody my age is the same. It's not death we're concerned with—it's this prospect of being bloody invalids. We're afraid of having doctors who will wire us up like chickens. Even a living will is not going to prevent you from bad luck if you've seen what can happen. For example, Alzheimer's can hit anyone. Iris Murdoch has it. Diagnosed about two years ago. She's completely gone and unable to work.

I have to say, the awful thing about death is the names crossed out in your address book. Awful. Last year was an absolute holocaust of people dying. Younger than me, even. People from the 1960s seem to be not long-lived. I notice all these people dying. Those old hippies. Have you heard of Lindsay Anderson, the filmmaker? He had a wake in the Royal Court, so we all went to say good-bye to Lindsay Anderson, and it was the funniest thing you can imagine. All the old stars of the Royal Court turned up. Everybody saying, "Darling, you haven't changed a bit." There we were—fat, old, gray. "You haven't changed a day." It was hilarious. A real comedy act, I'm telling you.

I read a lot, of course, and I'm interested in everything. Things I want to do? No longer. I've been to so many places, I don't need to do that. There's nothing really that I haven't done in my life that I still think I want to do. No. Not really. There is still too much to do in my work. But that's always been so, the too-muchness. Even at my age, I find myself doing it anyway. I was just looking at the sheer amount of work I managed to pack in, and now I just couldn't do it. I've got so many ideas in my head for books that

I shall never write. I've never been short of ideas for books, but now I'm short of energy. The ideas do sort of take you over. The last one I have done, my adventure story, took me over. I got so fascinated by it. I'm in love with it. It will be out next year, *Mara and Dann: An Adventure.* I've never enjoyed writing anything so much. I'm already sad that it's off and running. I can't bear it; I miss it.

About being afraid of dying, it's a thing of temperament. More and more, it seems a thing of temperament or makeup. Why is it, for example, that people one knows who are extremely religious with deep faith in the afterlife are scared stiff of death? Petrified. Whereas people who don't believe anything at all, fine. Must be something to do with their emotional makeup. Why is it that one person decides at age sixty or age seventy-five to become an old woman, and others get along fine? Has to do with some kind of emotional thing. Maybe they're lucky with their grandparents, as I think I have been.

I don't know what advice I would have for women my age. Would they need advice? If they're lively enough to want advice, they don't need it. For the ones who sit in their chair, "Get up and do something." ∾

One of the things that can be an advantage about living to the age of seventy is that you see enough "two steps forward, one step back" that you don't think two steps forward is impossible. And you don't think one step back is the end of the world.

ELIZABETH (BETITA) MARTINEZ

Elizabeth (Betita) Martinez

It has been a terrible century, has it not? In the sense of: awesome.
Not just bad, more like extreme. Such high hopes of profound change,
such setbacks—the clock of justice leaping forward then grinding in
reverse. Revolutions rising and falling, leaders rising and falling, hopes
rising and falling and rising again.

ELIZABETH (BETITA) MARTINEZ, "History Makes Us,
We Make History"

Profile

I've always loved dramatic-looking and strong-charactered women: Anna
Magnani, Melina Mercouri, Jeanne Moreau, Martha Graham. Women
who are themselves, on all counts, without apologies. I now have a new
role model—Betita Martinez. A woman with a dazzling smile who is
stylish, vivacious, and excited about life. "I have to show you my black
leather miniskirt before you leave; it's cool. I guess I like to be outrageous," Betita told me. She was justifying her purchase of a miniskirt
from her local Salvation Army outlet two years ago at age seventy. "When
I had it shortened," she laughed, "my daughter said, 'Mommm, you shortened a miniskirt?' I said, 'Yes, it was too long!' "

From the beginning, Betita was, in her own word, *atypical*: born in
Washington, D.C., to a Mexican father of Oaxacan ancestry and an Anglo
mother whose roots can be traced from the Mayflower. Both taught
Spanish for many years. Betita remembers being the only person of color
from primary school through her class at Swarthmore College.

Betita has lived through and participated in five international wars and six social movements in this land "where I grew up brown" and seven attempts to build socialism in other countries (most of which she visited).

As a young woman living in New York City in the 1950s, Betita worked at several places: the United Nations as a researcher on colonialism; the Museum of Modern Art as an assistant to famed photographer Edward Steichen, while spending her off-hours with the Beat artists on the Lower East Side; Simon & Schuster as an editor; and *The Nation* magazine as its Books and Arts editor. Then came 1963 and the Birmingham church bombing that killed four young African American girls. Her days of "normal" jobs ended as she went to work in the black civil rights movement with the Student Nonviolent Coordinating Committee, where she headed its New York office and was called "Liz." "I had been a volunteer with SNCC for several years," she recalled, "but the Birmingham bombing made it impossible not to go full-time." The first step was traveling to Mississippi for the 1964 Summer Project, when three young civil rights workers were murdered and hundreds of others carried on despite the terror. Concurrently, she was a single, very politically active mother, raising her daughter, Tessa, who is now an experienced stage actress.

In 1968 Betita moved to New Mexico and joined the Chicano movement. Perhaps best known for writing the book titled *500 Years of Chicano History* and codirecting the video documentary based on it, Betita is often introduced as "Mrs. Living History." On the one hand, she appreciates that people are being respectful. On the other hand, "It makes you feel this huge gap. Living history! All five hundred years of it!" She usually jokes, "Well, I'm not quite five hundred yet, but I'm working on it," at which point the audience is hers.

She says she has had "one long love affair with revolution and social justice and the infinite courage of so many people." In that spirit, she has taught and lectured at colleges and universities throughout the United States on women's studies, Chicano and Chicana history, racism, multiculturalism, and Latin American issues. Currently, her efforts as cochair of the San Francisco Bay Area–based Institute for MultiRacial Justice are of primary importance to her.

Betita lives in the Mission District of San Francisco in a ground-floor apartment that allows her to have a garden; her dog, Xochitl; and sun. We enjoyed the fallen fruit from her plum tree. "I've always had a little piece of land wherever I lived," she said, "even in New York City. It must be some Mexican peasant ancestry of mine," she laughed. "But it's also about seeing things grow. And change. Some things survive, and some don't. There's that whole dynamic of being alive. I come out in the morning and ask the flowers, "How are you, and how are you, and how are you?"

Being Useful to Humanity

Here in the United States, I spent about ten years full-time in each of three movements: the black civil rights struggle, the Chicano *movimiento,* and the Left effort to build a revolutionary party. If you think about the 1960s, there was the anti–Vietnam War movement, the civil rights movement, the women's movement, later the gay and lesbian movement, the Asian American student movement, and, by the early seventies, the Native American movement. I was involved in several of them; it was impossible to be in one thing only. I think that explains where a lot of the energy came from, a lot of the commitment and the belief that we were changing society, making history. And sometimes we did.

In some important ways, today is very much like the period after Reconstruction in the South when so much that had been improved in the Reconstruction period was undone. Taking away our gains of the sixties and seventies is similar to how the gains of black people in the South were destroyed. Everything stopped for almost a hundred years. When you think about the time between the post-Reconstruction period [1880s and 1890s] and the 1960s, it's a very long stretch without much change in the racism of the country.

One of the things that can be an advantage about living to the age of seventy is that you see enough "two steps forward, one step back" that you don't think two steps forward is impossible. And you don't think one step back is the end of the world. Which is not to minimize the importance I place on young people who don't have that sense at all. To them, it's today or nothing, and that's fine—that energy is necessary. That impatience is necessary.

One of the great outcomes of the book *500 Years of Chicano History* and the video is that they put me in touch with high school and college students—primarily but not only Latinos and Latinas—all over the country. Some of them say that book is like a Bible. When the video came along, it brought me into contact with the northern California movement of Latino youth that exploded in 1993 and still goes on today. I do a lot of workshops with youth and talk with some of them about their ideas, their plans and problems, like the sexism some of the young activist women run into. They are so sharp. I feel like my motor is constantly running on their gasoline energy—they are the "tiger in my tank."

It's probably a characteristic of getting older that you start thinking more about the next generation of leadership, beyond your own. Which doesn't mean there's nothing left for you to do or teach or read or guide. One of the things I've tried to do in an organized way recently is combat prejudice between peoples of color. There's so much of that in the schools, and the kids hate it. They see people getting killed, even in their own families, their own neighborhoods, over interracial issues. They know we're not going to change our society with each group struggling all by itself. That's where the Institute for MultiRacial Justice project comes in—as a resource center to help build alliances among people of color.

We had a party when the first issue of the institute's newsletter *Shades of Power* came out, and a lot of students came. They sat down with the newsletter and started to read it. When have you ever seen kids come to a party and read?! But they loved the pictures. "Oh, look, there's Malcolm X with Fidel Castro. There's Huey Newton in China." The Asian kids got excited, and the black kids got excited, and the brown kids got all happy. It was seeing these images of people together who looked like them. That's one of the good things about living in California. You're not going to see so much diversity on the East Coast, not yet. So that's what I'm doing now, working on educational materials like videos that people can use in their own organization or school to try to break down some of the ignorance and divisions between peoples of color.

The most consistent thread in my activism has been fighting for racial justice, which doesn't mean negating the class and gender issues. They're all so interconnected. The struggle against sexism is profoundly entwined with the fight against racism. You cannot put them in separate boxes.

Sometimes life seems to come down to great simplicities, like figuring out how to be useful to humanity.

There is no personal romance in my life at the moment. I wouldn't mind it at all! I'd be happy with some kind of regular companion. I was married twice and had a daughter, Tessa, by my second husband. She and I have improved our relationship 100 percent in this past year. I'm so pleased with that and I'm embarrassed to tell you how simple it was. I just had to listen to her. That's all.

In the course of seeing a wonderful therapist, I mentioned that my relationship with my daughter was very bumpy. Tessa got angry at me in ways that I couldn't understand. So she and I went to see the therapist together for three visits, and everything changed. I cannot tell you how grateful I am for that. She just talked about what I did that bothered her.

Tessa had felt that she was never my priority during all those years of my activism, and a lot of resentment built up, which she'd never had a chance to air. So I had to listen and implement some of her requests. It was extraordinary. Recently, I blew it again. She told me about a role she didn't like performing in a play, and instead of just sympathizing, I tried to suggest an attitude or action that might help. She was angry, but the next morning she came back, which never would have happened before, and said, "I want you to understand what was wrong yesterday. I didn't want you to problem-solve; I just wanted you to let me cry on your shoulder."

So, lesson number 97Z. But what a difference it's made. It's like another relationship, all because I started to listen and try to change. It also shows what a great person Tessa is, because she really didn't want things to be the way they had been.

Now in my life, I want to do something different, original, peculiar, whatever. Sometimes I call it my trip to Bali, where I've never been. I've been around the world twice, but it's a long time since I've been immersed in a whole new reality. About two weeks ago in Mexico, I met some people from a bus drivers' union and from there went to a housing project of fifteen thousand poor families who had built their own homes. In both cases, the people involved were very committed, very anxious to create a project that would be cooperative and good for working people. I was taking notes like crazy and thought, "I've got to write an article about this." It feels so good to discover and write about people engaged in struggles that are inspiring and difficult.

Other times, I think I should just take dance classes. It may have to do with wanting some things for my personal development, which I never paid much attention to. Learning something new, acquiring a new skill, gaining exposure to new ways of life. New input—that's how I define my desire at times.

I don't think in terms of slowing down, but it might be true. My energy is pretty much the same, except I do take a half-hour nap on most days. I had two hips replaced—they wore out, so I got new ones, plastic. They can't be recycled! Most of the time, I don't even think about those hips, but then I go to do something strenuous, like picking these plums today, all bent over and it isn't so easy. The fact is that there are some limitations. On the one hand, you are as old as you feel; on the other hand, there are changes in the body.

The psychological changes, I think, are not understood at all. Everybody's personality is different, to begin with. My mother was a tennis player. She was ninety-four when she died; she never talked about aging. A few years after my father died, she had a new boyfriend. "I've been seeing Jim and he comes by after church," she told me. "Do you think it's all right for me to be seeing a younger man?" I asked, "How old is he?"

"Seventy-six," she answered. She was seventy-eight. "I think it's OK," I told her.

On the other hand, you can get into too much denial about your aging, which isn't healthy and can lead to disappointments. So I'm arguing for some kind of balance between feeling limited just by what the calendar says and denial of real changes. Probably more people make a mistake in the first direction: "Now I'm sixty-five, so I'll sit back and watch TV." I'm more in the denial department, with my mother.

A lot of people came to reject their sixties' dreams and sometimes totally betrayed them. This, I refuse to do. Nothing in the world is going to make me think we can't have a better world, a healthier one, in all sorts of ways.

In the course of the sixties and seventies, I defined myself as a socialist. So I went to see what socialism was like firsthand: to Cuba several times; to Hungary, Poland, and the Soviet Union, when I was an editor at Simon & Schuster; to Vietnam during the war and China after that war. I also went to see Nicaragua twice after the Sandinistas took over. There were many problems, but I still have a fundamental belief in the possibility of living under a different system from capitalism that would offer people more justice, more hope for life.

At the same time, I see the process of struggle in ways that I don't think I saw before. I was sometimes dogmatic. There were things that I ruled out of my life or other people's lives as being unimportant. A commitment to social justice is my bottom line, but it also has to take into account things like the human urge for spirituality. I came to see that it was wrong to think of the political and the spiritual as opposites. Both are crucial to human life.

One of the things I've also learned is that impatience is very healthy. We shouldn't be patient about human suffering. Every homeless person you see on the street is a reminder. We also need to keep up the energy to work for positive social change without getting overcome by the difficulties of it. Again, it's a kind of balance. Balance is crucial, but let's never be patient about human suffering. ❧

℣   *One of the more important things I've learned in my life is that I*
think you can only add to what you have already. It's very hard to
say, "I'm going to learn this to be a better person." I've learned
to be happy with what I'm doing, not to be ambitious for other
things. It's terrific not to want more. I'm quite full. I learned that
about myself.

INGE MORATH

 Inge Morath

Profile

Photographing a photographer can be a formidable endeavor. Especially when the photographer is an internationally known and celebrated one such as Inge Morath. "Our theory was that a photographer is an invisible person," she noted. "I mean, we had no interest in being seen. You want to be behind the lens. In other words, you are the observer. So now suddenly everybody gets grants to photograph a photographer, I mean, really, truly!" she told me in mock exasperation. I assured her that I'd photographed only one other photographer, Mary Ellen Mark, and that I didn't have a grant, although I had to admit I'd received an advance. "Did that count?" I wondered.

Inge's own mentor (whom she was the first to photograph) in her study of the art form was the French master Henri Cartier-Bresson, whom she met after she joined Magnum, the famous photographers' cooperative founded in Paris in 1947. As a result of a challenge to take photographs from Robert Capa (one of Magnum's founding members), she took her first series of pictures on a rainy day in Venice in 1951, where she was on a brief vacation with her first husband. She finally used the old Contax camera that had been her mother's scientific research tool in Germany. Inge had carried this camera for three years without ever taking a picture. But in Venice that winter, she looked through the viewfinder while "people, columns, pigeons presented themselves in a rhythm," and she pressed the shutter. She said, "It was instantly clear to me that from now on I would be a photographer. At last, I had found my language."

Inge was born in Graz, Austria, to loving parents who were both scientists, and she came of age in Europe during the rise of Hitler in the 1930s and during World War II. In a written lecture about her life, which she gave in Berlin for the Bertelsmann Publishing Company in 1994, Inge painted a poignant portrait of what it was like to be considered a "degenerate" intellectual and freethinker living in a totalitarian state under Fascism during her university years. Harrowing—even for a non-Jew. After the war, she lived in Vienna, London, and Paris where she wrote, translated, and edited for magazines. She soon fell in with the group at Magnum Photos, where her first responsibility was to edit contact sheets of the various traveling photographers in their absence, especially Cartier-Bresson. Inge recalled, "I think that in studying his way of photographing, I learned how to photograph before I ever took a camera into my hand."

Her new passion helped her leave a marriage "that had been kind of a mistake from the beginning." She bought a used Leica and sold some photos under the "unintentionally Swedish-sounding name of Egni Tharom"—her name nearly spelled backward.

For a fee of $100, Capa assigned to Inge the Concours des Roses in the Parc des Bagatelles, where she found "older gentlemen in dark suits judging roses, smelling them, scrutinizing shapes and sizes." At first, she could not feel enthusiastic about such an "unheroic theme." But it wasn't long before she began to trust her eyes and realized that "when you really start to look, all of life is interesting."

Inge traveled with Cartier-Bresson, mostly in Europe, as his researcher, translator, and apprentice. She found that they talked little about photography but a great deal about the paintings they viewed wherever they went (painting had been Cartier-Bresson's first love), about books and politics and the ideas of the surrealists, whose thinking had influenced him very much. It was an opportunity to "learn a lot from watching."

In the mid–1950s, three founding members of Magnum died in the service of their work. It was a devastating loss, but as Inge put it, "We went on working, determined to keep going in their spirit—to do good, responsible work; be tolerant of different ways of seeing; cherish friendship; and love life."

Known as a portrait photographer of artists, writers, and actors, Inge prepares for a meeting with her subject by looking at that person's paintings or sculptures, reading their books or plays, or viewing their films. She feels that it is important to be prepared, "as the encounter itself is short and spontaneous and a facial expression is as fleeting as a shadow. I need to photograph people in their places of work or where they live, in the surroundings they created for themselves, in the old quest of capturing something of their essence by inviting them to be themselves."

"One dreams of the pictures missed," she said, slightly forlorn.

In 1962, Inge married the American playwright Arthur Miller. Arthur has two children from his first marriage: a son and a daughter, who are both in their fifties. The son lives in California and worked with Arthur on the film version of *The Crucible*. The daughter lives very near Inge and Arthur in Connecticut and is married to the sculptor Tom Doyle. Inge seemed genuinely pleased when she said of the daughter and Tom, "They're both great friends of ours, which is marvelous." Together, Inge and Arthur also have a son, as well as a daughter, Rebecca, who is married to the British actor Daniel Day-Lewis.

Inge admitted that marriage and children disrupted her traveling days for a few years, but she soon found that photographic discoveries could be made in her own backyard. In a joint project, she combined her photographs with Arthur's text to produce *In the Country*, a book about life in rural Connecticut. Inge spoke eloquently about her life and work in collaboration with her husband: "A writer's rhythm is different. He takes his time to think and choose his words. For a photographer, a missed moment is lost forever. But over the years, Arthur's way of thinking about an event has helped me to find other ways of seeing."

When asked about her day, Inge noted, "I get up very early. I'm up at six, do my yoga, start my day at seven thirty." Discipline is written all over her. One has the sense with Inge that whatever needs to get done will get done—and well. This is a woman who, after all, speaks several languages: German, French, Spanish, and Italian. She noted matter-of-factly, "I learned Romanian, a language with a Latin base and a Slav syntax, as a base for Russian. Then I learned Russian, which I love for the poetry. And Mandarin I learned in order to travel in China. I speak in those languages all the time with different people, and I read them, too. But from those I can actually understand many others." A knowledge of this many languages in one brain and on one tongue makes for an idiosyncratic mélange of accents and an utterly charming syntax, which Inge has.

She considers herself "a jack of all trades" and laughed at the memory of having to videotape an interview with Arthur because he didn't want the television crew and equipment all over the house. Just that morning, she had looked over some French translations of his plays and proofread them for him.

As I photographed Inge, I told her that there was something of the French actress Jeanne Moreau in her own dimpled smile and in the mischievous slant of her head. Of course, she knows Jeanne Moreau and burst out with, "I love Jeanne Moreau. She's a great artist. She's wonderful." Inge's enthusiasm for nearly every subject is infectious and accounts for her frequent use of superlatives and the overemphasis in her descriptions.

A slender, well-toned woman, her body speaks of years of training in yoga and the physical discipline inherent in the life of a photographer. Some people have a certain energy, a kinetic quality that simply makes them different. It's hard to describe, but it's palpable, and you feel it when you see such a person. Inge is one of those people.

We were in the midtown apartment that she and Arthur use when they are in New York City. Many of the objects in the living room have followed her from previous lives—both hers and theirs. The Spanish table she sat on was from the sixteenth century; decades ago, it was in her Paris apartment. "It's a beauty, isn't it," she marveled, stroking the wood as if it were the flesh of a beloved. "I love my little Catalan Madonna," she said of the sculpture that met her at eye level. "She has a beautiful smile. I haven't looked at her up close in a while. The little Jesus, the wood Jesus, has a great face."

"Be careful," Inge warned me, as I moved a ceramic platter across the table. "That's Picasso!" Not only does she have a Picasso—she knew Picasso. Hers has been a life filled with the notorious and the notable, and she has photographed most of them.

"Where is your hand from?" I inquired of the carved, well-patinated wooden hand that she wore around her neck on a gold chain. It was a gift from Arthur, one he made himself. "He does carpentry, too," Inge said, proudly. "He has a very good sense of proportion, which has also to do with playwriting—an economy of language in dialogue. He would be a very good sculptor if he put his mind to it."

It is fitting that a woman who has made her life's work through her hands prizes reproductions of them. "I love hands. I have a big collection of Buddha hands, and all kinds from around the world. But this one is my favorite. It is Arthur's hand."

A Certain Kind of Energy

I don't think about age terribly much. I don't mind getting older; you just have to. I have wonderful women in my family. My mother was great. She died at age ninety-six, two years ago. She just lived with what counts. She was a scientist, a brilliant woman. When my father died at sixty-nine, which was relatively young, I said to my mother, "Why don't you live with us?" Because my parents were very, very close, I didn't see her living alone. They married when they were twenty-two, had worked together all their lives, and they were really in love. So she decided that she would spend most of the summers with us. It was marvelous to be with her. Arthur and she were great friends, and for Rebecca, my daughter, to have an older woman of such vivacity around was very important.

You know, you get older, and you have to make all these decisions: Do you dye your hair, or don't you dye your hair? Do you get facelifts? I just decided to do nothing, because I think you make your own face. People can look wonderful with facelifts, but somehow or other then you have to work on it all the time. Soon it sags, and you have to go again. I can't see myself going to the hairdresser all the time, either. And then you have the crisis that they can't match your color. I sometimes listen to these conversations when I get my hair cut. "They stopped making number fifty-nine. This one is more pink!" It's a constant drain on your nerves. So we had a big conference with Arthur and Rebecca, and they said, "No, don't dye your hair," so that settled that. It started going gray in my fifties. It goes gradually, but you have to make up your mind.

So I'm for facelifts, but not for myself. I mean, then what do you do about your elbows? And your hands? You can't wear gloves all the time! You can exercise. I'm a big yoga practitioner—for decades—because I like the balance. I think you just have to admit to the fact that age is advancing, and there's not really much you can do.

As a European, I see this as much more of an American obsession. But the Russian women have the most facelifts! Already in 1989, everybody was having facelifts. I said, "Why on earth do you have so many facelifts?" It's cheap, but they're usually not very fantastic. In France I'm sure people have facelifts, but Arthur is always amazed at the elegance of the older women who still command a certain attention of men. Their whole being is graceful. They are not just a face. You see, here, in America, because of these myths you have, people start to efface themselves as they age. They can't face their physical changes. It's sad.

I think actually your inner strength has to do with your work. If you have a creative life, you are more concerned about other things than how you look. As you age, you become a lot clearer about yourself. Health is the most important blessing. And if you are lucky and have wonderful friends who stay with you and were with you all your life, there are marvelous things about getting older. It was wonderful that my mother lived with us at the end of her life.

Now I like to cook. I never cooked before I was married. I swore I would never cook, because I thought it was just women's slavery. I lived alone in Paris for many years. I had a wonderful maid who cooked, so it didn't occur to me. But then I married Arthur, and American life is very different from European life. First we lived in the Chelsea Hotel. Then when Rebecca was born, we lived more and more in Arthur's country house. Then he cooked, but I don't eat meat, and all he could do was steaks! So I got my maid from Paris to come, but she didn't like it in America, so she went back. Then somebody gave me a cookbook. The trouble is, cookbooks don't tell you how long anything takes to do. Finally, Arthur's sister gave me *The Joy of Cooking,* which was brilliant because it does tell you, more or less. The other thing is, I think if you've eaten in a lot of good restaurants, you have one leg up, because you can kind of reproduce dishes you liked.

So the gifts of age . . . I think you know more or less what you want. You know what you can do. If you have any talent, it helps, because you have embarked on the way toward realizing it, and you try to finish the things that you started. This is quite wonderful. I'm doing now a big story on New York. I worked in New York in the early fifties. It's great now to go back and do this again in the nineties.

It's Magnum's fiftieth anniversary this year, so each one of us had to have a special project. I'm fascinated by India and was going to go back there. Then I thought I really should do something here where I am. New York has changed. It's quite wonderful now. It's really the center of the arts in many ways. I am pleased that I can do this now thirty-five years later. I did the same thing with the River Danube. In the 1950s, I did the whole Danube from the Black Forest to the Black Sea, because to me it's the central European river. It goes through Germany, Austria, Yugoslavia, Hungary, between Romania and Bulgaria, and ends in the Black Sea, so it really does include all the civilizations from the Celtic to the Gothic to the Byzantine. It has everything. My Austrian publishers asked me in the early nineties if I had any project I wanted to do. I said, "Yes, I want to finish the Danube essay." I finished the book last year. So somehow I ended up doing things I started and did in the beginning of my career but felt that they weren't altogether finished. Which is kind of great.

One thing about aging—I think you feel the pressure of time more, and also I seem to be more busy than ever. I used to sit around in cafés in Paris, but I think it's also living in America—you're always busy. It seems to be part of the culture. That's why I like the contrast between New York City and the country. I do my own work in the country, but I also plant a vegetable garden. Contemplation can be combined with doing something, and gardening is perfect. It's very rewarding, and it's beautiful.

One of the more important things I've learned in my life is that I think you can only add to what you have already. It's very hard to say, "I'm going to learn this to be a better person." I think I've learned to be happy with what I'm doing, not to be ambitious for other things. I think it's terrific not to want more. I'm quite full. I learned that about myself. I always shared my life with people I like. But I also need a certain amount of being alone, which comes with my work. I work at home, but on most of my big working trips, I was alone.

In terms of my own mortality, when it's time to die, I'd like to have a quick death. That's all you can ask for. Long illness is the one thing you would like to avoid. If you do any meditation, you always think about death, so that's not a fear for me. It's part of life. There are actually lots of exercises you can do to relieve those fears. That's why I like the Far East. Their whole way of looking at life is so different, and I naturally like to be involved in that way of thinking.

Back to the question of age, it's funny—you don't think of your age; you don't. I celebrate my birthday. I don't lie about my age, because you have to remember too many dates. Why bother!? Arthur has a wonderful story about Stella Adler, who was a famous actress. So was her mother. Somebody said to her mother, "How old are you?" She said, "Sixty-two." And the interviewer said, "Well, your daughter Stella is sixty." She said, "That's her business!" I think you give that up. It frees your mind for more important things. The war was when the war was; that doesn't change. You did things at certain times, so it's important to keep your dates straight. But it's tempting, OK?

What do I want to do with my remaining years? Certainly to work as long as I can and then just plant gardens. I don't really see myself at a hundred. No, I don't think so. I don't think anybody makes it to a hundred in any comfort. It just happens. You can't think about it so much. If it happens, you hope you're in good health so you're not a burden on other people. That's the one thing I would just hate. I'd rather kill myself than just become some vegetable. I have all these living wills. But it's very hard in this society to have even that executed.

I use natural light. I think as long as I can see, I can photograph. The films are very sensitive nowadays. Occasionally, I've used a flash. But only when I really want to make a statement, "This is kind of artificial." Natural light is endlessly varied. See these flowers, for example—how different they look. One is in front of a wall, and the other is not, so the natural light by itself gives them totally different characteristics, and I like to find those rather than impose something else.

With a camera, what you basically do is to give form to a situation. With your own eyes and your own mind, you take out a moment. That becomes the picture. That's the endless fascination, because life is interesting. People's faces are interesting. There is something to see every minute. I don't set things up. Portraits are different; they are an encounter by mutual consent. Otherwise, I just photograph what I see.

That brings up photographing people without their approving of it. To photograph a person is a kind of relating. For example, I worked in Iran, which was very difficult. But I had a Polaroid camera in the fifties, which was just new, and I gave that instant picture to the people I photographed. Often, I had to give them a very good picture, but they let me do what I wanted. They didn't think the other camera was interesting at all. They were fascinated with that Polaroid. Also, I wore a chador to hide my cameras. To go with shorts in a country where the women are totally covered is kind of disrespectful.

I spent time in China. I learned Mandarin for that purpose, which took several years, but it made a lot of difference, because you've invested something in their civilization, in their culture, in their way of thinking. They do appreciate this effort. On account of this, you really get better work done.

Three years ago I went to Bhutan, and as for every big working trip, I prepared myself thoroughly. I read what I could about the country, the people, their religion. When you photograph a country and its people, you should at least have something inside as a foundation. You don't want to just go there and snap around. I would find that kind of unsatisfying.

My definition of *success?* There are two definitions. One, for me, is when I've done a job well, when I think I did it well, even if people don't see it right away. Then, actually it's very nice if you have the other kind of success, where you get wonderful reviews and people love your books—the success of acclaim. The best is when, over the years, the work you did and were satisfied with remains valid. This is the nice thing about having a longish life.

I never needed much reassurance. If you need a lot of reassurance, it's hard. I think that comes because my parents were great. I don't know that I needed to be reassured about anything, but then I was pretty stubborn! That's very important. You can get depressed. You can get angry. You can get all kinds of things, but if you arrive at a certain kind of harmony within yourself, you can get rid of those feelings. You know how to.

Photography demands discipline. Bodily discipline, because you have to be in really good shape to do the running around and the carrying. The discipline of taking care of your working tools.

Who were my influences? Cartier-Bresson, of course, is an artist who had a major influence on me. Louise Bourgeois is immensely inspiring. I love her work. I have photographed her over the years; I really follow her. I think friendship influences you; you become friends with people, because there is something in them that attracts you and that may in some way have influence on you. I didn't pick out role models. I like Madame de Stael. Lou Salome. A certain type of independent women. I work well with women. But I also like men a lot. I guess the role models who were around were the women who wrote novels and women who were themselves, I suppose. The wife of Alexander Calder, Luisa, had no profession, but she was wonderful. She ran a great house, she was inspiring, she was fun, and that's also something important. She had an enjoyment of life and liked to see other people enjoy life.

So . . . about marriage. We have mastered the art of being a couple. Arthur has a great sense of humor, which is wonderful. And because we work on different things, there are always subjects to talk about. There's an exchange all the time. It's never boring. I think boredom is an enemy of marriage. I have a profession and my own work. When Rebecca was little, I took her everywhere with me. I didn't leave her if my profession demanded it. Instead of going to Timbuktu, I photographed Connecticut. So she was part of everything. When I am with Arthur, we talk about what we see and discuss ideas: "You should look at that, and you should try and capture that." And I tell him, you should "see that." Basically, I think we're having fun. I'm lucky I live with a very interesting man.

If you don't have that, if your husband is a businessman and you wait around for him to come home and to tell you everything about his day, it will be tough. It's hard to come home from a trip and right away tell everything. It happens that nothing comes to mind. Then friends come two weeks later, and you're full of tales.

The advice I would have for women about aging is, "Don't panic about your age. Be yourself the best you can. Because if you aren't yourself, you are nothing. Be yourself, whichever shape or size you are." ✑

I don't judge things in nature. Old is not bad, blooming is not good. It's just the natural cycle, the way things are. I find peace with my aging process by looking at the cycles of the seasons, the cycles of birth and death and decay. This is how I prepare for my own life, and also for my death.

ANNA HALPRIN

Anna Halprin

🌿 Profile

The choreographer and teacher Anna Halprin believes that movement is an expression of the life force, that movement and dance have a magical power to renew, inspire, teach, create, transform, and heal. And when you are in her presence, you have no doubt that she is right. Anna's diminutive body is kinetic, the expression in her flashing blue eyes electric. She is both a wise crone and a childlike pixie.

Anna has been a pioneer in dance and New Theater. Her work has influenced theater, dance, and centers for enhancing growth around the world and blends ancient traditions, contemporary issues, and aesthetics. She is the founder of the San Francisco Dancers' Workshop, the co-founder of the Tamalpa Institute, and the author of several books on dance and healing: *Movement Rituals; Moving Toward Life: Five Decades of Transformational Dance;* and *Dance as a Healing Art.* Her numerous honors and awards include choreographer fellowships from the National Endowment for the Arts, a Guggenheim Fellowship, and the American Dance Guild Award for outstanding contributions in the field of dance. In 1997, the American Dance Festival gave her a lifetime achievement award in modern dance, the most prestigious American distinction in her field.

During her nearly sixty years as a dancer, Anna has developed an approach to dance that is a powerful tool for integrating personal and artistic development. Because she is convinced that everyone has the natural gift for dance, she has developed a process by which everyone can cultivate a natural sense of creativity through movement. Her approach emphasizes and revitalizes the whole person through the integration of the physical, emotional, mental, and spiritual dimensions. Anna's work is noted for its use of personal and collective myths and rituals and for large-scale community participation in both the creation and performance of dance. She is one of the first artists in the contemporary Western world to use dance as both a healing and a performing art.

As part of her research in dance as a healing art, Anna has directed "Moving Toward Life" for people challenging cancer, "Positive Motion" for men challenging HIV or AIDS, and "Women with Wings" for women challenging HIV or AIDS. For the last decade, she has created and led "Circle the Earth: Dancing with Life on the Line," a contemporary community dance ritual, using what she calls the Life/Art Process; the art confronts a community's real-life issues. In 1989, "Circle the Earth" was danced by more than a hundred people, and it focused on the issue of AIDS. "Circle the Earth," which has been renamed "The Planetary Dance," is now danced each year on Easter Sunday in thirty-seven countries on six continents.

In northern California, Anna lives with her husband of fifty-eight years, noted architect Lawrence Halprin. Their home is integrated into the sensual surroundings of the Marin County landscape, which, Anna said, has become her "theater." As we sat in a circle of giant oak trees on the Halprins' deck and overlooked the sacred mountain range of Mount Tamalpais, we listened to birdsong and were intermittently interrupted by Bear, Anna's black ten-year-old retriever-lab mix, who begged for our attention. It became difficult to distinguish among the fully integrated human, animal, and geographic landscapes. Anna observed, "I've found much inspiration in the way nature operates. The more I study nature, the more contact I have with the life force."

Anna is convinced that dance helped save her life in 1972 when she was diagnosed with colon cancer. She vividly explained to me how, after surgery, she used the arts as a psychological aid to recovery. Although Anna makes no claim that her work can extend the lives of seriously ill people, she is convinced that it can transform the quality of life.

As a sort of personal credo, Anna told me, "I envision a future where more of us call ourselves dancers and work together to make art concerned with the primary issues of life. I envision a future where dance is once again honored for its power to inspire, teach, transform, and heal. I envision a future in which all people dance together, where the circle is large enough for people of any color, culture, or spiritual practice. I envision a future when we will be asked to join the four-legged and winged creatures, instead of asking them to join us. We will dance with the mountains, the ocean, the sun, the moon, and in the forests. I invite you to join me in this quest."

Embodying Nature

Sometimes I see my life as divided into two sections, with my experience of cancer being the line between them. When I look at my life in that way, I can see how much I changed when I was forced to face my own mortality. I can also see two important strands of my life—work and family—weaving together in a new way. The experience of a life-threatening illness can bring about awareness at gunpoint. During the first half of my life, which I spent as an avant-garde dancer, I used my life in the service of my art. After I had cancer, I began to use my art in the service of life. This was a major shift in my motivation, my intention, and my perception of the world. I stopped playing the role of the contrary, who took actions to break down already existing boundaries. Instead, I became deeply involved in creating a useful art, one that would serve people in their lives and that had the capacity to create real change by approaching the boundaries of isolation and suffering that affect us all.

The early part of my life work had to do with opening up a larger perspective of dance. My collaborators and I questioned who dance was for, the role of the dancer, the role of the audience, and what actions we could call "dance." This trajectory often created unexpected humor, as well as moments of outrage. One example of this occurred in Rome in 1965. An Italian man in the audience became so exasperated with our performance that he marched down the aisle, stood right in front of the stage, and shouted, "For this, Columbus had to discover America?" He then stomped out of the theater, as the audience began to laugh and shout. Everybody thought this was wonderful. I couldn't ignore the outburst; I began to confront the audience right there. After this experience, a question began to play around the corners of my mind: How can I use the energy of the audience, rather than ignoring it? This inquiry led me in many different directions but ended up in a place I could not have imagined in that moment.

Another time during the same period, my company performed at the University of California at Berkeley. During our performance, a woman from the audience rushed up on stage, picked up a lantern (our sole light), and crashed it against a scaffold. The lantern broke, and the glass scattered, cutting one of the dancers and drawing blood. Then the woman ran up the aisle, smashed into the exit door, knocked herself over, fumbled with the door, and fled into the night. Twenty years later, I met somebody who'd been at that performance. He said it had been so startling and seemed so real. He thought the woman had been part of the piece!

Experiences like these fed my imagination and my intellect. I began to think about the relationship of the performer to the audience, as I was already thinking about the relationship of life to art. I sensed a hidden potential that I did not yet know how to tap. It was as if I had been handed a map that was written in a foreign language, marking the territory of an unknown place. I had the map but didn't know how to read it.

During this time and through our experiments, the dancer became a real person who could move, talk, make music, have feelings, and tell a story. Ultimately, I was interested in returning dance to the people and to its ancient communal origins, but I can only say that now, in hindsight. As I did all of this, I was following my heart, and my mind, and the momentum of the times. This was the 1960s, and boundaries of all sorts were being challenged. The structure of North American culture was changing.

I pursued a holistic approach to art. Not only did I seek to integrate my life into my art, but I sought to integrate the artist with her culture. I substituted regular clothes for leotards and tights and real-life issues for made-up stories. All of the artists I worked with shared their mediums with one another. We exchanged roles in order to expand our vocabularies and in order to identify more fully with one another. Performances took place anywhere—a street corner, a sandy beach, a forest, or a bus stop. The boundaries between real life and theater became blurred. I was quite young and innocent; I had no idea that my approach could stir up a controversy.

The holistic approach I was pursuing in my art was also reflected in the multiple roles I was playing in my life: wife, daughter, mother, teacher, dancer, choreographer, administrator, etcetera. This was not easy and, in retrospect, I think it was both a blessing and a curse for my family. It was a blessing because our life was full of excitement and richness. It was a curse because we were not in alignment with other families. My daughters grew up in a truly alternative environment. One of them said to me in later life that it was like growing up in a circus family. In other words, we were a bit freaky. I don't know what I could have done differently. I was obsessed with being the kind of dancer I was, but I wanted the other parts of life, too. This is the other way my life has been split—between the demands and desires for family and for work. Perhaps the expectations around women and their role as wives, mothers, and career people have been altered considerably in past decades, but in my own life, trying to have it all hasn't always been easy. I won't say it hasn't been worthwhile, because it has, but neither could I say it has been easily won.

I've been married for fifty-eight years to the same man. At a recent awards ceremony honoring both my husband and myself, when I told the audience we'd been married that long, everyone started to clap. I was amazed. In this day and age, I guess it's unusual for marriages to last so long, but among my peers, this is more or less the way it is. We grew up anticipating that marrying someone meant marrying them for life, and that is what so many of us have done. Still, it isn't simple to stay with one person for that long, and every marriage has its own kind of stresses and challenges.

I was nineteen when I met Larry, and he was twenty-three. We were attracted to each other for various reasons. We had a lot in common and ultimately a lot to teach one another. He was from New York, and I was amazed to find out that he was versed in dance. We were both Zionists. When we met, he was a painter, but he was also studying horticulture. At one point, he became very unhappy, and I brought him to Taliesin West, Frank Lloyd Wright's center, and he said, "Wow, I'm going to become an architect." Which he did. Sharing that brought us even closer. We've had more commonalities than differences in our fifty-eight years of marriage. We have grown together, our ideas emerged together, we've worked together, and we've supported one another's work.

I think our marriage has lasted and will continue to last because we like each other. We don't always get along, but we have a commitment to one another. We are both dedicated to our family, we come from the same Russian Jewish background, and we remain close to our cultural roots. We share similar interests as artists. He is an environmental architect and has approached his work with a broad scope and tremendous creativity. We have engaged in many creative projects together. Larry developed a process called the RSVP Cycles and wrote a book that describes this method for generating creativity [*The RSVP Cycles: Creativity in the Human Environment*]. For many years, this work has profoundly influenced the way I teach and choreograph. Larry and I have collaborated on many different projects together, and we support one another in the development of our respective careers. My work and my life would have been entirely different if I had not been married to Larry. When I think about the synergistic way in which our lives have evolved, I am so grateful and amazed.

Larry is eighty-two years old and hasn't slowed down one bit. This influences our lifestyle. He has no intention of retiring and, at the moment, neither do I. We have the same taste in where and how we live. We have shared a beautiful house nestled on the hillside of Mount Tamalpais just across the Golden Gate Bridge from San Francisco for over fifty years. This is the house where we raised our family and where we continue to welcome our grandchildren and our friends. Below our house is an indoor dance studio with a bridge leading to an outdoor dance deck where I dance surrounded by redwood trees, accompanied by the sound of birds and the light of the open sky. Larry designed this studio for me. This is the place where most of my work unfolded over the years. Larry and I share another home on the northern California sea coast, part of the Sea Ranch development, which Larry designed. It is one of the most beautiful and relaxing places I know. I love to stay there and walk along the beach with Bear, listening to the satisfying sounds of the ocean waves. I have brought groups of students and colleagues to the Sea Ranch over the last twenty-five years, and together we have danced in the environment of fog, wind, and sea. Some of the most ecstatic moments in my personal life and my life as a dancer have taken place at the Sea Ranch.

My family has always been my center, and I have felt so blessed by all the members of our small tribe. I always tried to incorporate them into whatever I was doing. I also created my work with my children in mind. I always incorporated my daughters into my performances, and together with my company, we toured around the world. We visited Venice and Rome and traveled to Poland and Sweden, as well. There was something remarkable about being able to continue on the path of my work and to have my children be part of this dream.

I was fortunate to have the studio beneath my house where I could work and still be close to my children. I taught children's dance classes for twenty-five years so I could teach dance to my children. My kids grew up around many other kids, sharing the joys of expressive movement and the beginnings of lifelong friendships. The children's classes, which were run as part of the Marin Dance Cooperative, were organized by the parents of the children who participated in the classes. I've always dreamed of a community in which dance would be an expression of its primary values. I wanted to live and participate in such a community. I've been nostalgic about American Indian tribal life because in that culture, mothers, fathers, children, and grandparents all dance together to celebrate, pray, and socialize. In that culture, dance is for everyone, and it takes place in the central plaza of the community. I have always wanted to live a life where dance was not just meant to be beautiful but was an integral part of life. Some of this took place through the Marin Dance Cooperative. All generations participated—girls and boys and their parents. Each spring, a grand celebration of creativity, community spirit, and celebration took place in a community center, followed by a feast in an outdoor setting. These were beautiful times, and in a way, my inspiration to be a mother fed my inspiration to be a dancer, and they came together in a happy union.

The better part of my life has been secure and exciting and filled with a great deal of joy. That is not to say that I do not struggle with my shadow. I have used my art to escape a confrontation with the terror of my own dark side and to avoid the monsters of my life. I am afraid I have always done this. My art has been both a blessing and a curse, a perfect and often inspiring outlet for my emotional needs, but one which has not always served my personal life. I have built a wonderful fantasy world around me, but my real world is often in turmoil. I have heard myself say a million times, "I wish I would take the time to experience and apply the Life/Art Process to my own life," but rarely do I allow myself the time. As effective as I have been in the dance world, I have been ineffective at times in my personal life. But I am lucky that I always had a creative process that I could use to engage with my dark side. Even today, at the age of seventy-eight, I still devote time to using the artistic and creative processes I have developed to work on my own personal issues. I enjoy getting together regularly with a group of artists and colleagues to continue to work with myself through the art process.

Here's an example of how I continue to discover truths about myself, others, and the world around me through dance. Currently, I've been exploring my aging process by designing scores (improvisational dances guided by specific directions) that require an investigation around this theme. Recently, I designed a score with an intimate group of colleagues in which we each made a time line of the high and low points in our lives. Then we set a floor plan creating a path on which we would each journey. One by one, we danced our time lines. The person just before me was a younger woman. During her dance, the long branch she was carrying broke. When my turn came, I picked up her broken branch and carried it on my journey. This simple action triggered an association to my sister who had died before I was born. For the first time in my life, I experienced the emotional impact of her death, and I danced the loss of my unknown sister, a grief I had hidden away inside of me for all of these years. The deep underpinnings of our psyches move us sometimes in ways we cannot expect. At the age of seventy-eight, I am discovering more and more about the personal myth that I have been carrying around since I was born and that has so fully shaped my personality. This wasn't a sad experience for me. It was deeply satisfying to feel I could complete something unresolved in my life. As I get older, it seems more and more important to find rituals that complete unresolved situations and that help me come to a greater sense of peace. It was such a relief to make this connection and to be able to dance it out. I feel so fortunate that I have dance as a way to experience this kind of awareness.

This reminds me of a time I spent with my father near the end of his life. When I was a child, he used to tell us stories of how he escaped Russia during the time of the pogroms. It was a story filled with hiding in attics and late-night border crossings. He always made it seem very adventurous and romantic. But on that day, when he was an old man and I was a grown woman, he told me the story again. This time, he cried and said, "I was just a little boy, and I was so scared. It was terrible." We held hands, and he cried some more. I understood my father's story better, and as he cried, I realized he had made contact with that small part of himself and had completed and come to peace with a part of his life that had haunted him.

I had a rare experience of completion with my mother and father before they died that has stayed with me ever since. I was commissioned by a conference called "A Celebration of Life!" to make a dance ritual dealing with the aging process. The theme I selected was the coming together of the generations. I wanted to place the elders in the context of their whole life, rather than separating them out as old people. I interviewed all the people who would participate in this ritual, and I asked them about the most important thing in their life, right now, at this time and at this age. I tape-recorded all of their responses. Then I created an activity in which people of increasing ages, starting with a mother and her six-month-old baby and leading up to the eldest among us, made a procession up to a figure on the stage who was turning continuously. She turned continuously for forty-five minutes while each age group did the dance they had created. As each group left the stage, another age group would begin.

Finally, the people in their sixties or older came up on stage. This included my father, who was in a wheelchair, and my mother, who was beside him. In his interview, my father had said that the most important thing in his life was love. He had said, "Now, I love all of you children, but Ida (his wife), I love her with my soul." He had gone on to say, "I haven't been out of this wheelchair in two years, but when I go up on that stage and do this performance, and when I hear what I've said, I'm going to get up and dance with Ida." And sure enough, when the time came and he heard his recorded words say, "I love her with my soul," he managed to get out of his wheelchair, call my mother to his side, and dance with her for a few steps before he sank back into his chair. I felt so good about having offered my father, through dance, the possibility of being witnessed in this final tribute to his wife.

When I came home from the hospital after my cancer operation, I honestly didn't know whether I wanted to live or die. At this time of confusion and pain, I had a rather mystical experience. I was in a daze, and a bird came to me. I was very frightened, because I thought it was the angel of death. In Jewish mythology, a bird comes at the time of death to take you back to Zion. I remember negotiating with this bird. Suddenly, I wanted to live. A great feeling came surging through my body, and I

remember communicating through my imagination to the bird. I said
I wasn't ready to leave this earth and that I needed to find more ways to
experience giving and receiving love. I made the bird a promise that I
would do this if I were to live. This experience epitomizes for me the
drive I have to continue in this path of mine, giving and receiving love
with my family and the people with whom I work, trying to move more
deeply into the power of love. Dance has proven to be the surest channel I
have for sharing my love with the people around me.

It was ultimately my experience with cancer that led me to a greater
understanding of how to use dance as a way to create healing and awareness in my life. When I was told I had cancer, I was terrified. I was taken
hold of, shaken, and pinned against a red-hot brick wall. No escape. I had
to confront the monster or die. I chose to fight for my survival. But my
initial reaction was to go numb, deaf, and blind. The doctor recited a litany
of statistics, and I blindly marched to the sound of his drum. I have never
been so passive in my art. In real life, I froze. I was so out of touch with
the situation that I went to a party on the same day I checked into the
hospital. I had an exploratory operation that would seal my fate, and
a radical operation that would alter my body forever, but in the face of
this, my only comment as I was wheeled into the operating room was,
"This is going to be the greatest performance of my life." Even as I was
about to face my own mortality, my first reaction was to use my art as a
form of denial, as a way to avoid life.

While it's not unusual to be stricken with cancer these days, the cir-
cumstance of my diagnosis was unusual. I have always been concerned
with the relationship between the mind and the body. Before the time of
my diagnosis, I had been exploring the use of imagery as a way of making
that link. I found it wasn't enough to create images in the mind's eye; I
wanted people to draw their own images, reflect upon them, and begin to
learn physically the language of these images. This process of connecting
with our internal imagery involved "dancing" the images that welled up
from the unconscious as another way of connecting the mind and the
body. It became clear that in learning this imagistic language, I was receiving messages from an intelligence within my body, an intelligence deeper

and more unpredictable than anything I could understand through rational thought.

While I was participating in what I termed the Psychokinetic Visualization Process, I drew an image of myself that I was unable to dance. This was a signal to me. Why couldn't I dance it? What was blocking me? I had drawn a round, gray ball in my pelvic area. I intellectualized that it was an embryo and romanticized that it was pointing the way to new beginnings. But some part of me was sure that this approach to my drawing was nonsense, because I couldn't put the drawing into motion. That night, when my mind was quiet, I had intimations that the image I had drawn had something to tell me, and that I was not listening.

The next day I made an appointment with my doctor. I asked him to examine me precisely where I had drawn this round ball. He diagnosed cancer. I went through the traditional operation procedures, and radical ones at that, which altered my body for life, leaving me uncertain about my future. Would I ever dance again? The doctor assured me I was just fine, which was funny, because I didn't feel fine! He also added that if I didn't have a recurrence within five years, I would be out of the woods. Three years after my operation, I had a recurrence. I knew then that I was going to have to make some very drastic changes in my life.

I chose to use the process I had been teaching in class to meet the challenge of my illness. I decided to draw a self-portrait and prepared myself to dance it. When I first drew myself, I made myself look "perfect." I was young and brightly colored. My hair was blowing in the wind. I was the picture of health and vitality. When I looked at the picture after drawing it, I knew I couldn't even begin to dance it; it just didn't feel like me. I turned the paper over and furiously began to draw another image of myself. It was black and angular and angry and violent. I knew that this back-side image of me was the dance I had to do. When I did it, I was overwhelmed by the release of rage and anger. I kept stabbing at myself and howling like a wounded animal. Witnesses said it sounded like I spoke in tongues. I had to have witnesses, because I knew that unless I did, I would never be able to go through this ordeal. My witnesses were my family, my colleagues, and my students, and they kept me honest, urging me to go deeper, reinforcing my sounds, calling out parts of the picture I was to dance. I danced until I was spent, and I collapsed and began to sob with great relief. Now I was ready to turn the picture over and dance the healing image of myself.

As I danced this image, I imagined that my breath was water and that my movements flowed through my body just as water would flow. I imagined the water was cleansing me. I had an image of water cascading over the mountains near my home and of the water flowing through me and out to the endless vastness of the sea, taking with it my illness. The movements of this dance started soft and small, and as I continued to dance, I added sounds from my voice. My witnesses again reinforced these sounds as the movements grew and grew, until my whole body was engaged in the image of cascading water. When I finished, I invited my witnesses to join me in a circle; I felt ready to return to my friends and family.

Soon after this experience, my cancer went into remission and has never reappeared. I don't tell this story to say that this is a way to cure yourself of cancer or that if you do this process, you will be healed. Rather, I tell the story because it was a miraculous and mysterious thing that happened to me and because I believe that the process I went through can be applied to many other experiences and provide much insight. I tell this story to encourage others to reach out and try some of these things. The expressive arts are a joyful and satisfying way to live your life, whether or not you are facing a crisis.

Much later, when I was developing theory and methods to apply to my art, I saw how this experience was the source of a healing process I had begun to identify. This experience gave me a new way of looking at healing, which I have used ever since as a guide to working with people with life-threatening conditions and in larger community contexts, in the form of rituals and group healings. In 1981, I began to apply this process to a whole community of people. I began to create large-scale rituals that addressed the different needs of the communities with which I worked, and I always applied this process of drawing and dancing as a way to generate what I call "resources." By 1989, one of the largest experiments using this process had evolved into "Circle the Earth: Dancing with Life on the Line," a large-group dance for and by people challenging AIDS and cancer. This piece, in which over a hundred people participated, was one community's response to the isolation and suffering caused by the AIDS crisis.

I've been grateful for all the wounds in my life, as well as the gifts. All of it is a great teacher. The journey to my own dark side gave rise to a form of dance that encourages and enables everyone to be a dancer. I reject any style that is not inclusive. One principle of postmodern dance is the use of everyday, pedestrian movement. This grew out of the philosophy that everyone has the right to dance. I began to create an approach to movement that was free from the artificial armor separating the heroes from the nonheroes. Everyone can become a hero. I began to create an approach to movement that gave people a place to be seen and to reveal themselves. Everyone needs to be seen and respected. I began to work with the emotional body. We need to know what people feel. I began to ask people to tell the true stories from their lives, rather than asking the imagination to make something up. People's lives are interesting—we need to listen to one another's real-life stories. And I began to want to hear from everyone, because I realized that everyone has a voice. My confrontation with death defined all of this for me, and I began to take this philosophy and apply it to my work in dance.

Creating movement that is based on people's individual responses, rather than a preconceived style, allows for open participation from all sorts of people, regardless of their backgrounds or social identification. It provides a forum for a cultural exchange and reciprocity that is impossible if I impose certain kind of movements on people. In this regard, a turning point in my career and personal life was the work I did with a group of black and white dancers. Our first piece, "Ceremony of Us," was a response to the Watts riots in Los Angeles in 1965. To make this piece, I worked with the group of black people in Watts and the group of white people in San Francisco. After nine months, I brought the two groups together, and we made a dance based on our real-life relationships among people in the two groups.

This experience was such an eye-opener for me. The battle between the white dancers and the black dancers, and my own unconscious bias, created an intense learning environment. The piece expanded my vision of dance, sharpened my awareness of my own prejudice, and completely changed my perspective of the world. I was made conscious of things I had never realized, and I learned something about dignity, soul, and passion in this process, which has enriched my life ever since. As I opened to people's differences, I became more compassionate and open personally, and this dance practice allowed us all to be more compassionate and open aesthetically. This was the beginning of my multiracial company, which I worked with for well over a decade. Even today, when I meet up with the people who worked with me on this piece, I am amazed by the deep feeling of recognition and family that still exists between us. In my own family, my grandchildren are themselves a model of intermarriage and ethnic mixture, from Native American, to Persian, to Anglo-Saxon.

I have learned that dance can provide a container for my fears, and through the safety of that container, transformation becomes possible. I feel that I can dive into the places I haven't been able to cope with in more ordinary reality. When I go to those parts of myself through dance, I now have a process that will take me from the dark forces of destruction to the generative power of life. The strength of the container, created by the boundaries of the exercises I make up and by my body itself, holds my fears and my distress sufficiently to promote and support change in my life. I have seen this happen with my students, as well. Over and over, these processes reveal themselves as reliable and effective.

I relate to my aging process through my experience of nature. Nature is so vital to me. I took a walk down to a waterfall near my house just a few days ago. I was looking at the new growth coming out and the blooming flowers and the full waterfall. Right next to the flowers was a rotting tree trunk. The colors were vibrant, the texture was beautiful.

I don't judge things in nature. Old is not bad, blooming is not good. It's just the natural cycle, the way things are. I find peace with my aging process by looking at the cycles of the seasons, the cycles of birth and death and decay. This is how I prepare for my own life, and also for my death.

Recently, I was on my way to lead a dance support group I formed called "Moving Toward Life" for people challenging cancer and AIDS. I stopped en route at a friend's house, and she said to me, "Why in the world do you keep teaching that class? Aren't you tired of it by now? Isn't it just too depressing?" In that moment, I had no response, and then I began to wonder why the group was so important to me. I would arrive to class each week a little tired and frazzled at the end of the day, and then would become so involved I would always run overtime, and would leave the class feeling refreshed and exhilarated. I realized then that people who are facing life-threatening and terminal illness are doing soul dancing. They dance with the greatest commitment and truth. They are not dancing around their issues as people so often do; they are confronting life and death. These people endure their pain, cope with their fear, and have the courage to continue. This is constantly revelatory and inspiring. It is a reminder to me of what dance is all about and how it can best serve our lives. I touched into some of this in my own experience with cancer, and as I said, I feel like that was a most pivotal event in my own life.

Working with people with life-threatening illness has changed my art and continues to change my life. I do not have a life-threatening illness any longer, or a terminal disease, but as my life passes by, I often question how I will live out my last days here. I don't ask this in a morbid, doomsday sort of way but rather with a sense of immediacy and opportunity. I imagine myself having enough time to answer this question in different ways, always learning and exploring, finding the maps to the territory, discovering the territory, discovering the next map. I tend to be a person who looks on the bright side of things, who sees the possibility and opportunity in every experience, and who tries to deal creatively with the punches life throws me.

For the most part, I would say I am and have been happy in my life. I feel incredibly grateful for a lifetime in dance and for the love of good friends and family that surrounds me. I care very much about creating a work of meaning, about finding ways that dance can be useful in our lives. But this has been a quest with great blessings. I have been able to pursue this question and have found many different answers to it over the years.

As I have grown and changed, of course, my questions and their answers have also grown and changed. I have lost some of my naïveté. But I haven't lost my thirst for life and for adventure.

Getting older may be about losing something, but it's also about gaining something else. I don't relate to being 78. When I look in the mirror, I know I'm 78, but inside I don't feel like I'm 78. I'm reminded of something a Japanese painter said: "When I was 5, I did things for the fun of it. When I was half a hundred, my paintings were worthless. When I was 72, I began to understand animals, insects, birds, and plants. When I am 80, I will progress a little. When I'm 90, I'll know the essence of things. When I'm 110, I'll know how things are. God of Longevity, give me the time." I identify with that. I'm just at the point where I'm beginning to understand the nature of animals and plants and insects and birds and the whole process of living and dying. When I'm 80, I think maybe I'll progress a little, but I'm looking forward to being 90, when I find the essence of things. At 110, I hope I'll be able to dance things as they are.

My mother's death left a huge gap in my life. She died on her hundredth birthday, when I was in my early seventies. She always wanted to live to be one hundred in order to receive a letter of congratulations from the president of the United States, who traditionally honors such a momentous occasion. When she left us, other than my missing her deep and constant love, my difficulty came from the sudden realization that I was now the grandmother in the family. The cycles of the ages confronted me for the first time, and I was quite unprepared. What was my role now? What did it mean to carry on? What were the traditions to carry on? What was worth keeping from the past, and what was worth letting go? The home? The holidays marking our Jewish traditions? Most of all, I wondered how I was to carry on the fullness of my mother's love.

Out of these deep questions came a dance that I dedicated to my four grandchildren. It was called "The Grandfather Dance." The dance was based on all the gestures, feelings, memories, and stories about my love of dance and my early relationship with my grandfather, which were stored in my body like a treasure chest. I thought my dance was a way to pass on to my grandchildren some of the traditions from my Jewish culture that had given me such a sense of belonging and security and family when I was growing up. After I had made the dance, I realized it was more than that. The dance was about how my grandfather and I shared our love for each other through our dance, but it was also a piece about how deep my love for dance really goes.

Through this dance, I wanted to be able to share my love with my grandchildren. It was in some ways the answer to my questions about how to be the grandmother of the family and how to fill my mother's shoes. It makes sense that the answer came to me in the form of a dance, because that has been my path for my whole life. The pull to make this dance was so strong; it was the first dance I performed publicly in more than twenty years, since my bout with cancer. In it, I came full circle, from dance icon-oclast to cancer survivor to teacher of people with life-threatening illnesses to ritual maker and back again to dancer, the stories of my life proving once again to be the map and the territory, the underlying thread that has connected all of my dances to themselves, and all of me to my dances. ᵒᶜᵌ

Something very important that I want to tell women is that it's never too late, but don't wait until it's too late, because you won't have the energy. You should do a little bit at a time. It's important to learn how to use your small bits of time. All those begin to count up. It's not the long amounts of time you have that are important. You should learn how to use your snatches of time when they are given to you.

RUTH ASAWA

 Ruth Asawa

✒ Profile

I was first introduced to the art of Ruth Asawa nearly thirty years ago, shortly after I gave birth to my first (and what would turn out to be only) child. I read an article (probably in the *San Francisco Chronicle*) about her life and work, in which the artist said that it wasn't until eleven at night after her six (!) kids had gone to bed that she would do her own work—on the kitchen floor. That example of a woman artist, who worked wherever and whenever she could, was profoundly affecting to me and has remained with me to this day.

So it was with long-held admiration that I went to visit Ruth and her husband, architect Albert Lanier, one week after they celebrated their forty-ninth wedding anniversary. They have lived in the same house in the Noe Valley section of San Francisco since 1961. Ruth said of this neighborhood, "We came when it was sleepy, blue-collar, working-class, but it's become very fancy now." Their multileveled and multidecked house was built in 1908 after the big 1906 earthquake, apparently for some couple's wedding present. Because the bride was a musician, she wanted the house to have high ceilings. Ruth pointed out the area in the center of the large living room where an organ once stood. "We bought the house for this room," she said, smiling at the memory.

Those high ceilings have not gone to waste in the Asawa-Lanier household. Many of Ruth's inimitable woven wire sculptures are gracefully suspended from the elaborately beamed wooden ceiling like a forest of trunkless trees in a Robert Wilson stage set. And she has other airy, constructivist forms that cast beautiful filigree shadows on the white walls of her large studio downstairs, where I photographed her.

Ruth Asawa was born in southern California of Japanese immigrant parents, who worked long, hard hours on their vegetable farm during the depression. Ruth remembers that she always liked to draw and felt that she wanted to be an artist. When World War II came, her family was uprooted and interned in a camp in Arkansas. As fate would have it, there were several Japanese American artists in the camp who had worked at Walt Disney Studios; Ruth's art education received a jump start.

In an attempt to earn a teaching credential in art, Ruth attended Milwaukee State Teachers College in Wisconsin. But after three years of study, she was told that she would be unable to find employment because of her Japanese heritage. Through college classmates, Ruth learned of Black Mountain College in North Carolina and decided to study fine art there. Aside from meeting her future husband, Albert, she received much more than she had anticipated. Today, she still expresses her love and appreciation for her formative experience at Black Mountain through her work and her spirit.

Ruth has spent her time in San Francisco combining her artistic creativity with a total involvement in community and family life. Her six children and ten grandchildren all live within a ten-block radius of her home. A major focus in her life has also been on art education in the public schools, where she taught art on a voluntary basis for more than thirty years. She has created major sculpture commissions in San Francisco's Ghirardelli Square and in the Grand Hyatt Hotel on Union Square. Her signature woven wire sculptures are in major collections, such as the Whitney Museum in New York City.

She no longer makes art on her kitchen floor—unless she is doing a project with her grandchildren—but more often than not, you can still find Ruth Asawa working past eleven at night.

Making Every Moment Count

I was at Black Mountain College in North Carolina for three years, including two summers. It was very intense and wonderful. Poets, actors, painters, architects all came together for an eight-week session during the summers. It was a very good education. You didn't teach there unless you were an artist. Each student was given one vote on school matters, just as every teacher was. So we exercised democracy in the raw sense. It was a good experience to have once, but I know it doesn't always work. It would be good if we could have government work like that, but it's too difficult. Somebody has to make final decisions. But it was a very good experience for students to have.

I had always been interested in art. I learned a lot at Milwaukee State Teachers College, but at Black Mountain College, I studied with teachers who decided to make art their life. That's what they really gave the students. The lesson that nothing is easy, that if you want to do art, do it, whatever may come. Art is taught like a business these days. You don't learn as much about art; you learn how to market it. At that time, it was not about self-expression so much but about doing something that meant a great deal to you. What was important was to find out what it was you wanted to do, what you were motivated to do.

During those years at Black Mountain, I think we learned how to live in the world. All of us had to do chores: dishes one week, farmwork the next week. We hauled coal from the train. We learned that everybody was responsible for everything. If you were lazy, you had a hard time there. You couldn't hide, because they would know that you hadn't done your job.

The teachers had to do as much as the students, so the students had a wonderful time doing dishes with their teachers. They might be washing dishes, but they would also be discussing a class or their poem or a problem. We all ate together at dinner or lunch. The teachers lived in separate houses with their families, and the students lived in dorms, but it was very natural for students and teachers to be working on the farm together.

It was a very poor school; we had no money, no endowment, weren't accredited. If you went there, you weren't there to get a degree. If that was important to you, you went to an accredited university or college. Black Mountain was an experimental school. You were only getting something from your experience; you weren't promised anything. Many of the students then became artists, but they also lived an artful life. The way they lived was very important. Some of the students later taught at universities and high schools and spread the Black Mountain philosophy.

We were taught how to see. Joseph Albers, one of our instructors, always taught us how to see, not so much how to be an artist. He wasn't interested in self-expression. "You do that on your own time. You don't need to come to class to paint. Better that time should be spent on learning." He told us not to be fooled or influenced by other people's work. He said you have to find your own way. He didn't want imitators of his own work, either.

I originally studied to be a painter. I didn't study sculpture, so my work with wire is like drawing a line and moving it out into space. I studied weaving just a little, but Albers taught us basic principles about positive and negative, background and foreground, that neither is more important than the other. The object is not more important than the background (the negative space). The transparency of my wire sculptures doesn't take anything away from what's behind them.

I work in bronze now. I did the Hyatt fountain on Union Square out of bread dough, because I was working with schoolchildren. I've done several sculptures with dough, which I then cast in bronze. It's an interesting medium, different from clay or plaster. I was working on objects in bread dough, but in four or five years, weevils would get into the dough, and it would disintegrate. It seemed too bad to spend so much time on something that would fall apart. I was working at a foundry and thought I could burn the dough out, but it left too much residue. Then the foundry made a wax mold from it, then cast it. Bread dough is a very easy material to use.

My work habit goes back to growing up on a farm where you learn how to work long hours. Every day, we would go to school, get out at 3:30, have a little snack, and go out to work from 4:00 until 8:00 P.M. Then we'd come in and eat and finally do our homework. That was the routine. In the summer, we worked even harder. We'd start at 7:00 in the morning and work until midnight. It has nothing to do with art; it has to do with the habit of working. It was a necessity.

I've spent a lot of time in the community—as an art commissioner, as a member of the California Arts Council, on the National Endowment for the Arts education panel, and teaching in the schools. All these experiences give me a perspective on what's going on in this city. How things don't change very much—they just get more complicated. Today's problems are harder than they were when our children were growing up. Age and experience give you a perspective.

Since my husband, Albert, and I have always been independent and largely self-employed, we've always lived a very risky life, by our wits, trying to make things work. I think that helps us now, in our later years, to be quite independent.

I think this has made our life more interesting, even though it may have made us often wonder about our future. Our time was our own, and I think as you get older, time is more valuable than money or success. Time becomes precious as you get older, because it's at the end of your life. Time no longer seems endless, as one realizes life is nearly over.

There is an interesting parallel—recognizing our own mortality, appreciating the time that we have left, and then seeing that limitation in our environmental resources. I've always composted, always wrapped newspapers up. I'm president of SCRAP, Scroungers' Center for Recycled Parts; we recycle industrial throwaways. We use these materials for schools and for community nonprofit organizations. I'm very aware of not wasting—

that comes from being raised on the farm. Farm life is all about recycling. On a farm, you recycle your boxes. You pick up your nails and straighten them out. Today it's not worth the time to bend down and pick them up. I still straighten out nails, pick up pennies, and do all the things that are a waste of time for most people.

I feel that I've done the most that I can do with my life. I didn't wait for retirement to start watercolors; I did it when I was thirty, when I was forty, when I was fifty. It's not like waiting for retirement. I don't know that artists retire. Probably artists do live longer, because they're doing what they want to do. My mother lived to almost ninety-six and my father eighty-seven. Who knows when death will happen? It could happen anytime. But I have a lot of ideas I still want to realize.

Individuals have to become personally responsible, because if day-care centers raised your children, then an old convalescent home is going to take care of you. It's not going to be somebody personal. If you leave your child at six weeks old in somebody else's care to go back to a lucrative job . . . I think you have to think about how much you are giving up. I'm for day care, and I'm for abortion, but not for me. I don't want it for myself. I wanted to raise my own children. I wanted to teach them, and the things they have learned, they've learned from us. How well they live is how well we hope for them.

For me, personally, I can't understand anybody else raising my children. I may end up in the convalescent home, but I think if you reject your children, you should expect to be tossed off at the end, with a once-a-month visitation. The child will do what he's familiar with. That's my feeling about child care or senior care. I don't know why anyone would want to do that. I've learned so much from my own children. I would advise parents to spend time with their children, because you learn a lot from them. I've worked with children in schools since 1968 when my children were in school. When women decided to go back to work, I went into schools. That was probably a less glamorous but more rewarding thing to do. I was an artist in the schools, as a volunteer. There's no teaching now of art or music. It's sad. My kids all went to public schools. I'm a firm believer in public schools.

I don't know whether I'll live to be my mother's age. But I'll be very busy in any senior center at any age. I'll probably be teaching; I love to teach. I don't worry about that so much, about where I end up. I still want to teach people how to use things around the house. Nothing fancy, but ordinary objects. Think about recycling milk cartons, egg cartons, paper. Make a sword out of newspaper. Those are my granddaughter's paper folds; I don't even know how to do them. I have a lot I could learn myself. I'm not bored.

Imogen Cunningham was a real role model for me, and a good friend. We were very young when we met her, and she photographed our family for about twenty-five years until she died when she was ninety-three. She didn't think I should have so many children. She was always trying to advise me. She had had three children in eleven months herself, twins and a single one. But it's interesting—that period of her life when she was confined was when she did her most beautiful photographs: magnolias, cacti, and plant forms. All that was done when she was taking care of her children, being confined, not able to go out. A time for observation, reflection. Imogen did the book *After Ninety.* She put my parents in it, although they weren't quite ninety. She did wonderful photographs of them.

I learned simple things from her. Our relationship was about putting up plum jam or making upside-down cake. It was very simple, not highfaluting. Albert's birthday was the same day as Imogen's, so we celebrated together. She was always interested in horticulture. My husband is also interested in plants, so there was a friendship through plants. It wasn't just about art. She never saw the fruits of her labor. Since she's died, her work has grown in recognition.

One day, she came to have dinner with us. I was working in this corner on a piece, and she said she was tired, going to lie down. And suddenly she saw the light come in and said, "That's such a good light. Hold it. Hold it." She took a shot, which she used, but she was that kind of very down-to-earth person who was aware of what was around her.

I wasn't as strong, physically, in my sixties as I could have been, because I was diagnosed as having lupus when I was fifty-nine, and I nearly died from it. It's an autoimmune disorder where the white blood cells eat your healthy cells. It was terrible. You get so tired, and you can't do anything. They finally diagnosed it. I had pains, I was itchy over my whole body. I would scratch it. There are twelve symptoms, and when four come together they call it lupus. They put me on prednisone and cytoxin. I didn't sleep for twelve days. I wrote, I drew, I went a little crazy, although it was a very interesting time. I don't take any medications anymore. They put me on cytoxin, which is a form of chemotherapy, and it destroyed the nerve endings in my feet, so I have pain in my feet now. If I hadn't had that bout with lupus, I would probably still be going pretty strong now.

This year, I've noticed that I can't balance myself. I have to find a different center in my body. I used to be able to bend over and do anything; now if I bend over, I might fall down. I have to learn about my body again. The doctor thinks it's just that I'm getting old.

I'm lucky that I'm still alive, in a way, because the lupus put me in intensive care. At one point, they asked me, "Do you want to live or die?" Five weeks in the hospital. I kept a journal in the hospital of every medication, every person that came to visit. I think it was the prednisone that made me a little manic. I have drawings that I did then. I could take this medicine, and in about twenty minutes it would start working, and drawings flowed like water. I could draw almost anything I saw. Then after the medicine wore off, my line got very wiggly, and I knew I couldn't draw anymore. Or I could do automatic writing. I wrote and wrote and wrote and wrote until my mind started getting confused. Then I would stop. It was such an interesting thing to experience.

But the lupus is the only thing that indicates to me that I might not live to be ninety-six. My life will be shortened by the illness. You always have it, and mine is in remission now. If it weren't in remission, I would be very sick. You're not supposed to have stress or sun. Sun gives you spots on your face. If you get stressed, you could get sick again. I don't have that much energy now, but what's happening is that I'm getting busy with my own work. More people want me to do commissions. I'm in an interesting position, because I don't have the same amount of energy, but I'm getting more recognition, and that happens when you get older—you get more invitations for work.

Something very important that I want to tell women is that it's never too late, but don't wait until it's too late, because you won't have the energy. You should do a little bit at a time, not only when you have a lot of time, but when you have a little time. It's important to learn how to use your small bits of time, your five minutes, your ten minutes, your fifteen minutes. All those begin to count up, because you could save all your nickels and dimes, and before you know it, you have a whole piggy bank full. It's not the long amounts of time you have that are important. Don't wait until your children are grown, until your husband is retired; I think that's a big mistake. You should learn how to use your snatches of time when they are given to you.

Maybe this is what you learned when you read the article about me when you were so young—if you can only get an hour at eleven o'clock at night, take it. But don't wait until you will have eight hours a day, because it might not come. That's so important.

That's how I was able to have a family and still do my work. By the time they were grown, all this work had been accumulated. It's like running. You run twenty minutes a day rather than once a month. You can't do it for that long, but you keep adding your five minutes. Then you add thirty minutes. Add a little bit each time. I think that's the secret to staying energized. It gets you to your next move. You never know what's going to make you turn left instead of turning right. I think you have to learn how to do that; you have to follow your impulse at the moment it happens.

These masks are of my family members. These were done when the children were very young. My son, Paul, was six then, but he's never going to be six again. (In fact, he is thirty-nine this year.) This mask is catching a moment, and all of these people were not this way a year from the time I did them. Using each minute.

I know everybody has had a sad childhood, but I don't like to dwell on my unhappy childhood. We all spend so much time on our unhappy childhood that we don't take advantage of a happy moment. I don't want to be influenced by my unhappiness. I want to be influenced by my good fortune of having gone to study with people at Black Mountain.

I didn't learn that so much at Black Mountain, but what I did learn was to continue a conversation that may have started in the classroom into lunch, where we all sat together. Then, during the chores we had to do, the discussion went on. Then it continued in the professor's living room. But everybody had a chance to say something. I think the important thing is not so much what a person says but that they have the opportunity to say it. Then that person can go on with his life, because he's gotten it out of his system; now he can go to the next thing. If things don't get resolved, like family problems, as you go along, then they become big problems at the end. That's one of the many things I carry with me from Black Mountain.

I find it easier to believe in the impossible now in my seventies than I did when I was in my rational midlife. I'm back to believing in the impossible. . . .

MADELEINE L'ENGLE

Madeleine L'Engle

Profile

A business consultant and dear friend of mine, Pat McAnaney, was over-joyed when I told him I was writing a book about women in their seven-ties. "Please interview Madeleine L'Engle," he said earnestly. As it turned out, Pat and Madeleine had been corresponding for some thirty years, since Pat had been a young boy and first read her books *A Wrinkle in Time* and *A Wind in the Door*. On hearing about their correspondence, I already liked her. As a writer myself, I know how precious writing time is; when a writer uses some of that time to respond to readers' letters, it means a lot.

L'Engle is Madeleine's baptismal name; her great-grandmother's married name. Because her writing addresses such themes as the conflict of good and evil, the nature of God, and individual responsibility, many consider Madeleine to be the American version of England's C. S. Lewis (the author who achieved wide recognition as a lay expositor of Christian apologetics and as writer of fantasy classics for children, such as *The Lion, the Witch, and the Wardrobe*). The author of fifty books of fiction, nonfiction, and poetry in as many years, she is best known for writing one of the top ten best-selling children's books of all time, *A Wrinkle in Time,* which won the Newbury Medal in 1963. A noted Episcopalian preacher and writer, she said, "What I believe in is outside the realm of proof. Most of the Bible is outside the realm of proof. It's a great storybook. A lot of people have trouble understanding that something can be true but not factual."

Madeleine is tall and elegant in her unconventional, long, flowing skirts and tunics and dangling earrings. Her gray hair is closely cropped in a Gertrude Stein fashion and reflects a no-nonsense attitude. She speaks somewhat tersely and to the point. The placid but pleasant expression on her face makes one forget that she was once an actress in New York after graduating from Smith College.

A rich and lifelong affection for books was formed when she was three or four and went with her family to the Norfolk, Connecticut, library reading room. To be in a room full of books was paradise. By the time Madeleine was five, she had written her first story. "I began to think in terms of story." She recalled, "My parents were the best. They were neither encouraging nor discouraging. I think too much encouragement is just as much pressure as too much discouragement. I was just allowed to write."

"Any advice for writers?" I asked the seventy-eight-year-old. "One of the main things a writer does is listen," she said of an author's relationship with her characters, meaning that the characters should dictate their actions to the author. "When you write, don't think. Write," said the woman who writes daily in her journal and works at her computer almost every day. "Writing is easy," she deadpanned. "You just sit and wait for the drops of blood to form on your forehead." But, she laughed, "It's also the most fun I know." And one more tip: "Write every day," and when you "get 'stuck,' swim or walk or do something else you like that is physical. Imagination is a divine gift."

Just before Thanksgiving in 1996, I met Madeleine in her office (a library reading room that had been left unused for some time) at the Episcopalian Cathedral of St. John the Divine in New York City. It must be a comforting and inspiring environment in which to work and a continual reminder of that day at the Norfolk library reading room that would shape this writer's life.

After forty years of marriage to her husband, actor Hugh Franklin, Madeleine was widowed in 1986. They had raised three children, who blessed them with five grandchildren. In her outspoken manner, she said, "In the last ten years, I have discovered more male chauvinism and sexism than I did in the rest of my life put together. I never bumped into it before. There was none in my marriage, none in my home growing up as a kid. After Hugh died, the bank accounts were frozen. I had to prove to the bloody bank that I was capable of having my own bank account. We'd had a joint account for years!"

In 1991, after a truck went through a red light in San Diego and broadsided Madeleine's car, she was left without a spleen and with health complications. She is still dealing with insurance problems and spoke at length about the state of health care in the United States. Having mostly recovered from the accident, Madeleine has no plans to slow down. "I have ideas in the slow cooker," she said. "When I finish a book, I see which next one seems to be bubbling the fastest."

The Divine Gift of Imagination

The person I was just talking to on the telephone is going to come and help me with the letters from my readers. Six times a year, I do what I call my general epistle, a one-page letter with a picture that tells more or less what's going on in my life, so I don't have to repeat myself to each individual. Then I add a personal note. Some just want to get the epistles. During my birthday and Christmas, the mail situation escalates.

Many of the letters I receive are absolutely marvelous, and I'm grateful for this. Some are so poignant. Two really shook me lately. One was from a young girl whose mother had had a stroke very early, was a vegetable in a nursing home, and her father had spent all his money. The only way for him to get her cared for was to divorce her. So I wrote back to that girl. Another was a woman whose little girl had fallen down the stairs and bruised herself quite badly. She was afraid to send her to school the next day because she might be accused of child abuse. I haven't had any relationship with these people. They just write to me after they've read my books. Every once in a while, I write enough to a reader so I make friends and get to know them, as happened with your friend, Pat McAnaney.

I spend much more time here in New York. I've now fixed up the little cottage in Connecticut, and I *hope* to get to spend more time there, but I spend far more here. And I have a lovely apartment built in 1912, when they still built well. When we first went into it, it was $218 a month for eight rooms, four baths, and twelve closets. Then we became a tenant-organized co-op, which we owned and ran. Then we experimented in solar heating. Our hot water comes from the sun, and our maintenance expenses go up and down, depending on what we've spent. So financially it's a very good deal. I brought up two families in that apartment—my children and my grandchildren. Those apartments on the West End were very spacious. And I have a kosher kitchen. Absolutely wonderful. A lot of those buildings were built for Orthodox Austrian Jews, so I have two sinks and all that lovely cupboard space. A six-burner stove and two ovens. I cook a lot and like to cook.

What's it like being in my seventies? I haven't really had too much time to notice. I have a very heavy schedule, which for years I said I would lighten up. It just hasn't happened. There are a lot more of us women who are single, either by death or divorce, and I have a wonderful circle of women friends. Quite a few are not in New York; they're all over the country. And it *is* very supportive. We all need support. I'm very good about not calling people at two o'clock in the morning, but they would let me. It's nice to know you could. At one of the writers' workshops I do, I made a lot of friends. Women with a *great* deal of talent who have never really known how to focus it.

I guess at seventy you're supposed to relax and enjoy your peace and quiet; that hasn't happened. I mean, I'm nearly eighty. I should try to relax and enjoy my peace and quiet. I'm always galloping on the white charger and trying to get something organized.

Our current political situation is depressing, isn't it? I mean, when did you last vote for somebody? In the '96 election, I voted against somebody. I very seldom vote for somebody. It's very hard.

Another problem that is going to make it worse is that we are so into the private life of everybody in politics. A result of this is that eventually we're going to end up with faceless nonentities with low IQs as our leaders. If you look through the history of our great presidents, they were not pure and sweet in their private lives. None of them. When my son was small, he would say, "Mother, I want to speak to you in privity." I think they ought to have some privity. We used to have real heroes and heroines, and now they are celebrities, and they bore me. There's a theory that older people tend to get more reactionary. The conservatives I find boring and mean. That's what got me about this last election; they were so mean. So negative. They'd say, "Tom Brown is the most terrible person in the world," and I'd hear about Tom Brown until I'd forget who I was supposed to vote for. It makes me want to hear something good. The Democrats were not quite as negative, but they weren't very good. They were just less bad.

In the last gubernatorial race, somebody on QXR Radio said, "Why are people so mean-spirited?" I thought, "Why are we?" I think one problem is that the media tend to make us believe that nice is normal, and if it is not nice, then it's not normal. But normal is not nice. Normal is like the weather—an unpredictable system.

This insurance business has been very disruptive. They're going to take us off our good medical insurance and put us on one of the bad ones. Five years ago in San Diego, a truck ran through a red light and totaled the car I was in and nearly totaled me. You always think that these things happen to other people. All my internal guts were ripped, and I had to lose my spleen and almost a kidney. The trauma team came in one day and said to me, looking terrible, "You're not ready to leave the hospital, but the insurance won't pay anymore. They're treating you like a simple splenectomy." I couldn't keep down any food, had to leave the hospital because insurance was making this medical decision, and they had to readmit me. Insane. Insurance people have no medical training whatsoever, and they are making medical decisions and not listening to the doctors. I have pretty much recovered, but I'm still fighting to get it paid for. I won't make money off it; they don't have to pay me for what I went through. I just want the medical expenses paid for. So I have a special empathy with what's happening to people. I mean, it nearly killed me. The insurance companies are in the business of making billions for the CEOs. The rest of us, they couldn't care less about.

Did I tell you the story about the three nurses who died and went to heaven? St. Peter looked at the first and said, "What in your life did you do?" She said, "I was an intensive care unit nurse." He said, "Oh, that's wonderful hard work for people who are sick. Welcome. Come on in." He said to the second nurse, "What in your life did you do?" She said, "I was a pediatric nurse." "Oh, you worked with children. Well, that's wonderful. Come on in." And to the third nurse, "In your life, what did you do?" "I was a nurse for an insurance company." "Oh, that's very hard work. Come on in, but remember you can only stay forty-eight hours." The only thing we can do is laugh about it.

My daughter-in-law is a primary care physician. They're having a terrible time. They're being forced to join something. A big, nasty mess. I don't know a doctor who isn't extremely upset by that. And I agree. People with no medical training should not be making medical decisions.

Have I been associated with the Church all of my life? Well, I was born into the Episcopal Church. I spent six years in Episcopal boarding schools in England. That's enough to finish you, so I left the Church totally. My husband was brought up as a Southern Baptist, so he left the Church. We had a child and thought, "What are we going to do? What are we going to tell this child about the world?" When I grew up in New York, my friends were everything. My closest friend was April Warburg, of the famous Warburg family. We were raising our kids in a little village where there really wasn't much else except damn Yankees. A lot of us were young and had kids and we didn't go to church to try to think things out. We were not popular, because we would try to think things out rather than just following everyone else. Living through the McCarthy Era, we saw so many actors who were targeted. I was frightened for my husband, the actor Hugh Franklin. Finally, when they said that Helen Hayes was a Communist, the whole thing fell apart, because she was so reactionary it made everybody laugh. But it was a horrible time.

I find it easier to believe in the impossible now in my seventies than I did when I was in my rational midlife. I'm back to believing in the impossible, if there's anything worth believing in. You can't prove God or disprove God. All being an agnostic means is that I do not know. It doesn't mean I don't believe—don't get it mixed up with atheism. I'm not an atheist. An atheist says, "That chair is not there." An agnostic may say, "I think that chair is there." I find the idea of God coming and living with us very fascinating, although we didn't seem to learn much about true Christian principles from Christ. It seems strange there's been so much damage done in the name of Christ, but every once in a while, something good happens.

I'm very much on the Fundamentalist hit list. *A Wrinkle in Time* is one of the ten most censored books in the United States, along with *The Diary of Anne Frank* and *Grapes of Wrath* and *Huckleberry Finn* and a few other terrible books. One thing that fascinates me—when *Wrinkle* first came out, it was hailed as an evangelical book, a Christian book. Now it is being deplored as a dreadful book. Not a word of the book has changed. So much else has changed in the world, though. It's not just that I'm growing older and saying things have changed. Something obviously has changed. We're more suspicious, more fearful. I still have hope. We've been in this kind of a mess over and over again throughout history.

My theology is basically reading particle physics and mono-mechanics, because they deliver the nature of *being,* and nothing happens in isolation. Everything affects everything else. I really like the theology behind this science. We cannot study anything objectively, because the study is changed by the observation. I never found any conflict between science and religion. All science can do is open up more discussion.

The best thing I got out of college was learning how to do research, so when I want to work on a new book—usually a fantasy—I do research for it. I may not understand all of it, but I'll understand enough. *A Wrinkle in Time* is based on Einstein's theory of relativity and Planck's quantum theory. Just as good science as I could make it. *A Wind in the Door* is cellular biology. *A Swiftly Tilting Planet* is theories of time. I love finding out about these things.

We tend to limit the feminine and the masculine; we have them marry and make love as characters in books. But it's much more imaginative than that within ourselves, within our smaller groups and our large groups.

There's one thing I just discovered last winter. And that is that the Fundamentalists are very afraid of the word *imagination.* In the King James Version of the Bible, it's always a bad word. It talks about "imagination of their hearts" as a conceit. I took my concordance and went all through it. Every time *imagination* is used in the King James translation, it has a negative connotation. So the Fundamentalists have taken that two-hundred-year-old interpretation and kept it.

Language changes. *Prevent* in King James means go before—*pre venire,* lead me. Now it means stop. Do you know the original meaning of the word *buxom?* Obedient. I get this vision of the Elizabethan tavern, the men with the velvet hats and the feathers and their swords clanking and these lovely young girls popping down their tankards of ale, and they say, "There's my good buxom girl," and you can see how it changes.

When I make up a word, I like it to be etymologically sound. I have a word called *Ecthroi.* I don't want to use Satan or the devil; they're so encrusted with meaning. *Ecthroi* is simply a Greek word that means the enemy. It's an enemy-sounding word.

People at the universities I speak at ask, "Do you believe in creationism—that God created the world in seven days?" And I'll say, "Oh, yes, of course. But was it Greenwich mean time or eastern time or mountain time?" Why would God use human time? Is he so literal? Besides, Scripture says a thousand years in our sight is but a moment when it is passed. I just heard a silly story in which somebody said, "How long is a thousand years for you?" "Oh, a minute." "How much is a million dollars?" "A nickel." "Could I have a nickel?" "In a minute." Literalism is very destructive. And the media wish to be literal so you'll buy more of the product.

I come from a very long-lived family. They say that the best way to live to a ripe old age is if people don't run through red lights. My grandfather lived to be 101 because he decided to be 100 and then die. My mother was cut down young in her 90s. My husband's family was long-lived, too.

While I am functional, there's no point in trying to prove that there are certain things I can't do as easily as I used to do. I was always clumsy; age really hasn't made that much difference. I can cook just as well. I don't notice my age most of the time. I've had eye problems since I was eight, so it never occurs to me it's got anything to do with old age.

One thing that was very important in my life—ten years ago, in the autumn when my husband died, my granddaughters were starting college in New York. One was in New York for seven years for college and graduate school, and she lived with me. My granddaughters were not about to let me get into any kind of a rut. I think my language is definitely looser than it might be otherwise. It's a wonderful way to keep fully functioning—to have young people in your life.

I've been to visit people living in these old-age facilities where you start out in your own place. I've eaten in the dining room. To be isolated with a lot of old people? I have very few friends my age, and none of them are in New York.

I'm friends with working women mostly. Interesting people. I haven't made young friends deliberately, but it has worked out nicely. And at the church I go to—All Angels Church—I am the only older person there. There are three Sunday services—9:00 is mostly young families, 11:30 is a lot of people working in theater and dancing, and 5:00 is mostly street people, a lot still on drugs. It's an Episcopal Church, but this one is unique. I think it's very good. There's a large population of homeless up here. And people you wouldn't normally think of as needing to be homeless. People who have had homes and educations. Something goes wrong, and we don't have any place for them to go.

One of the funny things . . . When we first moved to this neighborhood in 1960, I noticed the old women who couldn't cross Broadway on one light. I thought, "I'm going to make it on one light." I can still do it.

I would never want to be in a retirement home. I tell my kids to go put me out on an ice floe. It's in one of my books, which I wrote a good twenty, twenty-five years ago, and I had a letter from somebody last year saying, "You don't still feel that way, do you?" I said, "I most certainly do."

But there is a problem. Old Aunt Susie would be much happier if she weren't alive, wouldn't she? I don't think euthanasia can be legalized, but what used to happen when a baby was born with their spinal cord outside? They just didn't spank them. When an old person was in terrible pain, they just gave them morphine. Why let people suffer when they're dying? One doctor writes about their getting addicted. I say, "What difference does it make?" Where we're going after we die, I don't think it will make any difference whether or not we were addicted to morphine before we died. But we certainly need to think about the quality of life more. In our own consciousness, we have a little bit more to do. In the olden days, way before me, you had a choice about when you died. You decided to die. My grandfather died at 101. It was a sheer act of will.

We're so afraid of litigation, and we're so hung up on false guilt. "They'll criticize me if I let my mother die." When my mother died at ninety rather unexpectedly, I was extremely grateful. I loved my mother, but she was spiraling down. I had to call these billions of cousins and tell them. They said, "You sound so glad." I said, "I am. I'm so relieved. There was no place for her to go but down. I grieve for her. I loved my mother. But to keep her alive like this was not a kindness."

They are able to keep people alive so much longer now. We are living longer lives, and they're keeping people alive. When there's no quality of life left, when there is no brain function left, what is this we're keeping alive? If you have any sense that this is not the end, you're holding people back from going to the next level.

I don't really think we're looking at the issue squarely. But I also think it has to be decided one person at a time. Jesus didn't wave a magic wand and cure all the lepers—just one at a time. Another interesting and important factor is that the person in question has to want to be healed or to have their life prolonged.

What would my advice to other women in their seventies be? Go on living. There are people who decide they're old. That's a silly thing to decide. As long as your body is functioning well enough, you can still do what you want to do. ⌇

    I used to say, "When I grow older, I want to have a face that looks like Isak Dinesen's, full of wrinkles and crevices, all those marks of experience that would show the world that I had really lived."
I'm not so sanguine about it now!

ELINOR GADON

Elinor Gadon

◈ Profile

In her acclaimed book *The Once and Future Goddess: A Symbol for Our Time,* scholar Elinor Gadon critiques Western culture from the perspective of the sacred female, human and divine. The book explores our earliest knowledge of modern human consciousness while reconstructing the religion of the Goddess in prehistory, telling of her demise under patriarchy some five thousand years ago and her subsequent reemergence in the cultural mythology of the late twentieth century.

Elinor is considered a cultural historian in the fields of world religions, women's art and culture, and India. Her focus is on the analysis of visual images and symbols in their cultural context. Her approach is cross-cultural and interdisciplinary, and she uses the methodologies of art history, the history of religions, and cultural anthropology. She has taught at Harvard and the New School of Social Research in New York City and is the founder of the Women's Spirituality Program at the California Institute of Integral Studies in San Francisco.

I interviewed Elinor at Mills College in Oakland, California. She is a warm and lively woman whose energy can outlast that of many of her students. She spoke passionately about her professional work and revealingly about her personal life—her continuing sadness about her divorce some twenty-five years ago and the suicide of one of her four children.

The book Elinor has been working on for several years is called *The Wounded Minotaur: Reclaiming the Sacred Male*. In this male version of her Goddess book, she explores the myth of what it has meant to be a man in Western and American culture in relation to the explosion of violence in the twentieth century and in relation to the equation of men with violence. "Men have been just as victimized by patriarchy as women," Elinor said. "Men and women are in this together. We can't transform our culture unless we all work together to create new models for gender roles. I'm not a strident feminist. I wouldn't say that I keep quiet, but I'm not militant. Nor am I a separatist. I think women would be enriched and informed by having more meaningful dialogues with men."

Elinor ends the book on an optimistic note, because "despite the increase in violence, a sea change is brewing," she said. "Many men don't want to go to war, to be in the army. There is the new father, the nurturing male, and the possibility of intimate heterosexual relationships of equity, mutuality, and passion." The new book has the same format as her Goddess book, incorporating mythology and the visual arts within their cultural context and going from the Paleolithic age to the present. But, she noted, "It is much more profound than my other book, going into more depth on the ramifications for culture in which the myth of masculinity is tied to violence. We have to have a reconciliation between men and women, a healing from the gender wars."

Elinor is dedicating this book to her son Bill, who, "in his journals, documented how he struggled to become what he thought a man should be in our culture. He was good at sports, an expert skier and mountain climber, very sensual, highly sexual with women. On the other hand, he was a gentle, sensitive artist. He wasn't able to reconcile these two parts of himself. He died at twenty-five in 1981."

Elinor spoke in her excited manner about her future work and travel to India, a country that she loves and from which she has learned so much. In the beginning of our conversation, I felt that I received a private lecture on Goddess culture from one of the world's authorities. She went on to discuss ways for women to heal the traumas of their body images.

A Passionate Drive

After I finish the book I am working on now, I will be going to India. I want to explore some of the larger issues concerning the worship of the Goddess, and India is a perfect place to do so. Here, the whole subject of the recovery of the Goddess tradition in the West is so controversial, and we seem to be stuck in Western epistemological categories, while in the subcontinent, we have a documented case study of a continuing tradition of worship of a female deity that is five thousand years old and that can be traced back even further into the Neolithic culture of neighboring Baluchistan. We have evidence for ritual practice from the iconography of the Indus Valley seals and from the surviving practices in tribal and village cultures. Because of the inherent conservatism of Indian culture, we can with some confidence project backward about the meaning and nature of ritual practices.

What I am exploring is the nature of this female deity, which can be understood on many levels. It's very complex. In India, she is the One and the many. As the years go by and I work on different facets of the Goddess tradition cross-culturally, I am coming to understand this phenomenon in a different way. I have moved away from the popular concept of the Goddess who is the feminine god with *ess* tacked on, or as I say, "She's not a fat, pink lady sitting on a cloud." I was never really there, but some women within the spirituality movement are. I always saw the concept of a Goddess as different than that of the monotheistic God, because as creator, she creates out of her own body, unlike God the Father, who created by divine fiat out of nothing, out of the void. Because she creates out of her sacred body, all of her creation becomes sacred—it is all part of her being. This is very different from the monotheistic tradition, where a distant God has dominion over the earth and all of its creatures. Another important difference is that the God-dess is not transcendent, out there, but immanent, within. I could under-stand this, because it is the same in Hinduism. I have come to think of the Goddess as a force, a creative energy. In West Africa, the Goddess Oshun is thought of as an elemental force of nature, like the wind.

In India, it is understood that even if she has a thousand names, she is One. In fact, they say that every village has its own Goddess with her own name, as she is territorial, the Goddess of that particular place. Since there are three hundred thousand villages, that means three hundred thousand names right there. Of course, in practice there is a lot of overlapping and repetition of names. Devi is her generic name and, at some level of the tradition, the local Goddesses are all considered manifestations of her. But the understanding of Devi as One is of a different order from the jealous, monotheistic Father God of Judaism, Christianity, and Islam, where to worship other gods is heresy. Hinduism is pluralistic and tolerant.

In the Goddess course I am teaching right now at Mills College, one of the questions I ask my students to consider is whether there is a human necessity for a female God. After all, we were all born of woman. Mother is a natural image for the creator. In the image of the female divine, we can most easily embody life and death. For instance, in Christianity, the two most popular forms of the Virgin Mary show her with the infant Jesus and the dead Christ. The Pietà, as we know it in Christianity, was a devotional image long before Michelangelo's famous Vatican sculpture, going back to prehistory, and it was a popular icon during the Black Plague, when per-haps one out of every three people in Europe died.

To me, this is an ongoing fascination and mystery, and it has, from my point of view, enormous ramifications for this paradigm shift we all hope we're engaged in now, in which we move toward a culture and world that is more just and humane, both ecologically and socially. And we still have a long way to go. I can't even say whether or not we will survive as a species or a planet with an atmosphere in which we can live. I think it's perilous in terms of the new gene technology and the cloning of humans, which is inevitable no matter what laws we pass in the United States. If we can find some way to make enough people aware of this Goddess as an image or symbol of the interconnection of all of life and really understand deep down that this interconnection has to do with our natural resources—the rocks and trees, birds and flowers, as well as other peoples all over the globe—and the problems related to gender imbalance. Which is where we are right now. Nothing is right for anybody.

Because I'm a serious scholar, I want to do more than write about a dream or vision. I don't want to fault people who do that—there is a whole market out there for them. But my own compulsion and fascination are to try to find out how we got into this mess, to understand historical sources in their context, systemically, so we can work to change social and economic structures. We need to find a way to go beyond the rabid capitalism that is fueling our aggressive global marketing policies, which are working to transform the Third World into our notion of consumerism so that those nations can become our markets.

The first time I taught about the Goddess was at the Harvard Divinity School, twenty years ago, in a course comparing the iconography of the female in the Christian and Hindu traditions. I had five male ministers in that class, all of whom were middle-aged men in a midlife refresher program for ministers, and they latched on to Sophia as something they could understand. Then they could place whatever I was saying about the Goddess in India within the context of Sophia. Although I understood even then that they weren't the same, I wasn't able to articulate the problem of Sophia's disembodiment or the importance of the carnal, sensual nature of the Goddess. This is yet another way in which I believe that Christian theology has oppressed women in repressing the fullness of their bodily being and not honoring and sacralizing their life experience.

I used to say, "When I grow older, I want to have a face that looks like Isak Dinesen's, full of wrinkles and crevices, all those marks of experience that would show the world that I had really lived." I'm not so sanguine about it now! Certainly, my body has the stretch marks from childbirth and sagging breasts. So now, when I show slides of the Venus of Wilendorf, the earliest Goddess image we have, some twenty-five thousand years old, with her pendulous breasts, sagging abdomen, and fleshy hips and thighs, I tell my audience that when I first showed this image, women would tell me that no woman would have created that votive image, that no woman would ever want to look like that—she's fat. And now I reply that I look pretty much like that myself!

Part of women's healing has to do with accepting their bodies. And that's in the face of the enormous, powerful advertising that saturates our media, proclaiming that you can't be too thin, that thinness equals happiness. The disastrous consequences of this campaign is that eight- and nine-year-old girls are dieting, egged on by their mothers. The tragedy is our lack of understanding of the root causes of women's lack of self-esteem, despite all that's been written about it.

I don't see Sophia as a Goddess. I think she is an important female spiritual voice bringing the feminine into Judaism and Christianity, but that is different from what *Goddess* means to me. *Goddess* has to do with the female embodiment in the earth, in the "earthy," whether or not she's called an earth mother. The primary symbols of the Goddess are all taken from nature, like the spiral, the tree, the rivers, the lotus, the snake. These have to do with the life force, the life energy, and while they were all later appropriated by Christianity as symbols of the Virgin Mary, their meanings were reversed and transformed. Like the snake, for example (who represented the wisdom of the earth out of which it crawled—in the language of the Goddess—as well as regeneration, because it could shed its skin and grow a new one), became the dreaded symbol of evil in Christianity. The symbol of evil, which the Virgin could stamp out because she, alone of all humankind, was free from the stain of carnality. Or like the moon, a primary prehistoric symbol of the Goddess (because of the relationship of its cyclical nature to the three phases of womanhood—maiden, motherhood, and crone) symbolizes chastity in the iconography of the Virgin.

I keep going back to this kind of iconographic research, because of my passion to know and understand why our culture is so misogynist. This goes back to my experience of thirty years ago, when I was first in India. I wasn't there on any spiritual quest or mission or anything else like that, but I accompanied my husband, who was teaching at the Indian Institute of Management in Calcutta for MIT. Because I was trained as an art historian, the way in which I went about getting to know Indian culture was through the visual arts. We traveled widely, to every part of India that year, because as part of his assignment, he was to give seminars for high-level managers in government and industry. I was able to visit all the major sacred monuments.

Everywhere I went, I saw these powerful, sexual, sensual, beautiful, female sculptures carved on temple facades. I'd never seen anything like them. Thirty years ago, there were no books about the Goddess in the West. Something inside of me shifted and changed, because my primary way of knowing is to take things in visually. It isn't that I said, "I'm going to experience this bodily." I didn't even know what that was; I had never heard such language. But that is what I did.

Coming back home to Western culture was very hard. I decided I wanted to understand what had happened to me in India. Now, thirty years later and with a Ph.D. in Indian culture, I realize that I had gotten in touch with what the Indians call Shakti, the elemental life force, the cosmic energy that drives the world, understood as female.

What that connection did was to open me up to possibilities that had been suppressed for most women in the West, the validation of my sensuality and sexuality. It wasn't that I hadn't been sensual and sexual before, but there was no frame of reference for women to understand these instinctual feelings in a positive way. There wasn't any container for them calling them sacred, as there was in India. It was as if the veil was ripped off, and I saw things through a new lens.

Our children were with us. In all, it was a glorious family adventure. But the changes in me destabilized my marriage.

I had had four children, and I experienced each of their births as sacred. But how was I to know that I would feel this way? My mother had never spoken of the sacred; she was neither religious nor spiritual and had dreaded childbirth. I had wanted very much to have natural childbirth but couldn't find a doctor who was into it in the Boston area, where we lived. And New Haven, where the revival of this movement began, was 150 miles away. I didn't feel that I had the right to make a big fuss about what I viewed then as my personal issues around childbirth and demand to go there for prenatal care and the birth.

I now understand that the birthing process is a family matter, having to do with the ongoing relationship of mother and child, as well as with the father, now that he can participate in the delivery room. I've always felt that not to have given birth to my children naturally, fully conscious, as women had done since the beginning of time, was a great personal loss. But I didn't have the self-confidence then, the assertiveness, to act on my own instincts.

My first pregnancy was unplanned; my husband was just starting his first job, and money was very much an issue. I first went to a highly recommended women's hospital, but after listening to the obstetrician lecture me about all the precautions to take and things not to do during my pregnancy and feeling treated as if I were sick when I felt just fine, I said, "Uh-uh, not for me," and went to a general practitioner in a small town nearby who had delivered thousands of babies without any fuss.

Yes, labor was painful, but you forget about it right afterward. And what I did remember is the euphoria I experienced at each birth. But the first time, when I took my puny, beet-red, a-few-weeks-premature infant into my arms, I counted up her tiny fingers and toes and turned her over, noting that her backbone and buttocks were perfectly formed, and knew that I had created the miracle of life within my body. For weeks afterward, I felt that both baby and I had this halo around us, like a big aura. I was so absolutely high.

I tried to find words for it, to talk about it with my husband, who loved me and our babies, but found no vocabulary or frame of reference to do so—or any other women to talk about the sacred nature of childbirth or the need for rituals to mark it. There was no cultural container in which to put my feelings in the fifties. Later, in my children's early years, I joined other women in play groups. We lived in Providence then, near Brown University, and there were educated, enlightened women there, but we never talked about such things. We all loved our children, but most of us were typical fifties wives. A few actually had careers, which they had trained for and worked in before marriage. One woman, whom I had known as an undergraduate, was teaching at Brown and later became a leading historian and is now at the Institute for Advanced Studies at Princeton. But I didn't recognize her for the feminist she was, because I didn't know what a feminist was.

After the birth of my second child, I went back to work—very part-time, usually without pay—in public relations and fundraising for arts and social welfare institutions and local political campaigns. I still didn't see myself as having a career, although there lingered somewhere deep at the back of my mind a yearning to go to graduate school, to know more about the world of ideas, and to do something on my own that was respected.

But to get back to my travel in India, where I had a visceral experience of the Goddess, an experience that I connected to giving birth . . . It *is* connected. I never lost that experience; it was one of those major shifts in my consciousness. My sense was that the sacred body of the Goddesses that I saw everywhere was also mine. And that my sexuality was sacred. Now, I didn't come from a family where sexuality was repressed per se; it was just never mentioned. It wasn't that I felt my body was evil, which most Western women do, or that my sexuality was evil. But, again, it was discovering in India that there was some language and a symbol system, some container to hold my inner knowledge, that allowed me to access this knowing in my own cultural context, my own world. I had always felt that my sexual relationship with my husband—with whom I was madly, passionately in love—was sacred. We were both highly sexed and very well matched sexually. I felt that our lovemaking was the most sacred time in my life, an ecstatic mystery. In India, the sacredness of the sexual union was acknowledged in poetry and the visual arts.

Another insight gleaned from Indian culture was the cyclical nature of life and the universe. And this notion of time connects to our bodily processes as women—our monthly bleeding and its relationship to the cycles of the moon. It was clear to me that Indians understood this. They had a cyclical time frame in which the world was created, destroyed, only to be created again with no beginning and no end, as well as a seasonal festival calendar that was tied into what was happening on the land. This made much more sense to me than our linear time, which began with God's creation and would end in a fiery apocalypse on Judgment Day.

Indian Goddesses are not biological mothers. Pavati has children, but they were not born in the natural way. When Hindus call out to the Goddess, "Mata, Mata," which literally translates as "Mother, Mother," they are not referring to her as a biological mother but as the cosmic mother of all creation, the universal principle out of which everything comes. Mata (Mother) is honored as the source of life.

The theologian Paul Tillich's book *In Search of the Miraculous* had a phrase that is apt here: "the source of life and ground of being." Men, as well as women, honor the Goddess. I watched in awe and wonder as the men in crowds of hundreds and thousands called out "Mata, Mata" to the image of the warrior Goddess, Durga, during her nine-day festival.

The Durga Puja is the major pan-Indian Goddess festival held at the time of the autumn harvest. Every neighborhood in Calcutta had its own temporary shrine, *pandals*, huge, brightly colored tents with twenty-foot icons of Durga and her entourage on the altar. Not effigies. Hindus believe that if an image of the deity is properly consecrated, the living presence of the divine is embodied. They chide Christians, telling them that while Christians accuse them of idolatry, it is the Christians who are idolatrous, because the Hindus know they are worshiping the living God, but the Christians do not believe the God is alive within their sacred images. The gigantic images for the Durga Puja are made from clay and papier mâché on an armature of bamboo, with real hair, clothing, and jewelry. With music and incense burning all the time, it is all very sensual.

Durga is the cosmic warrior who slays the buffalo demon, thereby overcoming evil in the universe. In Bengal, Durga is conflated with Kali, worshiped as the Almighty Absolute. The Bengali mystics have a child-mother relationship with her; their devotional poetry is filled with intimate anecdotes about their encounter with their Goddess. This kind of intimacy between adult males and a powerful female is perhaps easier in India, where men don't break psychologically with their mothers, as they do in the developmental norm of the West. To grow up to be a man, you don't have to betray your bond with your mother. This, of course, has its downside in India, in complicating the marital relationship. An ongoing close relationship between a man and his mother is not considered pathological, as it is in the West.

Another thing that was so meaningful to me there was the family scene, a connection that I had longed for so much with my own children. As the Indians say, in the United States, we raise our children and send them out. If they don't leave home, we feel there is something wrong with them— and us. We've failed motherhood. These are things I think about a whole lot. The mother-daughter relationship in the contemporary world is so problematic. I hear about this over and over again from students and women in workshops. So painful on both sides. I have come to see the mother-daughter relationship as the fault line of the feminist movement. It isn't that all relationships are so marvelous in India—I do not want to glorify things there—but it's a society that respects older people. The family, the collective, has priority over the individual. The only people who no longer hold this view are those who are totally Westernized.

I would say that India is the best of all places and the worst of all places. In a population of more than eight hundred million people, it's probably a mixed bag. Most ordinary people seem much more gentle, much less aggressive than their American counterparts. When I came back to the U.S. after that first year, I had a bad case of reverse culture shock; everywhere I went, people seemed to have a mean look on their face. I later realized that while in India people's expressions were open, here they were closed.

Also, older people are respected. My introduction to this deeply ingrained cultural attitude was very poignant. Our closest friends in Calcutta were Indu and Suresh, colleagues of my husband. They had two small children. Her mother, an elegant woman who had spent most of her life in England as the wife of an Indian barrister, was now badly crippled by rheumatoid arthritis and lived with them. Her much-honored family role was to just love the little ones who shared her bed. Some years later, Indu called to inform me of her mother's death, saying how blessed she and her sisters had been to be able to be with their mother and to nurse her during her last days.

I think of how our mothers and fathers die in this day and age in our country, if not in a hospital, in a nursing home, all too often hooked up to all kinds of tubes. Both men and women feel burdened by the care of their elderly parents. There is much talk and writing about the sad plight of women caught between the care of their children and the care of their parents. Today, because of the AIDS epidemic, we have more tolerance and understanding of death and dying, but still a major theme that I listen to is the anguish of well-intentioned women who can't handle their old mother's total dependence on them, her constant demands. This is something we must relearn to do, to accept an imperfect world in which we are all interdependent.

We're responsible for each other. These aren't just words. We have to be there when other people whom we're connected to and love need us, and that's often inconvenient. Sadly, we've come to the ultimate extreme in an individualism that all too often puts the needs of the self first.

I feel that I have so much to learn. I have an ego. I see myself as an individual, far more individualistic than most women raised in Asia would be. But in my value system, I honor the collective, collaboration, which I hold as a woman's way.

One of the wonderful successes in the Women's Spirituality Ph.D. program at the California Institute of Integral Studies in San Francisco, which I created and direct, is the way we have bonded and formed a caring community in our years of learning together. Our culture is not competitive or egoistic; the women are willing to share knowledge and collaborate on research and the process of dissertation writing. There is a sweetness about this that I find very precious—not to have to be armored.

We rarely fully trust, because we are not brought up in a safe world. Without safety and trust, there can be no full disclosure, and this is where the generation of new knowledge about women's way of being begins.

It wasn't easy for us in the women's spirituality program to work out our differences. It took two years to learn how to handle and resolve conflict and really trust, knowing that our differences would be respected.

In terms of my own mortality, I'm not at all afraid of death, and I'm very healthy. I am most fortunate in having tremendous energy—far more than most people do who are forty years younger than I am. Also, I am passionately engaged in the work I do. I feel that I am at the height of my creativity and intellectual powers. I have all kinds of books to write. Two things drive me: curiosity about people and their ways, and my passion to make the world better. Not that I think I can do much on a gross level, but every little bit helps.

I have a wonderful role model, Lorna Marshall, my former neighbor in Cambridge and dear friend, a woman who is going to be a hundred in September. We share the same birthday. She's an anthropologist and worked on her most recent book well into her nineties, complaining that she wasn't as quick as she used to be, but Harvard University Press is now publishing it.

The problems of aging only came up for me for the first time this past year, when my children sat me down and told me that I've got to plan for my future. They are concerned about my financial security and don't want me to be dependent on them. Not that they said this up front. These discussions came about as a result of my program and position being phased out at the institute and my saying that I was thinking of relocating, perhaps going back East. Have I planned? Frankly, no. I'm not proud of it, but I've been one of those women who, despite having been on my own for twenty-five years, has never taken money seriously enough. For many years following my divorce, making ends meet was a great struggle. When I began to earn enough to live on comfortably, I began to travel, which is my great pleasure. And then I fancied I would remarry and that would take care of my old age. It is only recently that I have begun to save enough money to build a retirement fund.

I have two financially conservative children, a lawyer son and a doctor daughter, and my other daughter is an artist-designer who doesn't have any extra money. They all think that I should be more prudent in my investments. The artist is more forthright than the others.

Last Christmas, I realized that they had been talking among themselves about their concern about my situation. I had offered to take care of my six-year-old grandson so that my daughter and her husband could have a weekend holiday by themselves. I guess they were talking on their way about how to help me, because that evening they sat me down and told me they wanted to discuss their thoughts about my future financial well-being. I realized as I listened to them that they had an image of me that was in no way congruent with my own. I felt myself shrinking in front of them. I didn't realize it until I was on the plane coming home the next day, but it was as if I had shrunk down from this Me—who I am and how I feel—to this frail old lady, as they were talking to me. My daughter said she hoped that I would live some place that's convenient for her to get to easily so that she can come visit me in the hospital. She has this image of my mother in her old age, who was often in and out of the hospital.

But, you see, their notion of an elderly incapacitated mother is relevant to our time, when women live so much longer. My mother died at ninety-six, and I come from a long-lived family. My great-grandmother was ninety-two, and hers was not a natural death—she fell down the dark stairs on her way to the bathroom and fractured her skull. Longevity is in my genes.

The idea that one should retire never crosses my mind. I hope I'll always be writing and physically active. I climbed Mount Whitney when I was in my late fifties with a man who was my companion then. I'm no great mountain climber, but he felt I could do it, and Mount Whitney isn't a hard mountain to climb, although it is the tallest mountain in the continental United States—almost fifteen thousand feet high—so I felt very accomplished. There was a woman then who was in her eighties, a Mormon, who climbed Mount Whitney every year. She started at sixty-seven. I think I'd better try it again while I can still do it.

In terms of men, for me, the problem with an ongoing sexual relationship is that I would want it to be more than just sex, or at least I would want to have more and would hope that he would want the same. And as I have become more and more independent and always have this rush of things I want or need to do, I'm not willing to invest the time it takes to build a real relationship. There is a sadness about this, because I believe that not being involved in an intimate relationship with another is being less than fully human. It isn't that so many men come along anymore, but a friend fixed me up with a man last summer—a nice enough man. I keep meaning to invite him back for dinner, but I never do, because something else always comes up. I guess I wasn't really interested.

Many men my age lack self-confidence; they don't seem to be able to make overtures to a woman who doesn't first make overtures to them. From the time I separated from my husband in '73 until I came to California in '87, there was always at least one man who was *the man* of the time. And maybe a couple of others on the side, but I'm pretty monogamous, so that I really would have the one important man. I lived with one man for a year and a half and left him, because I couldn't really stand up to him when it came to any differences, and I was losing my power again, becoming depressed.

About the divorce . . . My husband and I were living in Switzerland, where he was teaching for the Harvard Business School, and he really wanted out from the marriage. I desperately wanted to hang in, because I was so committed to the well-being of our children, and they weren't fully raised. To this day, I continue to feel that our divorce was a disaster for them. They needed two parents at this critical time in their late adolescence and young adulthood.

Our older son committed suicide in 1981, and while his death was not directly connected, it was indirectly so, because what precipitated his depression was the breakup of our family. In his journal, he repeatedly wrote about his loss of the family life we once had and that the hardest time of the day for him was dinnertime, when he remembered our all being together.

It's not that I grieve over this all the time, or even think of it consciously, but it's there. If I could have had it my way, I would have wanted an ongoing relationship with the father of my children, so that we would live out our years together and continue to share in our children's lives and our grandchildren. Although we've become very different people now than we were in the years of our marriage, I feel that with tolerance for our differences, we might have grown together. But that hasn't been my life experience, nor for at least half the women of my generation. And the ones who are coming along don't even start out with that kind of trust. It never occurred to me when I got married that it wasn't for the rest of my life.

It never occurred to me that I wouldn't remarry, because I'm very gregarious and a nest builder. I love to cook; I like sharing. But what I realized was that I wasn't willing to commit. (Never mind; most of these men didn't care if we married.) It wasn't the ceremony; it was the commitment to them that I didn't want. When I think about it, and I've only recently come to this understanding, I realized that I was never willing to give myself away again. I didn't want to lose my voice in order to have my prince. Perhaps I could do this now, but it's taken me many years to get to this place of internalizing my own authority. Now I think I could have a relationship with a man who would be my partner, and I could hold my own. ♍

I just want to tell other women my own age, "Stop resting. Get up and help others. Go out and talk to your politicians. You can ask questions of them." There's no sense in being old and grumpy. There's no sense in resting. You got eternity to rest. No sense in starting now.

ENOLA MAXWELL

Enola Maxwell

Profile

Born in Baton Rouge, Louisiana, in 1919, Enola Maxwell arrived in San Francisco with her three children on July 4, 1948, in the hope of making a better life for herself and her children. That was fifty years to the week before I interviewed her at her bustling Victorian in the Bayview District of San Francisco near Hunter's Point.

For the past twenty-six years, Enola has been the executive director of Potrero Hill Neighborhood House, which is a multiservice, multi-generational community agency. The Omega Boys Club, the Potrero Hill Girls Club, the Multi-Ethnic Theater, the Substance Abuse Program, the Potrero Hill Neighborhood House Youth Choir, Head Start child care, Experiment in Diversity, the Senior Program, and the Developmentally Disabled Adults Program have all contributed immeasurably to the quality of life for both youth and seniors in the City of San Francisco. Focusing on education, health, and welfare, the "Nabe" (as the Potrero Hill Neighborhood House is affectionately called, as an abbreviation of *neighborhood*) prides itself on being a community resource from the cradle to the grave. It is a magnet for the young and old, for the active and frail,

bestowing its message of compassion, hope, and love on all who enter
its doors.

Who is the seventy-eight-year-old woman behind the "Nabe"? And
what keeps her vital and involved, even after undergoing heart bypass
surgery four years ago? Enola claimed not to feel any better since the surgery. Veins from her left leg were used in her heart, but because the leg
didn't heal properly, her foot suffers from poor blood circulation. "It's kind
of hampering my schedule," Enola complained. "But I still go to work
every day."

Enola is known for always wearing a hat. "I have a hat on all the time,
sometimes even in the house. People wonder why I do that, but I can't
stand to be without one. My nose gets stopped up." When I asked if she
might like to wear one for our photograph, she said with her characteristic good humor, "I don't know what good a hat would do me. I look
OK? When you get to be seventy-eight years old, what you gonna look
like? Now these doctors want to do plastic surgery on my leg. I said,
'I don't be wasting no money doing no plastic surgery on this leg of
mine, because they's nothing but drumsticks already. No way. What's the
use?' Shucks, that's terrible. Plastic surgery, if you please!"

One of the disadvantages of being older, for Enola, is that she no
longer drives a car. "I don't work very far away. My family drives me, or
the staff picks me up sometimes if I have to go early. I do feel underprivileged when I'm not driving. That's the only time I feel underprivileged.
It's been that way for many years. But I'm trying to get over it, if I can,
this underprivileged stuff, because driving is awfully hard these days. You
guys have your hands full. There's always traffic. I don't care what time,
what day. There used to be some times there wasn't as much traffic. People just driving any kinda way. Not enough consideration for others. If I
was driving, honey, I know somebody would just run into me to get me
off the street. Hah. I just could not keep up. So things have changed a lot,
and I'm trying to adjust myself to being underprivileged."

On a Sunday afternoon, I arrived on Enola's doorstep. Even on her
days off, she hopes to accomplish a lot at home. "Today, I haven't done
anything but a little bit of gardening, but not enough. I slept in kinda late.

Didn't worry about getting up too early. I should have been out there, the sun was so nice. I gotta do something with that garden; it's just too much. That's why I keep busy on a weekend, because if I don't, the weeds keep growing. All kinds of different plants. Peach trees are growing all over the place."

Every ledge, shelf, and table in her living room is covered with elephant figurines. When I asked their significance, Enola said, "That's my favorite animal. Have you ever heard of anybody picking on one? I won't be stepped on anymore in my next life. I'm coming back as an elephant. They don't step on many people, but they step on a few things in the way. They don't go out of their way to be mean or do harm to anybody, most times. Everybody gives me elephants. I've got some strange-looking elephants."

In honor of her seventy-fifth birthday in 1994, the city of San Francisco declared the week of October 2 to October 9 to be "Enola D. Maxwell and Potrero Hill Neighborhood House Week." In a statement made before the House of Representatives in Washington, D.C., Congresswoman Nancy Pelosi said, "Mr. Speaker, it is a privilege to bring to the attention of the Congress the achievements of a remarkable woman and a remarkable organization in San Francisco. On behalf of the Congress of the United States, let us join all San Franciscans in recognizing the outstanding achievements of Enola Maxwell, seventy-five years young, and the Potrero Hill Neighborhood House, which will continue to be a beacon of hope atop Potrero Hill for many years to come."

Celebrating a Multigenerational and Multiracial Community

As the executive director of the Potrero Hill Neighborhood House, I do a bit of everything. Our latest program, Experiment in Diversity, includes a group of ten teenagers and three adults, white and black and

Spanish, who are trying to create a better understanding between the different races. That's really nice. We have dinners every month, and for that month, we will study a different race. Last month we were studying Filipinos, so we had Filipino food.

At the Potrero Hill Neighborhood House, everybody kind of integrates with each other—the seniors with the youth, the various races. They all have the same program in the same house, instead of having the seniors in one building and having the youth in another. They're all right there together and get to know each other. Because of this kind of integrated program, the teenagers no longer make fun of the mentally retarded. Those that aren't mentally retarded aren't afraid of those that are. It's working out real well.

Nobody lives there, but the seniors come for lunch, games, and exercise. The mentally retarded people come for games, socialization, just to get out of the house. They would be shut-ins if they didn't have any place to go. So they go on field trips, to the library, learn to do things by themselves, and to socialize with other people unlike themselves. There are forty people in the mentally retarded program, thirty-five in the senior program, and hundreds of kids for various and sundry reasons, I guess, in summertime. We have about thirty in our school program. It's for the kids whose teachers get fed up with them and can't do anything with them. The kids can't adapt to the regular classroom. Sometimes they adapt to our school pretty well, and sometimes they don't, but it's the last resort for these kids, so everybody bends over backward to make them succeed. I mean, what are they gonna do if they can't go to school? Where are they going? These are the kids who end up mugging people and taking drugs.

I just can't see kids, fourteen, fifteen years old getting suspended from school. Does nobody any good. But a lot of that goes on. I wish they would enforce the curfew law that says every kid is supposed to be in school. It's the law until they're sixteen years old, and yet they put them out of school. Kids even make arrangements to get kicked out of school so they can go out and meet their friends and do stupid things. We're trying our best to get the school district to keep the kids in school. At least get the enforcement there, instead of the curfew at night; that's not going to do anything. There's nothing they can do in the night that they can't do in the day. So we work on that and a lot of other things to try and prevent delinquency. We also have a delinquency program. When young people are let out of the youth guidance center, they have to report every day to see that they're in school. It's called intensive home supervision.

That is the most hurtful thing, how those kids are just so lost. So much is expected of parents, but many parents are in such bad shape themselves— nothing they can do for the kids. I don't know the answer. I know the answer, but it's not legal; instead of locking those kids up, sometimes the parents need to be taken out of the home. How can you raise a child if you have no financial support, the husband is an alcoholic, the wife is addicted to drugs, the grandmother's an alcoholic? So what do you do? The answer is not incarcerating the children, I don't think.

Still, I really think it's going to get better, because I don't see how a country like ours could go on like this. People are going to wake up, and many people are now thinking differently. They need to *act* differently, too. I hope we can get rid of some of the present legislators. I just don't understand those people, where they're coming from. They're getting rid of the welfare system and putting nothing in its place. Nowhere to go. OK, no more welfare. And these women on welfare, some of them can't even live. They have no skills whatsoever, no education, and no income. Some of them have teenage children. Washington, D.C., is trying to get rid of the Summer Youth Employment Program. What are they thinking?

As an example, one of my doors just fell off the hinges, and getting somebody to put it back on is not the easiest thing in the world to do. It's such a small thing, but those who know how are busy. And the rest of them are too lazy and backward to know how to do anything. Can't even tell a screw from a nail. It's just terrible, the ignorance. Some of those things we cut out of school. We used to have shop. We have kids who don't know anything about operating a power saw, never held a power saw in their hands or any other saw. What can they do? They just don't know how.

Some kids don't even know how to wash dishes. In home economics, you learned something about cooking and cleaning. My children had a bank account, and they used to come and collect money once a week and take it to the Bank of America. They knew what saving was about. Nowadays, kids get a dollar and, I tell you, they just gotta go to the store and spend it on something. They just buy anything. It used to be a matter of needs, but now it's about wanting something that somebody else has. That's all it is. Need doesn't enter into it. "I want this because I saw it on TV" or "because a friend of mine has it," and if you don't get it, you're afraid to look out of it.

The truth of the matter is that I refuse to be old. I'll never get old. I can live to be a hundred, and I still won't get old. Old age is not good for you! But you can begin to think differently about age, and you can talk to older people your age. You can say anything. You can tell them about themselves, how older people are the most dangerous people you will ever have to deal with. "People, don't hit me. I'm old. Stop." Old people jaywalk across the street. I tell seniors, "Younger people don't like us. Their brakes don't know no age." Now that I'm not driving and trying to walk to the corner, I can see why they jaywalk, but it's not good. The closest I ever came to hitting anybody was seniors and small kids, because they always jaywalk.

So I talk to seniors about a lot of things. "Take into account, dear, that things are different." They say, "The politicians in nineteen-so-and-so . . . were better. Things were better back then." I can take a lot of things into consideration. That's how I survive, taking myself into consideration, looking within first before I look without. When something upsets me, I have a habit of asking myself, "Where was I? What did I do wrong? What should I have done?" Now when you get older, you can tell it to old and young.

Talk about respecting old people . . . I tell young people, "Don't you worry about respecting old people. What you do is respect yourself. If you respect yourself, that's enough for me, because you cannot disrespect me. Who are you to disrespect me? There's nothing you can do to disrespect me. But you can disrespect yourself." I can tell the kids that because I'm old enough. You know what I mean? I worry about these young. Some of these elderly people don't deserve any respect, and you can tell them that. "Why you want some young person to respect you? I teach my kids not to respect fools, so if you want to be a fool, you don't deserve any respect, and I don't want any kids respecting you." I'm so happy I can say that. They're so sure, older people. So we have a different philosophy.

When I first went to work at the Nabe, the older ones didn't even want the kids to go to the same bathroom they went to. My God, you can't prevent anybody from going to the bathroom! Everyone has to go to the bathroom. "You just have to share the bathroom with them," we tell the seniors now. "Either you can be afraid of every teenager you see, or you can be courteous to every teenager you see and get to know them, and they will be very valuable to you. Because they're not gonna mug you. And what's more, they're not going to let anybody else mug you." Of course, I tell the teenagers the same thing; it works out well. Some of the teenagers even open the door for the seniors, and when the seniors are passing them, they say, "I know that kid. That kid's all right." All because they had the courtesy of getting to know each other.

We had one old man, on a cane, if you please. He would carry on so terribly. He'd see a kid and start cursing. I looked at him and said, "John, I would like to tell these kids not to use that language, but the way you curse, I can't say anything to them. You're setting the example. If you can cuss them, don't know them no better than they know you, then they can cuss you back." So this multigenerational interaction is really valuable. It has helped us immensely. We have Filipinos—they're not afraid to come to the house. Black and brown, Samoans—all those people. They don't care who comes there every day for lunch. They all talk to each other. They're not afraid to come to the house, night or day, anytime they get ready. They feel like it's their house, and the kids feel like it's their house. I just wish there was a little bit more of this. A lot of people say this is the only community center where you find this kind of interaction.

I heard somebody the other day, "Ms. Maxwell, we're not going to have any summer employment program next year." I read about this in the paper, and Newt Gingrich wants to discontinue the summer employment program, but I didn't want to say this to the kids. I said, "Well, we have to try to see what we can do to get our legislators not to go along with that, not to support that. You guys have to encourage your mothers to vote. If you vote, it won't happen, but if you don't vote, then they do anything they want to do. You're not old enough to vote, but the minute you get to be eighteen, please register. You see to your parents' getting registered and voting, because that's where the power is." The kids don't have any power.

If America could take these kinds of things into consideration instead of helping to stir up this hatred, they could do something to eliminate it. But they don't do that. All over this country, they could have the same thing we have at the neighborhood house: diversity training, diversity living, teenagers from all these races working together. It should be a matter of fact in the school district. We say we have integration in the school district. This is not the case. They should have studies in diversity, teaching people how to live together, teaching people how to adjust to the society they are living in.

I don't have very much time to sit back and be old, because there's still so much undone. I tell old people, too, that we have to be the ones now to get in front of the bulldozers when they deny our people employment, when they start redevelopment. We should not leave it to the young people to get in front of the bulldozers. We didn't make the country a better place to live, because we haven't done what we were supposed to do. We did not see to it that affirmative action was enforced, or it would have been all right to discontinue it, because there'd be no need for it. We just sat there. We just dropped out and let things go backward.

And it's going backward fast, not just for blacks but for seniors and everybody else. They want to undo everything that benefited people. These congresspersons are messing with everything. Black people need to try to build alliances, because there's one thing—there are more seniors on Social Security than there are blacks, because for so long blacks weren't even paid Social Security. We didn't make enough money—no way. We have to see to it that those benefits are not taken.

Look what's happened since the unions have been taken away. They have practically destroyed the unions. Now you have grown men and women working for minimum wage, $5.75 an hour. Took the money away from the welfare people and are paying the corporations to hire them. Tax breaks!

But we allowed that to happen, so I have to keep on livin' as long as I can, and I have to keep on workin' as long as I live so I can get a few people together. I have to do that. I have to keep telling seniors that we got to go out there and do something. These promises that are being made, if they're not kept, do not leave it to the young people to get mowed down. Let us get mowed down, because we are old enough to die. We didn't do what we should have done. That's why I'm goin' on livin' and workin' as long as I can do a reasonable job.

I just want to tell other women my own age, "Stop resting. Get up and help others. Go out and talk to your politicians. You can ask questions of them." Every once in a while, you can go down there and make a statement to them. I've got some statements I want to make. There's no sense in being old and grumpy. There's no sense in resting. You got eternity to rest. No sense in starting now. ✌

Live as full a life as you can. Don't be self-absorbed; get involved in something larger than yourself. Find some way to be socially useful, and get involved in community life. Make a contribution. What really matters is kindness, generosity, and compassion. You've just got to find a way to use them in your life. Find some way that delights you.

MARGE FRANTZ

Marge Frantz

Profile

Marge Frantz has always been a role model to other women in living a life full of authenticity, meaning, kindness, generosity, and compassion. She has found a variety of ways to be socially useful, to be involved in community life, and to make a contribution. Nine years after retiring from her full-time employment as a lecturer at the University of California at Santa Cruz in the departments of American Studies and Women's Studies, Marge remains on campus, "still very involved with campus committees," teaching one course a year and offering her knowledge and support in independent studies with students.

As Marge sees it, she really had no choice but to be politically and socially involved. It was a legacy from her father, a radicalized professor of physics at the University of Alabama and a very early proponent of civil rights and unionization in labor. At seventeen, she was arrested for the first time by the soon-to-be notorious "Bull" Connor, the chief of police in Birmingham, Alabama; in the 1950s, he outraged people and polarized politicians throughout the nation when he turned full-force fire hoses on assembled blacks. Since then, her causes have ranged from civil rights to

People's Park in Berkeley, from opposition to nuclear proliferation to support for gay and lesbian rights.

Marge lovingly discussed her thirty-seven-year-long relationship with her partner, Eleanor. After twenty years of a traditional marriage and after having four children, Marge met and fell in love with Eleanor. In the social climate of 1961, even in Berkeley, where they lived at the time, there was considerable prejudice against lesbians. She admitted that it took her a long time to give up her marriage and the "safety it bestowed" on her. For years, she felt that her only recourse was to live a life of "subterfuge." She found, however, that knowing both forms of love—marriage and children, as well as a lesbian relationship—has been "the best of both worlds."

In *From Wedded Wife to Lesbian Life,* a book of stories published in 1996 about women who have left heterosexual marriages for lesbian relationships, Marge wrote an introduction on the history of lesbianism. In her well-researched and fascinating account, the reader is taken on a journey from the early 1800s, when "much lesbian history includes guesswork"; to the Victorian era, when contemporary "ideology held that 'proper' women simply weren't sexual creatures"; to the social change after the Civil War, as industrialization and urbanization grew and allowed for the possibility that women "might be able to live independently, rather than be forced into marriage, home, and domesticity"; to the feminist movement of 1890 to 1920, which afforded women further independence through intellectual education; to the creation of "all-female worlds" in the Women's Army Corp and various other branches of the military service; to the "lesbian hunts" during the cold war in the 1950s and McCarthyism; to the 1970s, which "saw the emergence of a newly energized, militant gay liberation movement."

The day we met, Marge and Eleanor were preparing to leave the rustic cabin in the Santa Cruz Mountains that had been their home for over twenty-five years. They had purchased two small condominiums across the hall from each other in a downtown Santa Cruz co-op. One would serve as more private quarters for the two, and the second would provide a living room for receiving guests and a study for Marge. At the ages of seventy-six and eighty-nine, respectively, these two were still curious about what life holds in store for them and were eager to be involved in yet a new form of community life in town.

The Best of Both Worlds

My life really changed when I was forty-eight. I went back to Berkeley to finish a B.A. But I'd been working as an editor at the Institute of Industrial Relations in Berkeley for twelve years, so I had already been in the academic community. While I was an editor in Berkeley, I started getting involved with the U.C. campus and auditing some courses in political theory. I became fascinated by Berkeley all through the sixties. It was a fascinating place to be. There was a very interesting group of political theorists on the campus, including Jack Schaar, who was just a marvelous lecturer. Although I audited quite a few classes, I never had time to do the reading, because I was working and also had four kids.

I was involved in pretty much everything that happened at Berkeley, at one level or another. In 1970, in the middle of the People's Park riots, I was working for the institute. Earlier, I had worked for the executive vice chancellor of the campus. He was the person responsible for putting up the fence at People's Park. We were close friends, but I was so upset about what was happening at People's Park that I quit the institute. It was completely impulsive, unplanned. At that point, I was editing manuscripts for a journal that came out of the institute, and my boss had said, "Marge, I want to go on early vacation. If you could get the manuscripts ready a few weeks early, it would be helpful." With no plan or anything, I said, "George, I'm so mad at the university, I'm not going to touch another manuscript until that goddamn fence comes down." I had no plans for my future. But the fence didn't come down, so I quit.

Then I had to figure out what I was going to do with the rest of my life! I was forty-seven at that point. My husband worked, and I decided for the first time in my life not to work. Our four kids were between the ages of thirteen and twenty. I continued auditing courses and doing serious reading on the heavy political theory classes. By that time, I knew most of the teaching assistants, and I just plunged into studying political theory for a year. I had a ball. It really was great fun. At the end of that year, the two most important teachers both decided to go to Santa Cruz. I felt as though the rug had been pulled out from under me. I hadn't planned to go back to school, but if I planned to go down to Santa Cruz to do some graduate work with them, first I had to finish my B.A. Luckily, one of their students, Hanna Pitkin, was teaching political theory, so I became one of Hanna's students and got admitted to Berkeley and finished my B.A. in political theory. I didn't want to get a political science degree, because there were various political science courses I wasn't interested in. I didn't want to do their behaviorist political science. So I did an independent major in the Western political tradition. Got my B.A. and came down to Santa Cruz. At that time, my husband and I separated.

My partner had one more year to go before she retired from her job as a librarian at the Berkeley Library. So the first year I came down here, I didn't actually move. I rented a bed in somebody's sitting room. Came down early Monday mornings, stayed through Thursday, and then went back home for three days. At the end of the first year, she came down from Berkeley, and we moved into this house in the Santa Cruz Mountains. We had met in the Unitarian Church in Berkeley, a women's group. We were friends for quite a while before we actually fell in love. I was thirty-nine and she was fifty-three when we fell in love.

In the long run, the situation couldn't have worked out better for me, because my husband was a lovely man, and he and I are still very close friends. We have all our family birthdays and holidays together. He has a woman friend, and we all get together, and it's very pleasant.

But when my partner and I first fell in love, we knew only one other lesbian couple in Berkeley. Nobody was out of the closet. It was difficult. We didn't have any support system. I felt pretty paralyzed. I didn't want to disrupt the kids' lives, so I lived a life of subterfuge for a while. I didn't know what else to do.

I've been very, very lucky in my life. I grew up in Alabama. My father taught physics at the University of Alabama, and my mother taught English at the University of Alabama. I had wonderful parents. I feel so lucky to be teaching. I still love what I'm doing. I didn't discover teaching—it's obviously my vocation—until I was in my fifties. My father was a wonderful guy. He was a very early civil rights person in Alabama, radicalized by the depression. He started his social activism when I was eleven or twelve and took me with him. I greatly admired him, and many others did, too. At one point in his work, he was kidnapped and beaten very badly by thugs hired by the local steel company, as he was fighting unionization in the South in 1937. They threatened to fill him full of lead if he didn't leave Alabama, and he didn't leave. My mother was pretty horrified by all these things. She married this fraternity boy, whom she thought would bring her security and whatnot, but she loved him and, with some reluctance, went along with everything.

In an effort to bring her along politically, my parents and I went to New York for a year when I was thirteen so she could meet other radicals from the East. There weren't very many in Alabama. My father had grown up in Birmingham and attended the University of Alabama and MIT. He was in the army during World War I and returned to work in his father's business. He was always something of an iconoclast, I guess, but not politically. He loved education. His mother supported his going back to school when he was thirty or so. He finished his B.A. and master's and started teaching at the Physics Lab at Tuscaloosa.

My mother had dropped out of Goucher College to marry him and went back to school when he went back to school, which was unheard of in those days—no such thing as a "reentry woman." But she was very smart; she became the darling of the dean of the arts and sciences and, eventually, head of the English department. She started teaching freshman English and sophomore literature as soon as she got her master's. She was a wonderful teacher, because she was totally charming and interested in people, lively and warm, enthusiastic, energetic. Students loved her, and she brought them home to dinner all the time. I thought that was the way teachers were.

I had a wonderful childhood, a college community where I could roam around at will. I used to hang out at the girls' gym or the football field in the years when the University of Alabama had the best football team in the country. It was a very small, easy community in Alabama. I was a free kid. It was a great way to grow up.

Then we moved to live in the woods, outside of Birmingham, just like this. I love the woods. My father started taking me hiking every Sunday when I was six and taught me the names of the trees, flowers, ferns, mushrooms, mosses, complete with field glasses and microscopes. We studied the stars at night. He loved the outdoors.

In New York, that one year when I was thirteen, I got very involved in political matters, student movements in the thirties—'35, '36. I made my first open-air speech at that time. When I came back to Birmingham to finish high school, I was editor of the school paper and started a League of Nations club.

I didn't do much politically until I went to college when I was sixteen at Radcliffe. I had a scholarship. I was basically studying American history, the history of the South. I wasn't a very serious student. I did well, but I had lots of other things on my mind. I was much more interested in political activism. I lost my scholarship, basically for political reasons, at the end of my sophomore year. I was too radical for Radcliffe. I dropped out of school and essentially didn't go back except for one quarter at the University of North Carolina in 1948, until Berkeley, when I was forty-eight.

When I went to college, I got very involved in political activity. I guess it was my freshman year, when I was home for the summer, and my dad was doing civil liberties and civil rights work in Birmingham with the National Committee for Defense of Political Prisoners. Bull Connor had just been made Commissioner of Public Safety (basically chief of police). He became famous for turning fire hoses on kids in the fifties. It was his first year in office, and he was given the job by the steel companies, which ran Birmingham lock, stock, and barrel. The police might as well have been hired by the steel companies. The police were supposed to stamp out any kind of dissent. One of the things they did was arrest anybody who was politically "suspicious." Ordinance 4902 permitted them to get anybody and keep them in jail incommunicado without the right to call anybody for forty-eight hours. Dad was fighting this ordinance and wanted to get a test case, so some of us went out to distribute leaflets about this ordinance, and they picked us all up. That was my first arrest, by Bull Connor when I was seventeen.

My dad was instrumental in organizing a group called the Southern Conference for Human Welfare in 1938—the first big interracial organization in the South since Reconstruction days—which brought together liberals and radicals and labor people and professionals from all over the South. Mrs. Roosevelt came down to speak, among others. This was the first major coming-together of such people, the first break in the monolithic South in the thirties.

About being in my seventies, I would say there are very few ways in which I feel my age at all, partly because in most settings throughout my life, I was always the youngest, and I still always think of myself that way. It's really weird. I was younger at Radcliffe. My friends have usually been older. Almost all of my closest friends have been somewhat older. Eleanor's older. Laurent, my ex-husband, is older. It's a habit to think of myself as younger. I'm older than anybody on campus. I don't think there's anybody my age who's actively teaching around there, but I don't think of myself as older. And I certainly don't think of myself as any kind of a sage.

I just don't think about age very much. Recently, I picked up Simone de Beauvoir's book *The Coming of Age,* which somebody gave me when I was fifty. I thought, "My God, what am I doing with this?" She presents this awful picture of the way society treats the elderly and talks about their poverty and decrepitude and silence. I just haven't experienced that, although I know it's true. But the older people I associate with, in groups like Women's International League for Peace and Freedom—they're all much like me. They've been socially active all their lives and are still active. In my view, it's an incredibly rewarding way to live, just the best way to live. You have a million friends and comrades that you've worked with all your life, off and on.

There are really two major disabilities for me about age. One is that your friends begin to die, particularly if, as I just said, you're younger than everybody. A lot of the people I care most about have died in the last few years—people that were very, very close to me. But I'm also very lucky because, having taught, I'm with younger people in school and graduate school. I have all these young friends, which is just great. I'm still in touch with many of those people, who are now teaching all over the country, and they're good friends. I'm glad to have all these young friends, but it's very painful for me when my friends die.

The second thing is I'm not very well organized and tend to be a procrastinator, and I've always sort of managed that by what I call "power bursts." You know, get up at four in the morning and clean my desk and get caught up. I can't do that anymore. That is a major disability. That started to happen gradually during the last year or two. Maybe a longer period. I can, every now and then, still do it, have these moments of feeling like I get a lot done in a hurry. Basically, it just takes me longer to do things, especially when I don't want to do them.

I so-called retired nine years ago when I was sixty-eight. I officially retired and started drawing retirement benefits from the University of California, because I didn't want to teach as many courses as I would need to teach to keep my medical benefits. I had an understanding that I could teach as much as I wanted, as long as I wanted, and I would get my medical and not worry about that. So that's what I did. I continued to teach two or three courses. Now I'm down to one course a year, but I still do independent studies with students and am still very involved with campus committees and things like that.

But the great love, the great joy I get out of retirement, is that I don't have to get out of the house first thing in the morning as I did for so many years. Now I can get up, take it easy, read the paper, go for a walk. I can think in the afternoon, not in the morning. That's just wonderful. I live a different life being older, but it hasn't really slowed down much. I mean, it's slowed down in the sense of how much less I get done in a day, but every day my datebook's still pretty full. I love it when I can spend a day at home, but that doesn't happen very often.

I don't think about the future a lot. I think when we move to town, we'll probably just wind down, but I don't really know that that's true, because there will be a lot of things to do. We may audit courses on the campus together. I thrive around other people. My husband used to say that other people collect stamps and coins and I collect people. I really love people; my mother was that way. That's one of the problems with teaching. Every time I teach a course, I end up with two or three new friends. I can't deal with more; it's too many. I can't incorporate them well. I feel I don't always come through for people as much as I should because there are just too many people in my life.

It's hard to know how we're going to slow down. I'm not sure we will. I think in some ways we have slowed down. We don't have too much company. When we first came down here, it was like R&R headquarters; all these people from Berkeley came down to Santa Cruz and spent the weekend. We started cooling that off sometime back, because it's great to have people for a meal, but a weekend takes too much energy. Everything takes more energy, that's for sure.

There's been a lot of talk about my retiring. It never seems to happen, though. I may stop after two more years. I'm not planning any big changes, but I do plan probably to try and write some memoirs. Not for publication but for my grandchildren and my friends, who are pushing me to do it. But I don't intend to put the energy into making it a literary masterpiece.

My health has been mostly good. I had a bout with breast cancer in 1976, twenty-two years ago, and had a mastectomy. There wasn't any lymph node involvement, and I'm fine. It was a useful experience in many ways, because it made me conscious of my body, and I started eating much more sensibly. Eleanor started dragging me to workshops and such on meditation and visualization, things that I resisted but that she insisted on, so I went. Actually, it really opened me up. It did not make a true believer out of me, but it was interesting. I was glad I did it. I went to a workshop by somebody who had worked with Simonton (who is a specialist in the treatment of cancer) on meditation and visualization, and I learned a lot. That was eye-opening in some ways, because I got in touch with feelings that I literally didn't know I had about feeling mutilated. I truthfully didn't. I thought, "I can deal with this." In general, Eleanor got me into reevaluation counseling and co-counseling. That turned out to be useful, and it broadened my views.

I was basically very healthy for a long time, and then a couple of years ago, I had a TIA [transient ischemic attack], a warning of stroke. Not serious. I had dizzy spells and severe nausea and visual symptoms. I went to bed one night and suddenly felt very dizzy. We had a digital clock on one side of the room and a PC modem with the light on. Both of them were wavering up and down. I didn't know whether to take it seriously or not, so I didn't do anything until the next morning. We looked up in the Kaiser handbook about when to call the doctor. It said if dizziness was combined with any of the following symptoms, call. One was visual symptoms. It was a wake-up call again. It's an interruption of blood flow from your heart to your brain, essentially, and probably a little piece of plaque chips off into your arteries and disrupts the blood flow. I did have continuing dizzy symptoms. Not in the sense of the room going around, which it was the first night. It was more like not feeling real secure on my feet. I never fell. They did tests, and everything was fine. It went away, and I haven't had any other symptoms. But those things scare you.

I've had lousy insomnia the last few years. I'll wake up at two or three in the morning and not be able to get back to sleep for a couple of hours. I just stay in bed. I've learned to live with it by thinking, using the time to think about how I would write about one thing or another. I find this kind of reflection fascinating. I really love it. So it's not a hassle. Sometimes I get sleepy in the middle of the afternoon, and if I go to a lecture I might fall asleep, but I try not to do it so visibly.

The longer you live, the more you learn to put things together and have a broader view and a little distance, to think more objectively. I don't like that word *objectively*. More dispassionately. Except for the loss of friends, I just feel unbelievably lucky to have work that I love, a partner that I love, children and grandchildren that I love, and to be comfortable and not have to worry about money. I don't have a very big retirement, but I have enough to live on.

Starting when I was sixty-three, we began traveling. I never had the money, time, and leisure to travel before. We always went to the mountains every summer, which we adored. Eleanor and I backpacked every summer for thirty years. That's our favorite thing, but we got to the point where we weren't that great at backpacking. At first, I had to persuade her to travel. She wasn't hot on traveling, because she's a voracious reader, and she had read all about every place she might want to go. And when people came back, like from China, we would go hear them talk about their trip, and she already knew everything they said. In general, she was better informed than the people who went. So she couldn't see the point. I persuaded her because I had never traveled in Europe, and she hadn't either. We had a fabulous trip in 1984. We had ten weeks, and she just loved it. She realized there was another dimension besides what she could read about and see in pictures. We both had a ball. Since then, we've done a lot of traveling. That's one of the gifts of age—the time, money, and leisure to travel.

We went back to Italy a couple of times. This last time, we went to Venice, then worked our way down to Rome. We went to Portugal one summer, and then to China. This time, we went on an Elder Hostel trip. (We love Elder Hostel for foreign trips.) By this time, we were ready to get somebody to deal with our luggage, not have to lug it ourselves. The next year, we went on a Quaker trip to Russia for a summer. Then we went on Elder Hostel to Sicily. The last Elder Hostel trip we did was to Turkey, which was just fabulous—about two years ago. We just had a ball traveling.

I bought a camper, which was a great comedown for us. We'd always camped. We did two trips all through the Northwest: Victoria, Vancouver Island, and we have various friends on islands off of Whidbey Island. One summer, we went back and concentrated on the San Juan Islands. Then we took a wonderful, wonderful trip to the Southwest in the camper, and that was thrilling. We have friends down there.

We also go back to the Sierras and "do" wildflowers. We were there last summer in the middle of June, and I guess this year it will probably be a month later, but everything was just coming out. Within three hours, we'd seen twenty-six different species just starting to bloom and lots that hadn't started blooming yet. It was just great. We did some hiking.

I think the thing that has kept us together is . . . First of all, we love each other very much. But also . . . in the early days, we had a lot of differences that we had to work out. Dogs, for example; she loves 'em, I can't stand 'em. She's a much more serious housekeeper than I am. But if you come down to it, you just ask the question, "Do I want to keep this relationship going, or don't I?" If the answer's yes, you work it out. Over time, you develop many methods and patterns for solving differences.

The main problem was that she retired down here in Santa Cruz and did not have a community. And I'd already been here a year, and I was totally absorbed with school. That was hard for her, and she just made her peace with it. She's been involved in various community activities since she's been here. And she has a circle of friends. Now we've got an enormous support system. We don't have a lot of involvement with the lesbian community here. We have a lot of lesbian friends, but it's not our main focus at all. We do have one Quaker lesbian group that meets once a year. We've gotten very close to those people. It's more important to me than it is to her, but it's nice that it exists.

What do I think about women leaving a heterosexual life for a lesbian life? Well, I think the main thing is that it's wonderful that there's a choice. There didn't used to be a choice; now there is. It's really a lovely possibility; I just don't think it was in my youth. I had one brief lesbian encounter when I was twenty with an interesting person who, unbeknownst to me beforehand, was a terrible alcoholic. My conclusion at the time was that things were so difficult for lesbians that that's probably how you would end up if you had to face all the social ostracisms. But the sexual encounter was very thrilling to me, and it was absolutely clear to me at that moment that, at some level, that's who I was. The books this woman gave me to read on the subject were not encouraging either. *The Well of Loneliness,* a famous lesbian novel. It's pretty awful in terms of what lesbians had to face—social pressures. So I decided that's not for me.

It's not that there are no serious pressures now; there are. But there's a huge support system to help you deal with them. It's not a question of giving up having children; you can still have children. I just think it's wonderful that that situation exists, and that there's a lesbian community out there that's really helpful. I know some wonderful lesbians, and I know some wonderful *young* lesbians, and I've learned a great deal from my lesbian students over the years. But I think I've had the best of all possible worlds. I was heterosexual, had my kids, and everything, and then I fell in love with a woman. A student I once had decided she was a lesbian when she was in high school. I thought, but didn't say, "Too bad for you."

Again, I've been incredibly lucky. Lots of things have come together for me. It's none of my doing. I was there. I've been part of many social movements that have been very satisfying and that have made a difference in my life. I've had work that I love. In my teaching, I could use all my life experience, and that infused my teaching with a lot of passion, which students like.

I guess my advice to other women is to live as full a life as you can. Don't be self-absorbed; get involved in something larger than yourself, whatever your thing is. Find some way to be socially useful, and get involved in community life. Make a contribution. What really matters is kindness, generosity, and compassion—those good things. You've just got to find a way to use them in your life. Find some way that delights you. Hannah Arendt has this great phrase—"public happiness"—and it refers to an intense joy and delight you get from participating in collective political activity and having community. It doesn't have to be political; it can be community activity. I think that's what makes a life worth living. If you do that, you'll be surrounded with people you feel very close to. It's just been very rewarding for me.

But you know, you can't prescribe for anybody else. People have to find their own way. You have to be able to take risks, have adventures. I haven't had to make a lot of decisions; things have just sort of fallen into my lap. They really have. I didn't plan to be a social activist; my dad put that in my lap.

For instance, my participation in the first major demonstration at Lawrence Livermore Labs (where all of the planning for the nuclear establishment happens) in 1982 was none of my doing. I've always been appalled at the whole idea of nuclear war and American foreign policy, starting with the cold war, which I was totally opposed to. In the beginning of the eighties, I was teaching a class on women in U.S. history. Livermore Labs is connected with the University of California. I and many, many other people in the university felt it was atrocious that the university should be sponsoring that. It's not that the development of nuclear weapons wouldn't have happened anyway, but having the labs connected to the university gave them a lot more prestige and made it easier for them to get the best physicists.

In '82, there was a big protest happening at Livermore. My students were going, and I thought, "I agree with them. Why don't I go?" I went to nonviolence training here in Santa Cruz and went up to Berkeley to be part of this group. We went out to Livermore at four in the morning to blockade the place, and we got arrested. We were in jail for two days and were charged with some minor infraction, less than a misdemeanor—like getting a jaywalking ticket. We had a very favorable judge and there were a thousand of us, about five hundred women and five hundred men. They put all the women into a huge gymnasium big enough for two basketball courts. It was an interesting experience. I was fascinated with part of it and appalled by part of it. Some of the kids were so young and radical and rebellious that I thought they were pushing the boundaries. It wasn't exactly my way of doing things, but I was learning. It was a whole new method of doing politics for me—by consensus. There was an enormous enthusiasm and a lot of spirituality connected with it. It was thrilling.

So I sort of absorbed all of that. It was just a two-day deal, and I came home. The next spring, I got a call from a friend of mine in Berkeley who was organizing a group called Elders for Survival, and she asked if I would please get a group of elders together in Santa Cruz to go to Livermore in June for another demonstration. It turned out I couldn't get enough elders, but I got a lot of people in their thirties and forties, as well as people in their sixties. We called ourselves the Salt and Pepper Brigade. It was a terrific bunch of people. We assumed we wouldn't be there more than two or three days.

We got to Livermore, over a thousand people got arrested, and the judge announced to us he was going to hold us only a couple of days in jail but we would be on two years' probation. If we demonstrated again, we would go to jail for two years. So in protest, we refused to even go to arraignment. This time, they put us in an old warehouse and erected huge circus tents on the ground and put barbed wire around the whole thing.

They couldn't treat us like we were in jail, couldn't control us the way they do in a normal jail scene, so we sort of took advantage of that situation and created our own "peace camp." We started organizing classes and workshops. We took charge of our entertainment and put on terrific entertainments in the evenings. It brought out all this creativity in people. Wonderful to watch these five hundred women. Just the most incredible scene. I felt as though my whole life had prepared me to be useful in this scene, helping to keep up morale.

One of the women suggested we have a Gandhi fashion show; we wrapped sheets around ourselves to see who could come up with the best sheet wrapping for dinner that night. We had an Emma Goldman birthday party one night; I talked about Emma Goldman. We had several good musicians but no instruments. We had a rock band made out of rocks. We formed these big circles in which we sang, and people took turns dancing in the middle. We entertained ourselves in the most delightful ways, and I taught some classes. I'd always been very wedded to notes in the classroom. I not only didn't have notes—I didn't have pencil and paper to make an outline. But I still taught. It was very liberating for me.

It turned out we were there for ten days before the officials broke down and said they wouldn't give us probation with two-year sentences. There were some unpleasant moments. We didn't have enough blankets. We were cold. But that was so unimportant. The food was god-awful. The National Guard fed us white bread and bologna sandwiches. But we didn't suffer in the least. We made the most of it, and we loved it. We became very tight, our group. We still get together periodically. It was one of the highlights of my life.

This new generation is really great. For the last several years, I've taught "Women in Radical Social Movements," a sort of historical survey from the abolitionist movement to the present. This class had 160 students— it was the biggest I've ever had. There was a degree of enthusiasm and re-ceptivity, which was thrilling to me. These students are really with-it, very serious young people who are determined to make a difference in the world. I think there's a new spirit in colleges now that hasn't been there in the last few years. I'm very hopeful about it. I think this country's a mess— don't misunderstand me. Corporate control is reaching out to everyone and being very, very pervasive, including the university in many ways. But I'm hopeful nevertheless. ∞

    I had gone to art school just fresh out of high school, and I thought I was going to have a career in art. But I put it aside. I let that dream go. But I always said to myself, "Someday when you have time, you should get back into it." When you're seventy or so, you realize you don't have all the time in the world, and if there is something you want to do, you'd better do it—get on with it.

JUNE SINGER

June Singer

I was guided by the wisdom of my own soul. When I paid close attention, things went well. When I did not, I met with difficulties. In the long run, I learned to forgive my trespasses.

JUNE SINGER, *Modern Woman in Search of Soul*

Profile

June Singer's earliest memories are of being about five years old. She liked to play that she was a tiger. She used to crawl under the grand piano in the sun room, and that would be her den. Then she would growl at people as they walked by. One evening, her parents were having a dinner party, and she thought it would be great fun to hide under the dinner table and bite one of the ladies on the ankle—which she did. The startled woman let out a scream, and June was promptly sent to bed. June's mother was an advanced thinker; in 1923, she was already reading Freud. She thought she had better take June to a psychoanalyst. "I will never forget this man," June told me. "He was something like Santa Claus. He had a beard and twinkling eyes, and he sat me up on his lap and didn't let my mother come in." He said he'd heard about June biting the lady's leg and asked her why she did that. June responded, "Because I'm a tiger!"

Years later, her mother told her that he had said June's imagination was running ahead of her ability to express herself in a socially acceptable way. He suggested that she be given some kind of nonverbal activity—

maybe art lessons. So her mother hired a local art student to come and work with June a couple of afternoons a week.

When she first came across the poetry of William Blake, June fell in love with his poem "Tyger! Tyger! burning bright / In the forests of the night. . . ." She tried to read everything she could of Blake's work, and she would come to understand him more and more as time passed. He felt to her like a kindred spirit. This preliminary reading worked its way into a thesis that she wrote for a dissertation at the Jung Institute in Zurich when she was training to become a Jungian analyst. Eventually, this led to her first book, *The Unholy Bible,* an anagogical interpretation of Blake's life and works.

June has always had an affinity for the tiger. She recounted an Indian folktale in which an orphaned tiger is raised by goats. He grows up think-ing he is a goat until a big tiger recognizes him and takes him away to teach him how to become a real tiger. "I think the part of my life after my analysis," observed June, "was growing up into becoming a full-grown tiger. And then, in my work as an analyst and a writer, I became the older tiger who is teaching young tigers to find themselves through analysis. But I don't have to go out hunting anymore. People will come, bring me a bone as an offering, and I'll give them what I have to say."

When June was in the prime of her professional life, she attended a shamanic workshop in which the participants were supposed to discover each other's totem animal. They milled around in a darkened room until somebody thought they had another person's totem animal. "This person who had never seen me before grabbed me—not without a struggle— and when he was asked what kind of an animal he had, he said, 'A tiger.' That was quite revealing. It's been a kind of theme of mine. Talk about coming full circle—this is the Chinese Year of the Tiger, so I feel I can really claim this year, whatever it will bring."

I met June in the California El Niño winter of 1997–98. She had accompanied her second husband of twelve years, Irving Sunshine (yes, it *is* his real name), to a forensic toxicology conference in San Francisco. Seventy-five-year-old June was the personification of graciousness and kindness.

I had often heard about June, who is a friend and colleague of several friends of mine who were Jungian analysts. Certainly, I knew of her books: *Boundaries of the Soul, Love's Energies, The Unholy Bible, Androgyny,* and *Modern Woman in Search of Soul,* among others.

We enjoyed a morning and afternoon together and were both disappointed that later appointments prevented our continuing on into the evening. As she told me her life story, it became clear how she sees fate as having directed her life and how those we love—in fact, most of those we come into contact with—determine our destiny.

One of the most intriguing parts was her retelling of the time she saw Carl Jung. He was very old when she went to Zurich in 1960 with her first husband, and Jung wasn't seeing people, except old friends. The day he died, she was allowed to view his body in his home in Kusnacht, because she was a student at the institute. "I walked up this big long stairway and went to the room with the open door and stood in the doorway. There he was, lying on his bed—a frail-looking old man in a white nightshirt with a white sheet covering him. There was a candle on either side of the bed on a night table, and no other light in the room. I just stood in the doorway, and I felt something come into me. Like some spirit, or just a feeling that my task was to carry his work on. It was a soul-stirring experience. I just stood there. Such an energy! I could feel it. A very strong presence. That was my only contact with him. Being near Jung was a tremendous experience, even in his death.

Modern Woman in Search of Soul

I think all my life I've been trying to prove that I could write by myself. I know exactly when I started writing. I was in fourth grade, and I wrote a poem to my mother and put it on my teacher's desk. She liked it. She suggested I write a poem every day. So I did. I put a new poem on her desk every morning after that. At the end of the year, I copied them into a little leather book and gave them to my mother. And she was very pleased, because she was a writer, a journalist, in the 1930s, when not too many women journalists existed.

When I was about twelve, we had a contest in school to write about thrift. I decided to write an epic, which I would call *Thrift Throughout the Ages.* It was during the depression. We were very conscious of the need to be careful with money. The prize was twenty-five dollars. I wrote this entirely in poetry. My mother happened to be sick in bed at the time, so I showed it to her. She corrected it a bit here and there, and gave me some suggestions. Damned if I didn't win first prize in the contest! As my mother worked for the paper, nothing would do but to print an article about me. I felt terrible. I felt so awful, because I had had help with this thing. My mother said, "Don't mention that I helped you. I didn't do much," but I felt like the worst charlatan. It was really a formative experience. My fear was that I had gotten something I didn't deserve. I think, in a way, this became a driving force in my life—to prove that I can do something by myself.

That feeling came up again for me during my first marriage. I was married to a brilliant man who was extremely competent, a very good public speaker, which I was not. He wrote, he spoke, he was one of those shining stars in that respect (and not in some others). I always had difficulty expressing myself in his presence and had the feeling that I could never do anything well enough. Maybe it was my nature to be quiet and introverted, but he certainly didn't help me to break out of it.

It wasn't until my analysis in my early forties at the Jung Institute in Zurich that I began to come into my own. I began to realize that I, too, had something creative in me but that I wasn't letting it come out. Part of the reason was that I was afraid of either overshadowing him or damaging his ego, which was rather fragile. So I had a real struggle to emancipate myself from the feeling of constriction. It was a difficult marriage.

So he returned to the University of Chicago, where he got his doctorate in psychology. I, too, went back to school and received my master's degree in educational psychology and vocational guidance. We were in our late thirties then, when he came home one day and told me, "I'm going to the Jung Institute in Zurich, to study to be a Jungian analyst." It was kind of iffy as to whether I would go along or not. But we resolved that I would, and I did. Our fifteen-year-old daughter went with us.

In Zurich, we had an unspoken agreement that I would stay home and keep house and maybe learn some German and not get any ideas about studying at the Jung Institute. Eventually, I decided to audit a course. I don't think he was terribly happy about it, but nevertheless I did it.

My introduction to the institute was attending a lecture that was given by Frau Doktor Jolande Jacobi. She was one of the earliest exponents of Jungian psychology and had written several informative books that were very well received. She started talking about the animus [the unconscious of woman, or the masculine principle] in women. This was in 1960, before anything of the women's consciousness-raising movement had yet started. She talked about how many women had this creative, dynamic aspect in themselves that they repressed because it didn't fit into the norm of middle-class society. Professionally active women weren't usually married. There was a glass curtain that made it hard for a woman to do anything creative outside the home. (Then again, I'd had my mother's example of a woman who had done a fair amount, even within a feminine sphere.) I heard Jolande Jacobi talk about how this repression of the animus can make for depression, for difficulties in relationships, for feelings of inferiority. I recognized myself, and after class, I told this to Jacobi, who soon became my analyst. Before I knew it, I was very deep in the process.

My husband and I had a stormy time in Zurich, partly because I was beginning to feel my oats. At first, I had no thought of becoming an analyst. None whatsoever. I wanted to find out what was the matter with me.

In Zurich, I discovered that I had a few problems of my own; they weren't all my husband's problems, as I had thought. In my analysis, there was an opening up of this great treasure chest of the unconscious. I don't mean *my* great treasure chest, but *the* great treasure chest—the potential that we all have. To get access to that was a fabulous experience. It was access to something beyond the world that we know. It's what I've later come to call the invisible world.

The unconscious is everything that we don't know or don't have access to. I regard what we know as just a tiny, tiny bit of the totality. My whole journey, I think, has been from compression to expansion, and to recognizing that every question we answer, every problem we solve, opens us up to a larger problem, another question. I don't mean *problem* in a negative way. I mean something to be solved.

I had a notion that I wanted to write about William Blake, the reason being that I had loved Blake's writing ever since I was a child and my mother read to me from his *Songs of Innocence.* One night, I had a dream that I woke up, and the whole outline of my thesis came to me, and I wrote it down. That was the dream. So in the morning I thought, "What a wonderful dream. If only I could remember it." I didn't remember what the dream was—just that it was important. I picked up my pad by the side of the bed and, by God, it was there. I *had* written it out, even when I was so sleepy. It was well organized and in the form of a complete outline. It was on Blake, Jung, and the collective unconscious. The next day, I took it in to my analyst, and she said, "This is fine. You can write on this." It went so smoothly that I actually finished my dissertation before my husband finished his. But we graduated at the same time. We went back to Chicago, where there were no other Jungian analysts at the time. It was 1964.

By then, I felt much more confident of myself. We had each started a small private practice, and we each had to have another job, because there were so few clients. Very few people in Chicago had ever heard of C. G. Jung. I took a position in Chicago in a nursery school for emotionally disturbed youngsters, doing therapy with the children and their parents.

Things were still not wonderful between my husband and me. One snowy day, he had gotten stuck with his car on the road and phoned me at work to say that he was coming home because he didn't feel too well. That night, he had a heart attack and died suddenly. We'd been back in Chicago less than a year. We'd sold our house and all its furnishings to get the money to go to Zurich, and we'd spent it all. We'd rented an apartment at what seemed to us to be an exorbitant price, and we had to buy furniture on credit. And there we were. Our daughter had not come back to Chicago with us. She took the money we had put aside for her college and went to New York to study drama. At his death, I felt frightened, yet in a strange way liberated. I was forty-six years old.

Then, my personal and professional development really began. My analysis, I discovered, had been only a preparation for what was ahead. I was very lonely at that time, as you can imagine. The people who had been seeing him as their analyst (about half a dozen or so) came to me to express their grief. They wanted to work through their feelings about the loss of their analyst, and we did that together. It was a painful experience, because his death was the cause of their suffering as well as mine, and I had to be with them through that whole process. As it ended up, almost all of them wanted to work analytically with me. So I had nearly a full practice, combining what he'd had and my own.

Meanwhile, I had settled into my position at the child development center as a family therapist. I had taken the position because it was the best one that I could find in the field of psychotherapy. But I had been trained as an analyst to help the individual become free from dependence on Mother and Father and not to confuse oneself with one's siblings. That was what "individuation" was supposed to be about. This was in the very early days of family therapy—actually, I had never heard of family therapy until I found myself in the middle of it.

Now my supervisor was telling me, "I want you to go and make home visits and see what the family interaction is." Suddenly, in my new job, I had to go into a situation to see how the parents treated the children, what the house looked like, what kind of taste they had, the kind of books they read, the kind of food they ate, how the mealtime was enacted—the whole thing. I was horrified at the prospect! It was *so* different, because I'd been used to sitting, as you and I are sitting, one-to-one in a small room, away from the context of the external world. The home visit was a revelation to me. It dawned on me, over time, that family therapists don't normally see people as individuals but as actors in a drama set in their environment. Nobody is isolated from the environment, and if you don't know the environment, you can't understand the plot.

I realized that, in order to be taken seriously—because Jungian analysis was rather beyond the academic pale anyway—I had to have a doctorate in psychology, in addition to my degree from the Jung Institute in Zurich. I had a very difficult time getting into Northwestern University. First they said, "We don't accept women over thirty-five in graduate school." Can you imagine that? They felt your learning years were over. Well, I had to fight and fight—and I can't tell you what I had to go through to get admitted. And *then* they said, "We'll take you, but you can't expect to get any kind of a stipend—and you better not try to work full-time while in school." So I said, "OK, I'll do my best. I'll accept this."

Now my daughter wanted to come back to Chicago and go to college. So we were both working and going to school. When she finished, she received a four-year fellowship to Stanford for graduate study in linguistics. She married a fellow doctoral candidate in graduate school.

I finished my doctorate in psychology in three years, while I continued working at the therapy center and building up my private practice. I also started a study group with people interested in learning more about Jung and his work. The group expanded, and soon we were offering public lectures. After a while, some people who were in analysis with me expressed a wish to get training in analytic work. By then, another couple of Jungian analysts had joined me in Chicago, but that still was not nearly enough to think of a training program. And there wasn't a Jungian training institute between the East Coast and the West Coast.

I went down to Texas to present a paper at a conference and found that there were three other analysts in Texas at the time. We were commiserating that we all had people who were interested in training but we couldn't do it because there weren't enough of us to make up a local training unit. I think it was my idea—I'm always coming up with outlandish ideas—that if the analysts in Chicago and in Texas joined together and formed one society, then maybe we could get the permission of the international Jungian establishment to form a training group.

We persuaded a couple of the most highly respected analysts in the United States to support this plan with the international organization. The international organization accepted it (I often wondered how much they knew about the geography of the United States), and we started the Interregional Society of Jungian Analysts. We were creating an American training institute that had no particular location! Jung talks about the self as an image, "a circle whose center is everywhere and whose circumference is nowhere." That was the kind of institute we developed, because there came to be little centers all over the country, but the boundaries of this group were . . . well, we didn't know. We joked among ourselves that the New York Institute could have the East Coast, and the San Francisco and Los Angeles Institutes could have the West Coast, and we would settle for what was in between. Our original idea was that when there were enough experienced analysts in a given area who had trained with the Interregional Society, they could spin off and form their own independent training institute. That was the genesis of the Jung Institute of Chicago. I worked in Chicago for seventeen years. I saw our little study group mature into the Jung Institute of Chicago.

Eventually, I felt it was time to leave. That came about when I saw that I'd had a part in the training of most of those analysts. It was a little thick; there were many projections, crisscrossing relationships, sibling rivalries. I was the "Great Mother," except when things didn't go well, and then I was the "Terrible Mother."

In the meantime, I began to take an interest in the developing field of transpersonal psychology, of which Jung was the precursor, because he had carried his psychology beyond the growth of the personal ego and was interested in the wider world and how it functioned, and in comparative religions, and how people's belief systems affected their behavior. Transpersonal psychology was just taking shape in the seventies, and it drew upon many different modalities. It addressed itself to the intellectual, emotional, physical, social, and spiritual dimensions of the person. Transpersonal psychology was also about breaking out of the confines of the consulting room and into more interactive group processes.

This was something we *never* had done at the Jung Institute. It was always the individual, and there was great resistance to working in a group. The concept of group dynamics had not yet evolved in Jung's time. He was still concerned with the darkest aspects of "mass" or "mob" psychology, and why wouldn't he be at a time when Hitler and Stalin and Mussolini were at the height of their powers? When people talk about the limitations of Jung, it's often from a position of where we are now. We need to consider how far ahead he was of the people in his day, to realize the context out of which he came. But psychology was moving on, especially in California.

At that time, Alan Watts had a significant influence on my development and my going to California. Many of my ideas came from talking with him. He had spent much time in India and Japan, studying and practicing Buddhism and Taoism and other Asian philosophies, learning the Japanese language and calligraphy. His books, lectures, and seminars brought a better understanding of the East to the West. He taught all over the country, but California became the focal point in the dialogue. Alan Watts seemed to strike something in me that sounded very right. I remember his saying, "June, you belong in California." That sounded right to me. It took me a year or so to work out how I could get licensed to practice psychology in California and how I could earn a living there. I was offered a position as clinic director of the internship program and faculty member at the California Institute of Transpersonal Psychology. I also became a member of the Jung Institute of San Francisco. I gradually built up a private analytic practice.

In the meantime, I had written several books. The one most widely read was *Boundaries of the Soul*. Jung was very discursive in his writing, and he would move around from one thing to another. His work wasn't all translated at one time, and then the translations that were available were not arranged chronologically, so you couldn't follow his development, much less the variety of ideas he dealt with. I had asked my analyst, "Dr. Frey, why doesn't somebody write a book systematizing the process of analysis, something that gives a picture of how it goes from the start, how you deal with dreams, and what these various aspects of the psyche that Jung talks about are—how they fit into a cohesive pattern—so that somebody who's not in analysis could get some idea of what it's all about?" She said, "That couldn't be done, because nobody who's not in analysis would understand it." I tucked that into the back of my mind, and from the time I began my analytic practice, I kept notes in preparation to write the book that wound up as *Boundaries of the Soul*.

In 1970, my daughter and her husband traveled to Romania. I never saw her again. He was on a State Department fellowship to study linguistics. Both of them were killed in an auto crash with a truck in the mountains of Romania. I cannot begin to tell you the depth of my loss. She and I were so close. After her father had died, we were able to have a relationship that had not been possible before. I hadn't been able to stand up for her against her father when he made unreasonable demands upon her as she was growing up. But when she returned to Chicago, she and I became very close. We were both working and studying and providing companionship and loving support for each other.

She was only twenty-six when she died. Beside losing her, my only child, what was especially hard for me was being around people who would be talking about their children and later their grandchildren. I felt that even beyond the joy of having children was the sense that one's immortality survives in the children and grandchildren that follow you. Now my line stopped with me. Empty of hope. As I tried to understand my feelings, I realized that my attitude was an attitude of possessiveness. Children are *mine,* and this is *me* going on. Fortunately, my work gave me the opportunity to connect with people on a very deep level. I gradually came to the realization that *all* children, the world's children, are my children. Immortality is not what you give to an individual but what you give away in terms of your creativity, books, or working with people, or friendship, or healing, or making something of use to someone. You don't have to be a genius to do this. You don't necessarily have to be recognized. This immortality is not the immortality of the individual but the immortality of the life force that makes for growth and change and an expanded consciousness.

Let me backtrack to Irving, because that has to do with my life in Ohio now. I was born and raised in Ohio, and I lived there until I went away to college. I have a sister in the Cleveland area with whom I'm very close, and over the years we've kept in touch. I've come back frequently to visit, and she would come visit me wherever I happened to be. On one of my trips to Cleveland in 1985, my sister and her husband were invited to a

New Year's Eve party that they went to every year, and they asked me to come along. I wasn't very eager, because I thought it would be all couples, and I would be a fifth wheel. But I went.

There was this man whose wife had died a couple of years earlier and who seemed like a lost soul wandering around. He'd always gone to this party with his wife. My sister and brother-in-law knew him just slightly. I did meet him, and we got to talking. We had both been great travelers, and we compared notes about the different places we'd been to and the different things we liked to do. We were chatting, and it was pleasant—you know how a New Year's Eve party is. So at the stroke of twelve, everybody is hugging and kissing their spouse. He's over there, and I'm over here, and we start drifting together. "One enchanted evening . . ."

After a very short time, we thought we had found each other. I was sixty-six then. It's funny—over all those years, I did have relationships of various kinds with various people, but they never were quite right, and nothing permanent came of them. I don't know that I really wanted a serious relationship, because I was so busy with my career. But now I was getting to the place where my career was "been there, done that." He was at loose ends, too. I lived in California, and he lived in Cleveland, so we hadn't met many times before we decided we would get married. The biggest difficulty was where would we live? He had been in Cleveland for thirty-five years, where he was chief toxicologist in the coroner's office. He had many caring friends in Cleveland. My group was the Jungian and transpersonal community, about which he knew as much as I knew about toxicology—zero. In my first marriage, I had suppressed so many of my own inclinations that I knew that if I were ever to remarry, I was going to marry as an autonomous person with my own ways of doing things. If the man couldn't accept me as I was, I wasn't going to pretend to be something else or compromise my real nature. At the same time, I wouldn't expect him to compromise his own way of being. We talked back and forth; this was a long discourse. I was pretty insistent on staying in California and thought that he should come out there. Cleveland was home to him, and he had his position, but he was getting close to retirement. The breaking point came just when we thought we couldn't resolve it. He said, "Why do you want to stay in California? Why don't you move to Cleveland?" I said, "If I go, who will water the flowers?" He was an ardent gardener. He loved the garden I had. I don't know if that did it or not, but we ended up in California.

We had some great times in California. Living in Palo Alto, we could drive to the ocean or the mountains or to San Francisco in less than an hour. The culture was vibrant with new ideas in every area from the creative geniuses of Silicon Valley to the pioneers of the human potential movement to the explorers in genetics and biotechnology to the environmentalists—I could go on and on. At one time or another, I worked with people in all of these areas and learned much about what goes on behind the scenes in the bellwether state. I had many dear friends and colleagues. I had a full analytic practice and was still director of the clinic, but every time I climbed the steep outside steps to the third-floor Transpersonal Center, I realized that I was not as young as I used to be. I began to cut back on my activities there. I remember my mother saying, "The time to go is when they still want you to stay."

We returned to Cleveland more frequently to see family and friends. We felt a sense of stability there. People we knew were mostly still in their first marriages. Families remained in contact, even though their children might have moved away. Friends were friends for life. One thing that had struck me, when I first went to California, was that so many people seemed to be in a state of transition. Relationships were quick to form, quick to dissolve. When I opened my analytic practice, I was dismayed to find that people would shop for psychotherapists as they might for real estate agents. They would interview several psychotherapists and, often, even when they had made a decision, they would not stay in therapy very long. My experience with people in the Midwest had been that there is generally more commitment. And not only to psychotherapy. My sister is still friendly with people she's known since high school. They've all grown up together and shared their experiences and watched each other's children grow up. It was a solid community. I had been on my own for a long time, but now I felt that as you get older, you need more of a support structure. You don't want to feel that you have to keep proving yourself.

Margaret Mead talked about the three kinds of marriages a person should have: one for the passion of youth, one for bringing up a family, one for your older years—companionship and mutual support. I missed the middle one—that was career time for me. But now Irving has been unbelievably supportive and caring and never asked me to do anything that I didn't want to do. Anything I want to do is OK with him. I feel the same way about him. If he wants to go to Italy for a meeting, I could either come along or not come along, as I wished. He could go or not go—his choice. It is a very permissive, caring relationship without being clutching or demanding in any way. I think for someone of our age, that's the only kind of relationship that would work.

My marriage with Irving is very different from my first. There just isn't any question about it. There's a mutual respect for the differences between us, and that's very heartwarming. A feeling that the other person is OK just as he or she is. You wouldn't *want* them to be any different. Also, that people are what they are. If you don't really care for something in the way a person is, then don't get married to them, because they are not going to change. When people are in the second half of life, they're already formed. They have their relationships, and you need to recognize that you're marrying the whole package: their past, their present, their future. Irving has two boys and five grandchildren, so, after having felt that I never became a grandmother, I became an instant grandmother. That pleases me very much.

After ten years together, we decided to leave California. When we returned to Cleveland, I fell into a horrible depression. I was so miserable. It was a real identity crisis. I'd been in California fifteen years. I was well known as an analyst and writer. There were many people there that I had grown to love. I missed them, and I wondered how my analysands were doing. I felt sad about leaving them, many in the middle of the stream. We've been in Cleveland now since 1995. I found a house. It had appealed to me—it had certain nice vibes. It had a lot of land around it. Probably more than we wanted, but still it was better than a tiny place. But when we got into the house, it had everything in the world wrong with it that hadn't been obvious at first sight. Everything that could go wrong did go wrong. The carpet was tacky, the wallpaper was garish. . . .

But then my personal identity crisis was far more upsetting to me. I didn't know who I was or who I was supposed to be. I was "Irving's wife" when I was with his friends. I was "Sue's sister" when I was with her friends. But where was June Singer? Was I an analyst or not an analyst? Was I "just a housewife"? This troubled me and made me very uneasy. I was seventy-six. I think people who don't move or undergo other traumas in their seventies may not realize that your ability to adapt to changes is diminishing. As long as I was on familiar streets going to familiar stores in familiar neighborhoods with familiar people, I was just fine. But when all that shifted, I didn't know the language. It was like being on Mars.

I didn't know, as I made new friends, whom you don't call before nine in the morning, whom you don't call after nine in the evening, who doesn't eat seafood, who keeps kosher, who's vegetarian. When you grow up with people, you know these little things without ever thinking about them. But as you get older and find yourself in a different context, you don't know whether women wear dresses or slacks. It sounds so superficial and picky, but it's like you don't know the language. Do you take something to their house when you go for dinner? Do you come on time, or do you not come on time? Social conventions are important, but we take them for granted. It's not as superficial as it appears to be.

So, finally, I resolved it. With all my concerns about "Who am I?" I concluded, "Who cares? What difference does it make? Who I am is myself, and the labels don't mean anything." That epiphany was a big relief— a *big* relief.

Then I also found that people of my age become much more concerned with their health. It becomes more a topic of conversation, which is boring. I do not enjoy it. My experience is that there is much more consumption of culture than production of culture. I'm talking about going to the theater, going to musical events, going to classes, learning the computer. I don't know if it's typical of this stage of life, but I am not consumed with consuming. I get more pleasure out of the simple act of creating.

In Cleveland, I started getting involved in art and painting. I had gone to art school just fresh out of high school, and I thought I was going to have a career in art. But I put it aside. It was the depression, and I needed to do something a little bit more practical. Besides, I didn't think I was good enough as an artist, so I let that dream go. But I always said to myself, "Someday when you have time, you should get back into it." When you're seventy or so, you realize you don't have all the time in the world, and if there is something you want to do, you'd better do it—get on with it.

Of course, it didn't happen quite that rationally. I went to an art show in a neighborhood art center, and there I saw paintings done by students that I thought were awfully good, and I liked the ambience, so I signed up for a couple of courses. Another part of it was that I wanted to do portraits. One of the main reasons was that I wanted to have a portrait of my daughter. That was the motivator, to learn enough so that I could do that. So I took a course in portrait painting, and I loved it. What I like about painting is that it's producing something, not receiving. I like to take in— I don't have anything against it. But I think there needs to be a balance of taking it in, processing it, and then giving it back in a new way.

Painting portraits has a certain relationship to analytic work because, first of all, it's one individual trying to capture the soul essence of another individual. Also, as one gets older, the memory for verbal details is not what it was. That was one of the reasons I wanted to slow down my analytic work. It was very hard for me to keep in mind all the details of a person's whole life. And I became impatient with endlessly trying to interpret the past, because I realized you can't do anything about the past. I certainly didn't *want* to do anything about the past. I wanted to deal with the immediate present. I want to have a person right in front of me and deal with where that individual is in this moment. That's the real stuff, not what *was,* because "the past" is a story we have developed over the years. All of what I've told you today is really just my fantasy of what happened. Somebody else could tell it differently. But being present in the moment, that's real, that's where it is. And trying to give expression to the moment is a living process.

That's the wonderful thing about getting older. You can let go of the clutter in your life and just be with what is and enjoy it to the fullest. You can see where you're needed and do that. Just be there, show up. A child grows up being spontaneous and follows the inner impulses until somebody says, "Don't do that." Then you learn to hold back, and the real essence can get buried awfully deep. I think it's a great privilege to be able to bring that essence back to the surface. To find out what it is on this earth that you're here for. I think I've done that, but it took a long, long time. My first husband never did find out; he didn't live long enough.

What I want to do now is to improve my painting. I've been learning about painting. After a couple of years of instruction, I found that I could look at something and put down what I saw, but I didn't have the foundation of structure and anatomy. So I put my painting aside for a short time, and I've been drawing skulls and doing life drawing with a really tough teacher. We do "gesture drawing," where in one minute you have to get the whole sense of how the body is moving. So now I'm eager to get back into painting to see what effect my drawing is having. I'm hoping in the spring to paint some landscapes. This may sound antithetical to portraiture, but it's not.

I've learned that my idea of a portrait is not a picture of the head of a person, because people don't exist from the shoulders up; and, furthermore, a person doesn't exist in a vacuum or a mush of color. We are in a place. There's a landscape around the body, and the body is in that landscape. We are not superimposed on a landscape. We're part of our environment in both a psychological sense and a physical sense. We do not exist alone. We're always interacting with the light, the way light makes us look. Wherever you sit, whenever you move, the light changes. That's what the impressionists discovered. Let's take Renoir, for example. In his portraits, the people are always interacting. They're in a place, and you feel them as part of the whole scene. You feel that the place is as important as the person, and that they are as one. The place is filled with the people, and the people are filled with the place. To go back, this is what I learned when I was forced to do family therapy at the beginning of my practice. People don't exist as isolated beings. That's where I've had a reservation about the analytic process. Not that it excludes the environment altogether, but it doesn't *see* the environment, except through its representation by the client.

I can't do the things that I did in the past. Who can, when you get to a certain age? But it's being part of the cyclic process of life that I recognize. I look at my life in terms of chapters in a book. It seems to break down into finite periods, one merging into the next.

It's hard to say something about the gifts of age. A long-view perspective. Recognizing that what people think is new and wonderful has cycled through many evolutions and revolutions. Plus, when you get older, at least as I get older, this long view feels natural to me. Just as fingers are part of the hand and can't function without the hand, the hand can't function without the rest of the body. But the hand is not the fingers. This is a spiritual understanding. There is something that guides the whole organism; it's not just the process of things happening one after the other and evolving in a random fashion. There seems to me to be something behind it all. An organizing principle. It's awesome and wonderful. It's what some people call God and I call an Absolute.

This is a view that troubles many people. They say, "Everything is relative." There's a real semantic catch here, because the question is, "Relative to what?" How can something be relative unless it's relative to something that is not relative? I was thinking of the relationship of a single life to eternity. A life span is linear—starts here, ends here. But the Absolute, which you might say is eternity, is cyclic. It's like the forest and the trees. The forest can exist indefinitely, but the trees are relative to the forest, because they come and they go, while the forest remains. Our lifetimes are relative: we come, we're here for a while, we go. We live out this life; we are transformed into something else. We have a lot of ideas about what that something else might be, but we really don't know. The Absolute cannot be comprehended by the relative, but the *relative can* be comprehended by the Absolute. We are experiencing the Absolute all the time; we just don't recognize it. The followers of Jesus asked him, "When shall we find the kingdom?" He said, "The kingdom is spread upon the earth, and you do not see it." We're interested in why something is the way it is. Yet we have to look beyond experiences and realize that what is *is,* that it's the product of everything that's gone before it and what's going to come after it.

In California, my consulting room faced out on the garden, and I would sit with my analysand so that we could both look out on the garden. Outside the window, there was a persimmon tree. We would watch it. Analysis is a long-term process, and we would watch from early spring when the leaves came out and the blossoms were almost the color of the leaves, so you had to look very hard to see them. Then, as we continued meeting throughout the summer, we would see the leaves begin to harbor these little persimmons—very green, like olives—then get bigger and bigger. Then in September, as autumn came, they began to get an orangey color. By October, they were a deep orange, and in November they were a deep persimmon red. Then the birds and the squirrels would start to eat them. The persimmons would be so luscious and ripe looking, so heavy that they would pull the branches down to the ground. My clients would wait for the persimmons to come into their ripeness. I'd pick the persimmons and give them to my analysands. They would always go away with a few ripe ones.

We would use persimmons as a symbol of the analytic process, of how it would reach its fullness after a long period of growth and then finally ripen. Some would fall down and get squashed, and some would be eaten and enjoyed. Then the whole cycle would happen over again. The persimmons would be eaten or die—their life cycle would be over—but the tree continued. It went through its stages. When the leaves dropped off, and the tree finally got bare in the winter, I'd think about how some of the leaves dropped early and some later. It reminded me of our lives—some people are cut off early in life and some later. To try to figure out why is senseless. That's just the way it is. My analysands and I learned to accept a lot of things as we watched that persimmon tree. The great wisdom, if you want to call it that. There is always something in nature, it seems to me, that mirrors on a larger scale the process that is going on in our lives. ❧

It makes me impatient when people worry about getting old or looking old. Just seems very odd to me. It's really a pleasure to be living beyond seventy. Maybe one shouldn't be too greedy.

MITSUYE YAMADA

# Mitsuye Yamada

Masks of Woman

This is my daily mask
daughter, sister
wife, mother
poet, teacher
grandmother.

My mask is control
concealment
endurance
my mask is escape
from my
self.

<small>MITSUYE YAMADA</small>

 ## Profile

All her life, Mitsuye Yamada searched for her cultural heritage—until she discovered that it is within her. It's in her poetry, in her work with multi-cultural groups, and in her work for human rights. In poems such as "Masks of Woman," Mitsuye confronts the invisibility of Asian American women in American culture. This poem could also have been written for every aging woman in America of any ethnicity who struggles with her feelings of invisibility in a youth-oriented society.

I met Mitsuye through our mutual friends, Allie Light and Irving Saraf. In 1981, they had produced a documentary on Mitsuye and her friend Nellie Wong called *Mitsuye and Nellie: Asian-American Poets.* When Mitsuye and I met in early 1997 at her house in Irvine, California, it was just weeks after her son-in-law in Boston had died of cancer, and Mitsuye was deeply saddened. At that time, Mitsuye lived with her husband, Yosh, and her mother, Hide, then ninety-six. Their daughter Hedi lived separately but had her business office in their home, and their daughter Jeni was a frequent visitor. This made for an often multigenerational household, which is consistent with her childhood experience.

Mitsuye, who was mostly raised on the West Coast until the outbreak of World War II, told me about how her family was moved to a concentration camp for Japanese Americans in Washington and Idaho. Several years later, she wrote *Camp Notes and Other Poems* about that painful experience. Tillie Olsen, a much-admired feminist writer, gave that book the following appraisal: "Deep, hard-wrung poetry, out of mature comprehension and passionate caring. Individual poems tenaciously remain and work within one like tears, like illumination—or with the force of a terrible blow."

Mitsuye founded the group Multicultural Women Writers and, in 1990, she coedited an anthology of the group's work, *Sowing Ti Leaves: Writings by Multi-Cultural Women.* She is a former board member of Amnesty International and is currently the chair of Amnesty's Committee on International Development. She is also associate professor in the Asian American studies program at the University of California, Irvine.

At age forty, Mitsuye was misdiagnosed with terminal emphysema and didn't believe that she would live much longer. She remarked, "People are always worried about getting old. I was told that I had about a year to live in my early forties. My younger daughter was only three or four years old. So when I turned fifty, people asked if it was traumatic. I replied, 'No, it was wonderful.' I thought, 'God, I'm still here!' Perspective is everything."

A Poet Speaks Out

In a discussion with my two daughters during the filming of *Mitsuye and Nellie* in 1980, I mentioned casually that I might have prolonged my graduate school years at the University of Chicago because I was in a state of indecision about what to do with my life. In 1950, feeling the social pressures of being an unmarried twenty-seven-year-old woman, I decided to get married. Since I wasn't sure what I would do with my degree in English after graduation, getting married that year felt like a convenient option. And having a child right away, given my "advanced age," seemed to be the right thing to do. (Our older daughter, Jeni, was born in November 1951.) I was thinking aloud and was not prepared for the responses of surprise and wonder on the part of Allie Light, the filmmaker, and my older daughter, Jeni. Her sister, ten years younger, was shocked almost beyond words: "What? Weren't you and Dad in love? Didn't you want to get married? Didn't you want to have us kids?"

They had just heard their grandmother, Hide Yasutake, talk about how her engagement to Grandpa was arranged by their respective parents, and they laughed over her story about how she had not realized he was shorter than she because he didn't stand up until the engagement ceremony was over. I had to reassure them that of course our marriage was not like that. We had three glorious dating years while studying for our degrees, and we were devoted to each other. I said, "I am happy to have been married, and my greatest joy today is our four children and our four grandchildren," and meant every word of it.

However, how does one explain to young people today who have so many choices open to them that in the 1950s, there didn't seem to be an option for women not to marry and, when married, not to have children? Certainly, in the 1920s in my mother's generation, there were even fewer options for women. The circumstances of my birth in Japan to Japanese immigrant parents who were residents in the United States at the time were entirely set by a lack of alternatives on my mother's part.

I was born in Kyushu, Japan, in 1923 and grew up in Seattle, Washington, until the outbreak of World War II. My parents had settled in Seattle in 1920 and lived there with my two older brothers. When my mother became pregnant with me, she had a two-year-old son and a five-month-old baby. My dad just about "had enough," he said, with two babies and another coming along, so he decided to send my mother home to his parents, where she would have help with the new baby.

About a month after I was born, Tosh, who was a year old by then, became very ill with encephalitis. Failing to get adequate medical help for him in this small farming hamlet where her in-laws lived, she took Tosh to Osaka to a hospital. She left Mike, who was by then three years old, with our grandparents and left me with a nursing mother, a woman who had a baby around my age. Mother returned to Seattle for further treatments for Tosh, whose recovery took several years. I was about three years old when I joined my parents in Seattle. Mike returned a few years later. A younger brother, Joe, was born when I was nine years old.

The upshot of all this is that my three brothers who were born in Seattle are American citizens, while I was the only one among the children in our family who was a Japanese citizen because I'd been born in Japan. The Japanese, those born in Japan, were not eligible to become American citizens at that time. (I became a naturalized citizen in 1955 after the passage of the 1952 McCarran-Walter Act, which made this possible.) I think that being Japan-born had quite an impact on the way I grew up. For as long as I can remember, my parents, my mother especially, made me very much aware that I must behave like a "proper Japanese lady."

When I was about nine or ten, two of my brothers and I accompanied Mother to Japan to visit her relatives. She left me with an aunt and uncle to attend school, but my Japanese-school education in Seattle had not adequately prepared me for grade-level work in Japan, so they hired a schoolteacher to tutor me for a year and a half. When I returned to the United States, I quickly caught up with my classmates and entered my own grade level within a year. My parents were insistent about my not losing the education I received in Japan; I continued with Japanese school every day after American school and had classical dancing, calligraphy, flower arrangement, and tea ceremony lessons on weekends. I must have complied rather reluctantly, because I am not proficient in any of those areas, unfortunately. By the time I was in high school, those activities fell by the wayside one by one.

Unbeknownst to my parents, I became actively involved in the high school debating team and editorial staff for the creative writing magazine. I believed that I was growing up like other somewhat assimilated *nisei* [first-generation Japanese Americans] in Seattle. So much so that when the evacuation orders came in February 1942, during World War II, it was as much of a shock to me as to other *nisei* that the U.S. government would actually remove us from our homes. Our father had already been arrested by the FBI on December 7 and was in detention. Mother was dazed and helpless, Mike was in bed with a prolonged illness, and Joe was only eight years old. So there I was, a senior in high school, and Tosh, a freshman at the University of Washington, trying to assume family responsibilities we'd never had to deal with before.

I remember during the year and a half that I was in the camps in Puyallup, Washington, and Minidoka, Idaho, I couldn't get too involved in the social activities that were going on around me. In Minidoka, working the night shift in the emergency clinic at the camp hospital was a way out of making excuses for not attending dances and other functions. I wrote in my journal, which I called *Camp Notes,* during those long nights at the reception desk of the emergency room.

The desert was unbelievably quiet those nights. One could hear oneself thinking. I felt somewhat removed from my peers, whose conversations revolved around applications for jobs or colleges on the outside, and from my mother and her *isei* [the first generation of Japanese-born to emigrate to the United States] friends, whose daily concerns didn't interest me. Every day, I was receiving letters that read, "We regret to inform you that . . ." from colleges in response to my applications.

As small groups of young people were receiving permission to leave this concentration camp, I had visions of being stuck there with the older folks and little children because I was an "enemy alien." When my older brother, Mike, was accepted by the University of Cincinnati, he asked a Quaker worker to look into the possibility of my getting a job in Cincinnati so that

I could leave with him. Thanks to our Quaker connection, I was able to leave camp with a secure job working at the University of Cincinnati cafeteria. Once out of camp, I was accepted at the university, spent two undergraduate years there, went on to New York University for a bachelor's degree, then on to University of Chicago for graduate school.

I met Yosh, my husband, in Chicago, where he frequently visited friends while studying for a Ph.D. in chemistry at Purdue University. His interest in and knowledge of both art and science were an intriguing combination. Together, we visited almost every museum and gallery in the city. We were married in Chicago in 1950. Our oldest daughter was born in Chicago, where my parents had settled after camp. After Yosh's graduation, his job took us to New York for seven years, where our two sons were born. I was thrilled to be back in New York. When he applied for another job in Chicago and suggested we move again, I made my first independent decision in our married life—I refused to move to accommodate his career ambitions. By this time, my widowed mother had come to live with us. I was happy among my friends in New York and very satisfied with the school where our older daughter was in third grade. Yosh said the job was such a "good deal" that he was willing to commute between Chicago and New York, which he did stoically for a year and a half, flying home every weekend. One weekend he came home and said, "The company is moving me to California. I think that's a bit too far for me to commute, don't you?" So we moved.

We lived in the foothills of Sierra Madre, near Pasadena, in the 1960s, but I was having serious respiratory problems, because of what was thought to be a deteriorating lung condition and the increasing smog in that area. My condition was diagnosed by a general practitioner as "terminal emphysema." Incredibly, neither Yosh nor I thought about seeking a second opinion by specialists or even moving out of the area, because that would have meant he would have to quit his job, and the children's lives would be disrupted. I firmly believed that it was more important for my children, who were ages 13, 7, 5, and 3, to feel secure in familiar surroundings, in case they became motherless within a year or two, as was predicted. As if some Asian genetic code was in operation, Yosh and I resignedly set about making the most of this situation. He installed an air filter into the furnace mechanism. We bought an air purifier for our master bedroom. I visited a respiratory clinic almost daily and carried an oxygen tank around with me wherever I went. Seven years later, when I was forty-eight years old, I went to an emphysema specialist and learned that I had been misdiagnosed.

We decided to move permanently to Irvine, where I taught English at a local college. It was very stressful, because essentially I became the sole support of our family, which left even less time for my writing. But the air quality was better, and I was no longer commuting so far.

When people asked me in early 1993, "How do you feel about turning seventy?" I felt like screaming, "I am so lucky. Thank God I'm still here!" For my seventieth birthday party, my four wonderful children and their families came from Boston, San Francisco, Seattle, and Aliso Viejo for a gala family gathering. There I was, still alive and active at age seventy, with my mind still intact, in good health with great kids, and gorgeous grandchildren. Also, my husband of forty-three years hadn't given up on me yet, my ninety-four-year-old mother was still in relatively good health with perfect hearing, and she was still minding my business. My three brothers, two in their seventies, were, as always, loving and caring. And I had many loving and loyal friends. The decade birthdays that many people worry about—turning fifty, turning sixty, and now seventy—for me were great celebratory events.

Life for me started at age forty-eight. My heart aches for my son-in-law, whose life ended a couple of years ago, exactly at that age. I would have given anything to share with him a few of those additional years of life that I was given so that he could have seen his sons grow up and spare my daughter these past two years of intense grief. It sounds like a platitude to say that one only appreciates one's life when faced with a crisis. I know that I consciously thought to myself at that time, "I must do something worth-while with these additional years that God has granted me." Occasionally, I do have a sense of regret that this piece of wisdom did not come sooner, and I indulge in "if onlys"—if only I had started writing at a younger age (when I had nothing else to do except to raise four children!), if only I didn't have to work full-time just when my social consciousness was beginning to kick in, if only I had more time to write.

My new awareness prodded me on to try to incorporate my political views into other areas in my life. It affected the way I taught my English classes at the community college in conservative Orange County. I scraped around for materials to have students write about sexism and racism in the English language and in literature. Because I was an active member of Amnesty International by that time, I had my students write about human rights issues. Some students started to complain that I was teaching mostly sociology and philosophy instead of English composition and literature.

In the early days of my teaching career, I would get very upset when students turned in papers that were racist or sexist or made racist comments in class, sometimes as a joke. I learned how to confront students and colleagues. Gradually, I learned to be more proactive and chose reading materials for my classes that focused on social issues. I realized that it's not enough to be a passive antiracist, because the racists on their side are working very hard to disseminate their views. It was very important for me personally to help my students understand this.

At the same time, my own writing career blossomed. I was a little nonplussed when Alta, the publisher of The Shameless Hussy Press, the first feminist press in the country, offered to publish my poems. Me? A poet? It took several years before the poems were collected in my book *Camp Notes and Other Poems* in 1976, but just the mere suggestion that my poems may be publishable gave me the courage to submit some of them to publications and write to women writers whom I admired. Nellie Wong, Merle Wood, and I gave readings together at colleges and universities on the West Coast, billing our readings as "Three Asian Americans Speak Out." These two highly gifted women drew out the political voice in me that I never knew I had. I met Audre Lorde and Tillie Olsen through our correspondence. I am grateful to Audre, especially, though she was younger in years and was already an established writer when I was just beginning. She encouraged me not to listen to senior editors but listen to my own heart! Her astonishing courage through her illness in the last years, encouraging women writers to form coalitions, inspired me to form the Multicultural Women Writers group in 1980. Although her stunning works survive her, her death in 1993 is a tragic loss to our world that needs her strong voice for justice and peace. I have lost a truly valued friend.

Multicultural Women Writers started out as the Asian American Women Writers group, for I felt a need to form a group of women of kindred spirit, but by 1983 we expanded the group to include women of all ethnic groups. The group applied for and received a grant to pay for the publication of an anthology of our own writings in 1988 entitled *Sowing Ti Leaves*. We were pleasantly surprised that more than our own family members and friends were willing to buy the book from us. This year, The Feminist Press will be publishing a third edition of this anthology. In the introduction, we claim that the metaphor of the ti leaf

> recalls an array of images to reflect the textures of our separate lives. We are women whose lives have been formed out of a variety of cultures. . . . Our dominant image is sowing. When we hear ti leaves, we hear sowing, planting, dispersing, broadcasting, and even squandering with abandon. We picture sewing, piecing together patches of fabric from our lives as women have done for centuries or patching things up, another activity that has been part of our traditional role. We taste ti leaves, edible leaves which women in the Pacific Islands will use to make neat packages of wrapped rice, vegetables, and meats for family and friends, putting things in neat order, gathering and nurturing those around us. Or we savor the more familiar tea, a mild beverage women were expected to serve during leisurely afternoons along with casual conversation and amiable company. On the other hand, the tea ceremony ritual—pouring and drinking—is a solitary inward journey into oneself in the company of others.

Our next project is a collection that includes writings by women outside our group, also to be published by The Feminist Press in New York. My coeditors (Sarie Sachie Hylkema and Helen Jaskoski) and I are in the process of getting the manuscript prepared to send to The Feminist Press for the second time around. The subject that we chose initially was to be about our own relationships with our mothers or older women in our cultural groups. I felt very close to this subject, because my mother lived with me for many years until she died a few months before her ninety-eighth birthday last year, and I have thought a great deal about her aging process. We expected a greater variety of writings by women in different cultures, but interestingly enough, many writers sent us stories and poems about how women of all ages struggle to adjust to a different culture or a hostile environment. *Motherland* to many women means a comfortable and safe place to be. We yearn for such a place and settle for metaphors that would give us a secure home within our own minds. I have learned a great deal about my own relationships by reading various writings by ethnic women and women of color who write of strong women in their cultures.

I first read Tillie Olsen's short story "Tell Me a Riddle" in a collection of best short stories in 1964. I was so powerfully moved by her characterization of the proud strong woman whom the husband and children merely tolerated that I sat down and wrote a poem about my mother and sent it to Tillie. I realized for the first time that Mother's strength was what my father called her "ganko na seishitsu," her hardheaded nature. My gentle brothers, Mother's three sons, make light of it. When Mother was younger, her strong opinions about everything in our lives, such as how the children should be disciplined, often grated on the nerves of my three sisters-in-law. My brothers would simply dismiss her sharp criticisms with, "Oh, don't let it bother you. She's just old." As she got older, her strong opinions became a source of much amusement to them. I, on the other hand, took her seriously and often corrected her if I felt her comments were not acceptable. When I got into an argument with my mother, my brothers would say, "Why argue with her? She will never change!" But through the years, even they had to admit that in some instances she *did* change, that she was capable of change even in her eighties.

This is an exciting thought, as I pass my halfway mark in my seventies. I am capable of change. The world is capable of change. I could not go on working on behalf of my friends who are political prisoners in the United States if I didn't believe that. Many of them, accused of sedition and conspiracy, have spent almost twenty years in prison with very little hope of unconditional release. Every time I visit these women in the federal prison facilities at Dublin, California [about thirty miles north of San Jose, California], I come away awed by their stalwart spirit. In an environment that daily works to break them, they retain their dignity and humanity. They maintain a highly developed sense of social justice and morality. If I accomplish nothing else in the life I have left, I dearly hope that Carmen Valentin, Marilyn Buck, Dylcia Pagan, and the others will soon be out among us. ❧

You're a success if you stay alive. Success isn't the operative word. It's doing what you want to do, what you're able to do, even something you're not so good at but something that intrigues you, because failure doesn't matter anymore. Success and failure are out of your vocabulary, I think—or they should be.

BETTY FRIEDAN

Betty Friedan

Profile

What better way to celebrate my fiftieth birthday than to spend it interviewing Betty Friedan? On my way out to her home in Sag Harbor on Long Island, New York, I imagined a pleasant, stimulating tête-à-tête with a catalyst of the second wave of feminism. An earlier telephone call had made me anxious about what to expect, when she was unfamiliar with me, my work, and the purpose of my upcoming visit. I had often heard from those who had previous experience with her that Betty was "difficult," but just what that meant, I hadn't known, exactly. So I had attributed her uninformed state to an overly hectic schedule.

"Are you George?" Betty asked me when she opened the door. "Not the last time I looked," I answered, somewhat puzzled. It wasn't until we sat down in her living room that I understood: "George" was *George,* the magazine of politics and popular culture, which was also interviewing Betty that same week.

My immediate impression of her was how small in stature she is. A larger-than-life icon also has human proportions, physically as well as psychologically, but that's often easy to forget.

Betty had recovered from the heart valve surgery she had had the previous September, and she was trim after having lost nearly twenty pounds. (Actually, that very day after our visit, she would be meeting a personal trainer at the local health club.) The heart valve, Betty wise-cracked, would outlive her. "I'm fine," she said when I asked about her health. When I told her that it was my birthday, she began to recall vivid images of her own birthday, twenty-seven years ago.

"Well, for God's sake . . . on my fiftieth birthday, the women's move-ment was just exploding. Nineteen seventy-one. In my early years, I never buckled down to be a serious academic. My academic career began after my fiftieth birthday, so questions like tenure never bothered me. I just went in at the top at my own inclination or disinclination. You can't judge anything by my life. Whenever I had time to think about it, I thought I never really had a career." She mimicked whining. "Well, I won this big fellowship to go for my Ph.D. in psychology. I didn't take it, so I didn't become a Ph.D. in psychology, although by now I have received seven honorary doctorates. I got fired from a newspaper job and was pregnant with my second child. I loved working on a newspaper. I would have been very happy to have been the women's page editor of the *New York Times* and see it evolve into something else, and so on. But I entered aca-demic life at the full professor level after publishing my book *[The Femi-nine Mystique],* and I could write what I want to write, so what's the question?" she said, remembering her irritation.

"What do I have to look forward to in the next twenty-seven years?" I asked again.

"What you can look forward to is liberation from the limitations. You don't have to prove anything to anybody, do you? And you've ful-filled whatever roles were prescribed for you. If you've gotten married, if you've had kids, raised the kids, that's finished now. So the rest of your life is just where you want to take it. I had this discussion with myself lately. I'm all for new adventures, but I get my life so filled up with things that I'm asked to do, expected to do . . . They're not bad, but they don't leave me any room," she said, echoing a sentiment that I had heard over and over from women in their seventies. Women who thought their lives would calm down and hoped they would be able to relax more but who instead found even more responsibilities and interesting activities that they wanted to do and that were expected of them.

The American feminist revolution of the 1960s, or the "second wave" of the women's movement, began among white, middle-class, educated women who became aware of the many inequalities that all women in American society suffered. Betty Friedan's book *The Feminine Mystique* articulated the discontent of women frustrated with their plight. In 1966, Betty Friedan founded the National Organization for Women (NOW). The National Women's Political Caucus was founded in 1971 by Bella Abzug, Shirley Chisholm, Gloria Steinem, and Betty Friedan.

In 1993, the publication of *The Fountain of Age,* her fourth book, did nearly as much for the "age mystique" as Betty's first book had done for the "feminine mystique." She began writing *The Fountain of Age* at age sixty-eight. In the preface to the book, Betty admits that she "didn't even want to think about age. I was locked in my own denial before I could truly take in and exult over the stories of the surprisingly many women, and also men, . . . continuing to grow, and living with vitality at a different kind of age." One of the great gifts of *The Fountain of Age* was its offering of role models of people "living with vitality" into what she calls "the third stage" of life.

Our interview had a rather rocky start, including a few accusations on Betty's part that I felt were unwarranted: "You obviously suffer from ageism"; "You're operating from an obsolete concept"; "I said what I said, not what I didn't say." We came to realize, however, that we shared more interests than she had previously thought. The conversation jumped from topic to topic, and I discovered a woman alive with concerns and curiosity. Later, we had lunch together at a dockside fish house, where our talk continued in a patternless form, touching on sailing, doctoral programs, literary gossip, Alicia Mugetti (a New York–based dress designer), the current state of feminism, food, travel to the Easter Islands. It eventually became the fiftieth birthday tête-à-tête I had hoped for.

Doing Something New

I don't know that women suffer the brunt of ageism. All this seems so obsolete to me. Obsolete. Women that I know are not invisible in their seventies. They're more vigorous. They have established themselves in whatever field they're in. You're operating from an obsolete concept! Women are *not* perceived as invisible in their seventies. Today it depends on what a woman is doing. Years and years ago, if women were only visible as nubile sex objects, then they're invisible after they're no longer nubile sex objects. But that, my darling, has not been true for a long, long time. Women are visible in the world in whatever field they're operating in and however they operate. They may also be, at various times, daughters, mothers, wives, granddaughters, grandmothers—different roles in the family. But they're not invisible even there, not when they're grandmothers, and certainly not when they're great-grandmothers, which more and more women who are living longer lives are becoming.

Age has certain bonuses. They are a result of what you've been doing. All right? You see things more holistically, if you continue to develop intellectually. It's not programmed—decay and decline after forty, or develop and evolve. Depends on what you do or what you don't do. But if you continue to be involved and continue to have purposes and projects and face challenges and you have built up a lifetime of experience, you develop a certain kind of wisdom, I think. And an ability to see more complexly than linear thinking, or either-or, win-lose thinking. More contextual.

Success previously has been defined in monetary terms or in terms of status or material advance. I say in my lectures lately—and this is not just in terms of women—QOL, which is quality of life, has to replace GDP, which is gross domestic product, as our priority and our basic measure. I think in terms of America generally, but it's certainly true with people in what is considered the new third of life after midlife.

Turn-of-the-century life expectancy was forty-five years. Now it is seventy-two for men and eighty for women. So there is a new one-third to one-half of life that people didn't even have before. And in this third to half of life, the conventional measures have been fulfilled, for better or for worse. You either had a success or have it in your career, or it doesn't matter to you any longer, or you're burnt out, or you've fulfilled your role: wife, mother, husband, father—whatever. You've finished your parenting years, so the territory is open. What do you want to do?

I've been thinking lately. A friend of mine was head of Small Business Administration and he's generally been concerned with financial deals and things like. He's a big burly Irishman, but the kind that reads James Joyce. Big reader, insatiable intellectual curiosity, which I love about him. So he decided he was going to write a play. Got fascinated by the Holocaust. Was going to write a play about the Holocaust. I said, "First of all, it's not your material, so take a course in playwriting." He did; that was really very good advice. So he's written a play, first about the picking of the Pope, which *is* his material. Then he said, "Now can I write a play about the Holocaust?" I said, "Yes, all right, OK." He's having a reading of the play in Washington, and I won't be back there for it this month, but I'm so proud of him and envious of him for doing something new like that, something new seriously. Taking the course in playwriting, writing the play.

I'm thinking, "What can I do that's new?" The trouble is I have so many demands, requests, opportunities, just to keep on doing what I'm doing. You do it in new directions or with new questions, but I'd love to do something really new. There are some intensive art courses offered on a barge or something that I could sign up for. It would be *fun* to do something that I'm no good at, that I've never done before, to do something different.

That's it. Doing what interests you, but also trying new things. Maggie Kuhn had a motto: "Do something outrageous every week." And then she changed it to "every day" at the end of her life. I've got to do that, something outrageous every week, and I've got to do something new, you see. That's got to be my motto—to do something new.

When you do these new things that suit you in this new third of your life, when you don't have to worry about success, failure, what anybody else is going to think, how much money you're going to make, and so on, status is not the important thing. Imagine a banker becoming an emergency room nurse, which is a case I write about in *The Fountain of Age.*

The word *success*—what does it mean anymore? You're a success if you stay alive. Success isn't the operative word. It's doing what you want to do, what you're able to do, even something you're not so good at but something that intrigues you, because failure doesn't matter anymore. *Success* and *failure* are out of your vocabulary, I think—or they should be. You're a mother, you're a grandmother, you're a friend, you're a lover—whatever. You deepen the relationship. Maybe the relationship will evolve in surprising ways. But the idea of success—no.

As far as my work goes, I wish I didn't have this memoir that I have to do hanging over me, but if you interview me a week from now when I've really gotten back to it, I'll be all right. When I'm actually writing, it's OK, but the dread . . . If I didn't have this goddamn memoir on my back, I could fool around with something different, like a novel or a detective story.

Advice? I don't offer advice. Not my business. Your life is what you make it. What do you want to do? Even if you're not rich, if you have Social Security . . . I interviewed women living on Social Security who were still adventurous, so they managed to plunk themselves down in something unusual but cheap. Like a ski lodge. There is the woman in California who is driving the bus in some little mountain town. She went there to ski and ended up staying there. I loved finding people like that. I know how many there are.

My impression today is that women I know have a lot more vitality than men. Most of my friends are younger, I must admit, at this stage of the game, because I'm so very involved in everything. A lot of women and men in their seventies are, but some aren't. You need to make friends that are younger. I have to say that in the last couple of years, three of the men in my life have died, and the women are still going strong.

What do I see for the women's movement now? I don't know. I was thinking about this question recently when I was reading something. Women are now getting equal numbers of professional degrees as men, so that means that in another generation, two generations, the playing field will be level. There's equity now at beginning levels and even at mid-levels. I think the glass ceiling will disappear as the pool changes—if 40 percent or more of the law school class and the medical school class are women. There are going to be so many bright, well-trained women in every field, every profession. And according to demographics, because of baby busts, there's going to be a shortage of skilled, trained professionals. You can already see it, except at the very top.

So I was thinking, women could declare victory and move on. For me, the main questions now are not, "Women alone, or women versus men?" We could declare victory and move on, except for one thing—we will not have achieved equality until children are considered equally the man's responsibility. The change now has to happen with men. If children begin to be seen as man's responsibility as much as women's, and as more and more men have the experience of hands-on parenting, as they are, as my son's generation is—hands-on parenting from the diapers to the teenage angst—and men are doing this as well as women, not only will equality be more real but it will be very good for the men. In fact, I think new research shows that men that do hands-on parenting live longer. They used to die eight years younger than women. So they'll live longer. That's good. There are skills, qualities that are not measurable according to male yardsticks of success that come from sensitivity to life and dealing with kids.

I wish I had gone to law school. It would have been fun for me, but I don't think I can do it at seventy-seven. I don't think anybody's going to let me in. On the other hand, my mother lived to ninety. But I could have done it ten years ago. I got to do some of these things. In June, I did so much traveling. In Paris, I spoke at a conference on the longevity revolution. The ambassador to Switzerland asked me to keynote a conference for the women of Europe in Bern, Switzerland. I was there two, three weeks. Since they knew I was coming over, the embassies asked me to speak at Madrid, Barcelona, Amsterdam. Fine. Visited friends for five days in Italy. Stayed in Paris nearly a week, just to play and shop. I tootled around Europe for three weeks. On the other hand, traveling is a drag—too much packing and unpacking. What I'm now looking for is some really interesting expedition, like a cruise, where you stay on the boat but get off and explore places, but you don't have to pack and unpack everywhere.

What do I see for the twenty-first century? Exciting times. Change is happening so rapidly and so completely, and yet it's imperceptible. You can't extrapolate into the future beyond about five years, it seems to me. Unpredictable events can change things enormously. Like, take this question. There's no dissent in this country right now. And there's a growing income disparity. But who's confronting it in any way whatsoever?

We had a lovely party here in Sag Harbor on July 4; it's given every year. We lowered the British flag, raised the American flag, read from the Declaration of Independence, and then anybody could give a little patriotic reading or say something. I always choose to say something. I was going to read the Declaration of Women's Sentiments of Seneca Falls, written 150 years ago. I put it down somewhere and couldn't find it, so I had to improvise. I gave a little speech about the power of America, about here we are at the new millennium: Oughtn't we be having a national dialogue about national purpose? I think Clinton should call such a thing. When I get back to Washington, I might try to institute a national dialogue. Every community should have one as we head for the millennium. What will be the purposes and values of this nation and all its power?

I go to different colleagues and say, "What could it take to get this country moving again in a progressive direction? We're mired in the culture of greed, aren't we? What would it take?" Nobody thinks it will happen without a depression or a war. Isn't that something? Isn't there any way that this country could be moved to some progressive politics again? Depression or war? Look around, and I must say, the Democratic Party tries to sound more and more like the Republican Party. And nobody even thinks at all about the poor. In fact, what did I just read that confirmed this? That HMOs were refusing to take Medicaid cases, or that they were trying to get rid of the elderly and the poor. Just cold-blooded. And there's a lot of elderly and poor now, and there's going to be more, because society's aging.

At the Fourth of July, I said a few mild things like this: "Just where is this nation with all its power and all its riches on the verge of the millennium?" Nobody's dealing with the growing income disparity. Everybody came up to me afterward as if I'd said something really radical. "Oh, Betty, thank you. That was wonderful."

In that yard were a hundred people, plenty wealthy. When you say we have to deal with the growing income disparity, everybody was on the upper end of that. But they were also very influential people, and a lot of my friends here are from the media. Oughtn't we be talking about these things? There hasn't been a progressive political movement in a long time dealing with this.

The last one began in the late sixties, and then it was the seventies and the eighties, but by the end of the eighties . . . People now say the women's movement is dead, and I say, "No, the women's movement is a part of society." As I said before, we could pick up our skirts, declare equality, and move on. Yes, women are only making seventy-four cents to the dollar, but I think that's bound to change with women getting an equal number of professional degrees. Plus, the discrepancy begins with the child-rearing years, so the only real question that remains is that children should be considered the male responsibility as much as the woman's and society's. And we're a backward nation—we don't have a national child-care program. To me, that's the main question.

I gave a talk, maybe the end of last summer. I used the term *culture of greed* disparagingly. A couple of people were commenting afterward, and I heard, "But what's wrong with that?"

Women who are in their thirties have been raised with just taking for granted the equity that now exists. They don't even know what it used to be like. That's what I think. They really don't know that women didn't always have it this way. Unless they've studied it, of course. That's my experience. Then they say, "I'm not a feminist, but I believe a woman's going to be president someday." So why do they say, "I'm not a feminist"? Because feminism to them means antimarriage, antimotherhood, antifashion, anti–beauty parlor.

The Christian Right did this for a dead serious and dead evil political reason. The Christian Right is against feminism, and they want women to go back home again. They don't dare say that aloud anymore, so they pick on abortion. "I'm not a feminist, but . . ." is popular culture. Feminism means you're anti-man, antifashion, antimotherhood—whatever. Feminism has been given a bad name. There are incredibly more women now in their seventies or in their sixties who are surely going into their seventies than there've ever been. Life expectancy of American women today is eighty years. That's average. Not eighty senile years, but eighty effective years. ∾

As I've told widowed women friends that I'm getting married, the response is always the same: "Wonderful. Does he have a twin brother?" I think almost all older women would want this. I guess the only advice then is, "Don't be shy. You have nothing to lose by taking the first step." Our generation was taught to feign indifference and coolness to protect ourselves against rejection. You don't have to sit back and be coy at our age.

LEE ROBINS

Lee Robins

Profile

The first thing that struck me about Lee Robins when I spoke with her by telephone was her laughter. She had a young woman's laugh, which made it difficult to picture her as seventy-five. A giggle repeatedly broke through as she told me of her upcoming marriage to a doctor at Washington University, who was also seventy-five. "It's never too late for romance," I said. She agreed, "I'm proof of that!"

I was intrigued by this woman, who is widely known in the field of sociology. She has spent much of her life writing interview questions. Through those questions, she has revolutionized psychiatric epidemiology, the study of the incidence and origins of mental illness. She equipped researchers around the world with precision tools to detect in the general population the psychiatric symptoms that physicians see in their patients. The surveys she designed to diagnose psychiatric disorders have gone beyond their original scholarly use and have found their way into hospitals, prisons, and doctors' offices. Since 1980, she been part of the task force that updates the *Diagnostic and Statistical Manual* for the American

Psychiatric Association. When we finally were able to arrange a convenient time and place to meet, it was at a Beverly Hills hotel in April 1998, where Lee was attending a select meeting of experts on drug use and dependence. On the nightstand in her room lay a Patricia Cornwell murder mystery, *Unnatural Exposure.* I commented on Cornwell's female detective, Kay Scarpetta, and Lee told me that in her own work she felt herself to be a bit of a sleuth. For two hours, Lee shared with me details of her public and private lives.

Born in New Orleans, she attended Radcliffe and Harvard. She married at twenty-three and had her first of four children (all boys) at twenty-five. The expanding family moved from Boston to St. Louis, where her second son was born. Although Lee had collected the data for her dissertation before they moved, she had not had time to write it. Due to the redesign of the social sciences department at Harvard, Lee was given one year to complete her doctorate or lose her standing. "That got me off the button," she recalls. "I borrowed the apartment of a bachelor friend of ours every morning, hired somebody to take care of my two babies, and wrote. I got it done!"

Lee and her husband wanted four kids, so after she finished the dissertation, she got pregnant again—twice. "That was fine, exactly what we had intended to do. I thought as long as I was going to be home with babies, I might at well do it all at once. Then I would be able to go to work when the youngest entered school."

But destiny had its own timetable. She was given an opportunity to do a child guidance clinic follow-up at the Department of Psychiatry at Washington University School of Medicine and went back to work part-time when her last child was nine months old. Her first book, published in 1966, was *Deviant Children Grown Up: A Sociological and Psychiatric Study of Sociopathic Personality;* medical researchers and social scientists consider it to be a classic. "I've spent most of my life studying people who were antisocial kids and finding out what happened to them later on," said Lee. This book challenged prevailing notions of why people become sociopaths, repeatedly losing jobs, committing crimes, abusing drugs, and wrecking their marriages. What she found was that the strongest predictor of such a lifestyle was not social class, economic status, or intelligence, as some believed, but antisocial behavior in the early school years.

I asked what effect her research may have had on raising her own family. "It was probably good for the children in some ways," she responded. "I would sometimes get really upset with them when they weren't doing what I thought they ought to be doing, but then I'd think about the kids I was studying who had really serious problems. Then my kids didn't look so bad to me. So what if they made a mess or punched their brother? Worse things can happen."

After her husband's death, Lee never expected to remarry. But at a dinner party in the home of friends, she ran into a recently widowed emeritus professor from the medical school where she has done her research. Because he was thinking of selling his house, she invited him to see the condo she had recently moved into. "When I asked him over, I thought he was very attractive and would be a pleasant escort; that's all I was looking for."

"So you have fallen in love again?" I asked.

"Oh, yes," Lee beamed, as her giggle got the best of her. "I'm crazy about him."

Love, Again

My work has been particularly satisfying. The first thing that was tremendously satisfying was making contact with people from all over the world after my first papers were published. I was amazed to get letters from people in Europe and everywhere, really. That was fun.

The studies I've done have been very interesting. Finding subjects thirty years after they attended a children's clinic was a little like being a detective. You get very good at it. I have one story in my book about how we found one of our normal control group kids who lived in the same neighborhoods as the clinic patients, whom we picked out of school records at random. Of course, those people didn't have any connection with the clinic and were not always cooperative. We usually had to go through relatives to find them. One guy wasn't in the phone book, and we couldn't figure out what had happened to him. We did locate a sister, who was very angry with us for trying to get hold of him and said, "Well, he has enough trouble with his family and his dogs without your bothering him." So we thought, "Hmm, dogs." We called the American Kennel Club and, sure enough, he was a member. He raised dogs in the country. He was delighted to be interviewed; it was his sister who was being protective. It was fun being able to locate more than 80 percent of these people after so many years.

One of the most interesting studies I've conducted is on drug use among nine hundred Vietnam veterans. I hired the National Opinion Research Center in Chicago to do the interviewing, but I wrote the interview and ran the study. We needed a staff of professional interviewers, because the veterans were scattered across the nation, and we wanted them all interviewed in four months, so that all would be interviewed after being back from Vietnam about the same length of time. We picked nine hundred men who had returned in September of 1971. They were extremely cooperative. They wanted someone to listen to them. Ninety-six percent were interviewed when they had been back ten months, and 94 percent were reinterviewed when they had been back three years. We were able to find virtually everybody, because we had access to their military records, which includes names and addresses of next of kin.

We found that, contrary to what everybody believed, almost all the men addicted to heroin in Vietnam just took themselves off. Very few had any problems with heroin after they came back. That's still a controversial study, because people aren't willing to believe that heroin addiction is often short-lived. And, of course, it isn't for some people. Some of the critics thought we hadn't followed them long enough, because "once an addict, always an addict." A young woman who was originally a postdoctorate student with me, and who now is part of our faculty, has just finished reinterviewing this same group twenty years later. They still have not been readdicted to heroin.

I don't know much else about the twenty-year data yet. They're pretty new. The tapes are being readied for analysis, so we don't yet have a complete picture. Still, it's reassuring that our original results have held up. One of the reasons is that study subjects are amazingly honest. The Vietnam veterans didn't know that we had access to their military records. Yet when we asked them about their use of heroin in Vietnam, of those who had any notation in their military record about heroin use, 97 percent admitted that they had used it. In addition, many more told us that they had used it, when there was no notation in their record. The army had no idea how high the drug use actually was. The rate we found was more than double what the army knew about. Forty-three percent of these enlisted soldiers had used heroin or opium.

We asked them why they did it and what they thought about those drugs after using them. That was very interesting, too. The reasons they gave for using them were not the ones that were popular in the press. It wasn't because they were terrified of combat, which was one of the theories. That just wasn't the case. Most who used it began as soon as they arrived. Right away, they were offered it by other enlisted men or by Vietnamese working in the camp. It was easy to get and was very cheap and pure. Many of the users saw little or no combat. You think of these guys as being cannon fodder. Some of them were, but a lot of them were working as clerks, in the kitchen, printing newspapers, or doing any number of things. There just wasn't much connection between being on the front line and using heroin. They told us that they used it because they enjoyed it and had nothing else to do—they were very bored. It helped them pass the time, helped them be less irritated by army regulations and all the "hurry up and wait" that was life in the military. It was a way of coping with army life and being one of the guys.

We asked them what they thought of the war, too, to see if that was connected to their drug use. Some of the users were very antiwar, but most of them weren't, just like the soldiers who did not use heroin. Even men who used heroin without having any problems as a result and who were able to quit using it still thought it was the worst drug in the world.

They felt it couldn't be used in a controlled fashion either in Vietnam or in the States. It seemed that each man thought his own ability to use it without problems and to discontinue its use was unique.

In terms of my personal life, my husband died three-and-a-half years ago. He had been sick for a very long time with multiple sclerosis. A tough experience. Hugh, the person I'm going to marry, lost his wife a little over two years ago. He is someone I had known slightly at the medical school for a long time. We also had some friends in common, but we didn't know each other very well.

I had lived in the same house for almost thirty-five years, and two years after my husband died, I moved to a condo near the medical school. Some friends had us both over for dinner. Hugh was beginning to think about selling his house, so I said, "Maybe you'd like to see my condo," and he came over. I hadn't seen him for a long time before that. Last December, we started seeing each other and decided in April to marry.

We're almost exactly the same age. When we exchanged curricula vitae and I saw the date of his birth, I said, "Did you know you're dating an older woman? I'm five months older than you are." He said, "That's all right. I'm used to dating older women. My wife was two months older than I."

We have gotten along extremely well. We have lots of parallels in our lives. We married only a year apart. He and my husband both did their residency training in Boston, at the same hospital, though we didn't know each other then. Being academics, we have gone to meetings in Europe, which led to our visiting many of the same places. We both have four children and now have a slew of grandchildren.

We had seen each other only four or five times when Hugh told me he'd like to marry me. I was incredulous. I was not ready to decide that quickly. But by April, I was. I hadn't understood why getting married was important to him. I understand it now; it will be much more comfortable introducing each other as, "This is my husband/wife" and not having to make explanations or use ambiguous terms. It is much simpler. People don't have to wonder whether to take the relationship seriously. And, yes, it's making a public statement.

Before agreeing, I interviewed friends, some who had married late in life (but not this late), and some who were living with someone without being married. I asked what they thought about a late marriage and, of course, everybody thought that what they had done was right. I found that the people who had not married felt differently about their relationship. They were not as wholeheartedly committed as the married ones. One said she wouldn't marry the guy because he had a problem son and she didn't want to end up responsible for him. There was always some "but" or "if." I didn't feel that way; I was making no compromises. I thought, "This man is wonderful. So why not marry him?"

How different is love in my seventies from when I was in love as a young woman? It's not terribly different. In some ways, it's a lot simpler, because when someone is our age, there are no unknowns anymore. I know exactly how Hugh will turn out, because he has already done it. Hugh and his wife had a happy, successful marriage. He enjoyed his children. There's no mystery here. I know he's going to be a great person to live with, because he did it so well before. Not having to wonder how it's going to turn out is a great asset. I know what I'm getting, and I like everything I see.

Another advantage to a late marriage is that there is little competition at this point in our lives between loving and other concerns. At least for me, and I think for most women, there was a good deal of competition when I was younger. Not between marriage and a career, because I wasn't that committed to a profession early in my life. But there was a lot of competition between the needs of children and the needs of a husband. My husband was the one with a conflict between career and family. I used to be unhappy about his working late and not being available when I wanted him to be, keeping me waiting. I don't have that problem now; Hugh is as free as I am. We can let the other person come first without question.

Yes, I know the study that states that marriage is good for men but not for women. I think the evidence for that is pretty good. The main evidence is that married men survive longer than unmarried men and that married women don't have any particular advantages compared to single women.

I think that women don't show beneficial effects because, traditionally, women who stayed single had often chosen between marriage and career and were strong, positive women. They did what they wanted. On the whole, they were a particularly competent group.

For me, being female was generally a big asset. This career that you've heard about was possible because my husband supported me. I could work part-time, so I could still spend a lot of time on children and the home. Working part-time allowed me to do research, because I didn't have to do all the things that most people who have academic appointments do. I didn't have to go to committee meetings, and I didn't have to do a lot of teaching. All those things are very time-consuming and interrupt research. My pay was correspondingly small, but that didn't really matter; my husband was making enough to support us.

You asked what love is—an interesting question. It's everything together. I'm sure it's partly the chemistry between us. Hugh is an easy person to be loving toward, because he's such a loving person. We share interests. We enjoy being together. I also enjoy his social grace and his good looks. That is much easier for me to recognize than it would have been in my youth. My "high principles" made it sort of indecent to care about how someone looks. Now I think it's fine to enjoy everything about someone. Being bright and virtuous and witty are essential, but grace and beauty are tremendous pluses. I think I've learned to be tolerant of all my tastes. I'm less prissy than I was in my youth.

There is always some concern about illness. You can't help that at this age. You know you only have a limited amount of time. You don't know who will be the first to have something devastating happen to their health. Hugh's father lived to eighty-six, so I'm very hopeful that he'll be long-lived. But I don't think in terms of how much time we have. Each day is a gift. I would take nothing for the pleasure we've already given each other. It's so much more than what either of us expected. He had been grateful for the long happy marriage he'd had and thought, "That's it." As he described his life after his wife died, he said, "Well, I wasn't unhappy, but I wasn't positively happy. Now I am." It's a terrific sense of power to be able to make someone that happy. I love it.

One of our priorities right now is to share friends who have been important to us in our individual lives. That's a big job, because we both have a lot of friends. I want him to know mine, know my past. You have a tremendous amount of past to share when you're this old. We spent the first few dates talking compulsively, trying to cover all the history. You want to know all about the other person, and you want the other person to know all about you, too, to understand what particular people mean to you and why they play an important role in your life.

The other important task for me is cutting back on the amount of time I work, though I probably will never completely retire. It's difficult for me, because I have obligations to many colleagues that I feel that I must fulfill. A frequent task at my time of life is writing recommendations for colleagues and for young people I have taught or who worked for me. They depend on these letters, and I owe it to them to write them. Before I left for this meeting, I owed reviews of six papers sent to me by journals. It's a privilege and an obligation to urge the publication of excellent papers and to weed out poor or misleading ones. Here, I feel less indispensable than with letters of recommendation, because others can take my place.

I'm reluctant to stop working, because work was really a wonderful thing for me while my husband was sick. He went to sleep early. We couldn't travel. The things we could do together were very limited. I would have gone crazy if I'd not been working. But once you get so involved in work, it's hard to pull out. I doubt that I would have had a major career if he'd been well. In the early years of our marriage, I was bringing up kids and being the gracious hostess once my husband became head of the department. We would go out several times a week, and I traveled with him to meetings. Life was very full. When he resigned because of ill health and found travel difficult, work filled that void for me.

My husband-to-be is officially retired but stays very busy. Like me, he doesn't say no very easily. He's on several boards, serves as a hospice volunteer, and is writing a book. So even at this advanced age, we both have to be sure to leave enough time for each other.

Having fallen in love at this late age has been rejuvenating. It's wonderful. One of the things I've always loved is dancing. My husband was an excellent dancer and hated it. Wouldn't do it. I never could understand how anybody could dance well and not like it. I don't know with Hugh yet, but he's such a sweet person, he's volunteered that he would be happy to take dancing lessons if I wanted. That would be fun.

I adored my husband and greatly love and admire my husband-to-be for many of the same reasons. Both nonjudgmental, free of snobbery, open to a great variety of people, loved by everyone who knows them, and interested in a huge range of things—food, the arts, sports, books, music, travel, and science. It's amazing to get many of the same assets over again; I really didn't think that could happen.

When you ask for advice for other women about aging, it's hard to give, because us old folks don't feel aged. The women I know best who are my age feel no internal correspondence to what they see in the mirror. For a long time, even the mirror was kind to me, but that's changed. I clearly have baggy skin now and all the other signs of age. It sounds vain, but to give you an example, I went to my fifty-year college reunion at Radcliffe. When I checked in, I said, "I'm here for the class of '42" and the person issuing tickets said, "You must mean the class of '52." People vary in how much they show age, but it always gets you sooner or later.

But no matter how you age, being elderly is very different from what I expected. Life is much more challenging and changing and varied than I expected. I thought that everything would be settled long before now. And it isn't. Nothing's settled. We live in a sea of changes, unfortunately made up more of deaths than new, wonderful starts.

As I've told widowed women friends that I'm getting married, the response is always the same: "Wonderful. Does he have a twin brother?" I think almost all older women would want this. I guess the only advice then is, "Don't be shy. You have nothing to lose by taking the first step." Our generation was taught to feign indifference and coolness to protect ourselves against rejection. You don't have to sit back and be coy at our age.

One of the most important things for people my age is their relationship with their children. The children are middle-aged now and past their struggle to prove their independence of their parents. You no longer have to pretend to be the model for what you want them to grow up to be. Now they can just be your good and intimate friends and an important source of knowledge about how the world is changing. Hugh and I have similarly warm but nondependent relationships with our respective kids. This is another reason I admire him so much.

One of the worrying things about aging is that your friends begin to die off. You can become isolated. A late marriage helps this, because the new spouse brings with him or her a host of new friends, who will take you in for their old friend's sake. Of course, they too will die off in time, so it's really important to keep a new supply coming. Old people don't always feel like making the effort. Then, there's a lot of age prejudice, so that some younger people avoid making friends with old people.

I've really been very lucky here. There are several young women in my life to whom I've been important. One reason, I think, is that they've all had difficult times with their own mothers. I'm lucky that they sought me out because, like with seeking romance, older women tend to be too passive. Because I had all boys, I'm particularly open to daughter surrogates. I've loved these young friends and my daughters-in-law. It's important to keep a flow of younger people into your life.

I have some very good friends who tried to persuade me to move into their retirement residence. It was the nicest such community you could possibly imagine, but I realized I didn't want to live in such a place, at least not without a spouse, because it's too age-uniform. It limits your access to young people. I have enough trouble now feeling I'm part of the contemporary culture. I often feel baffled by current movies and music. Having younger friends bridges the gap, at least in part. It reminds you that people of any age think the music in their youth was the right music and the books they read were the right books. Young friends and offspring help to keep you from being hopelessly stuck in your own era. ✑

My great-aunt passed without ever really finding what her niche was. I think that's true with most people now. They don't know where their niche is. What they want. All of a sudden, you're staring at the ceiling in the hospital and you say, "Now, wasn't there something I was gonna do?" So I want to do it now.

BETYE SAAR

Betye Saar

Welcome! You are about to abandon your preconceived notions about what is sacred and for a time embrace the conception that where the spirit is invited there it shall be.

NADINE DELAWRENCE, *Receptacles of the Spirit*

 ## Profile

Purple hair? At seventy-one? That's Betye Saar. No excuses. The diminutive, trim, curly-haired artist and grandmother of five has a girl's voice and a quick, optimistic manner. Her beauty echoes that of her role model, Lena Horne. Betye's artwork has elements of the mythical, autobiographical, historical, cultural, political, and metaphysical. Her interest in the occult has moved her to study palmistry, tarot, voodoo, phrenology, and shamanism. This interest can be recognized in many of the titles of her artworks: *Palmist Window, Nine Mojo Secrets, The Liberation of Aunt Jemima, Wizard, Eternity, Spirit Catcher,* and *The Domain of Chance.* Her dreams play an active role in her work, as reflected in the title *Dreams: The Flowering of.*

Betye's process of creating art is a ritual in itself. She considers her collages, boxes or assemblages, and installations to be not merely objects but objects of power. She calls herself "a junkie," because she zealously and lovingly collects her art materials at yard sales, thrift shops, flea markets, swap meets, and botanical gardens. Although her work has a certain sophistication to it because of her academic training at UCLA and USC, there is still the naive child behind it all—much to the delight of the be-holder. Betye's works are intricately cross-cultural, inspired by her exten-sive world travels and the materials she finds in the markets of Africa, Mexico, Asia, Europe, and the Caribbean.

When most people look carefully enough at their early life, they usu-ally discover an experience or series of experiences that they believe to have formed their character and perhaps even their vocation. For these people, it's as if there is a straight trajectory from their childhood to their adult world. Betye Saar is such a person. Growing up in Los Angeles in the 1930s, Betye would visit her paternal grandmother during the sum-mers with her two younger siblings. Her grandmother had a house in then-rural Watts on a triangular lot that was two blocks from the railroad track. Betye remembers how "the railroad track went right into the town of Watts, which came from Long Beach and San Pedro up into L.A." She and her brother and sister would walk along that track to go to town to help their grandmother with her marketing.

It was about that time that the architectural visionary and Italian immigrant Simon Rodia began to build his three highly decorative one-hundred-foot spiraling mosaic towers from the Watts neighborhood detri-tus, using glass, shells, metals, tiles, mirrors, rocks, and pottery on a base of steel rods, wire mesh, and concrete. They came to be recognized world-wide as the Watts Towers, but to Betye they were "a fairytale palace." Betye never got close enough to satisfy her curiosity until she later had three children. She has a photograph of herself there with her two eldest daughters, Lezley and Alison Saar, who are both artists. Alison has told her mother that when she starts her lectures, she shows that slide and says, "This is where I became an artist."

Betye has created her own "fairytale palace," complete with a lush forest, courtesy of Laurel Canyon in the hills above Hollywood. An artist's property is always a magical place for visitors, but because of the nature of her work—primarily mixed-media collage and assemblage—hers is a ver-itable fantasyland. Everywhere a visitor looks, treasures are to be found. She is especially proud of her daughters' art pieces and the "art" of her grandchildren.

Motherhood (and more recently grandparenthood) has been her most passionate concern. We spoke about an exhibit I had seen of her and Alison's work at the UCLA Wight Gallery in Los Angeles in 1991. It was open on Mother's Day, and Betye and Alison decided to make it a special event. "Alison and I gave a talk on Mother's Day. It was really special. Later, we got so many letters from young women saying, 'I took my mother' or 'My mother took me there. I'm an artist but she does dressmaking' or something like that. It allowed so many people to be aware of the mother-daughter relationship in a very different way."

Finding Your Niche

I'm winding down after about five years of travel. Every time I get home after a trip, it's really valuable to be at home and get my house together, get my garden together, and to start making work. So this year's a bit calmer. I've retired, so to speak, although I took some trips abroad and made several trips to New York.

Do I still have any unfinished business? Well, I would like to go to Egypt and go down the Nile. I feel a pull to that place. Most of it would be places to go, places to see. I feel really blessed. My life is complete, because I have a fabulous family. I've had a really easy life.

About three years ago, I started three new projects. One was public artwork that I collaborated on with my daughter Alison for the Public Art Fund. It was a garden for kindergartners at an elementary school in Queens. When I went there one winter for a site inspection, it was all asphalt, and I thought, "We could make this better." So we redesigned the garden, and that opened in May.

The second project was a print that I was doing for a book on the Persian poet Rumi from the thirteenth century. I had just one thing to do, but it was hard to get the proofs made and the plates made and everything. So I finally signed that last spring, too.

Then, all through the last three years, I've been working on a CD-ROM about my art. That's beginning to be completed. It would have been finished, I thought, last January, but then the company that was producing it was bought out by the partners, and there was a big mix-up. So it's been very difficult to get it finished. For me, it was sort of a challenge, because I'm a really tactile person. I collect materials and make things out of those materials, and I had to deal with a little machine by pressing little buttons. It took a lot of work with the designer to integrate the way I felt the work should look. But it should be out by the first of next year, so look for it.

Now, when I say I'm retired, it means I'm living on my Social Security, my Keoghs—things like that. My retirement doesn't have to do with work; it has to do with finances. And also with the work I accept. I don't want to do any more public artwork. I don't want to teach at all anymore. I can just say no to a lot of things and pick what I want to do and spend more time doing my art.

Doing art is a real pleasure after raising children. Especially when they were students, it was hard. Their father helped—we split all the expenses and everything—but still I had the main responsibility. Now that they're married with kids and have their own homes and families, I finally get to exhale. Of my three daughters, two are artists and the youngest one, Tracye, is interested in writing. She has a two-week-old baby, brand-new. So if she's like her elder sister, that will just open up her creative energy, and she'll start producing what she wants. That happened with Lezley.

My youngest daughter (who's thirty-six now) has moved out. She was like my right hand. She's a good cook, so we would switch off cooking and housecleaning and chores. Also, she would travel with me when I had an assignment somewhere. Now that she's started her own life, people go, "Aren't you really lonesome? Aren't you suffering with empty nest syndrome?" I say, "No, finally it's my nest, and I can arrange it the way I want.

Nobody to say, 'You're not going to put that there, are you?'" So it has brought about a lot of independence. Personal independence.

I was doing an interview yesterday with an art critic about my exhibition, and she asked, "How are you feeling in your seventies?" I said, "I feel really independent. It's my house, it's my garden, it's my body—I can do what I want with them. If I want my hair purple, it's purple."

My hair is a funny story. In 1981, I went to a Halloween party, and I dyed my hair pink for it. One of those put-it-on-and-wash-it-out things. And I liked it: "This is sorta fun." By then, I was teaching at Otis Art Institute, and punk things were in—fuchsia and magenta were in. I said, "This isn't punk. It's just pink. It's mellow, and it looks nice with my skin color, and it's sort of pastel." I enjoyed it. And then when I became a grandmother eight years ago, I said, "Grandmothers do not have pink hair. Just go back to the natural gray." But I got bored with that, so I tie-dyed it a mixture of magenta and purple. The color moves. Now it's only on the top. Before, it used to be all around. So this way, if I have to go to a conservative place, I just put a little hat on.

You know, when you get older, it's like, "I'm gonna do what I want." One day, I was over at my daughter's house, and I was having some brownies. And they said, "Do you want milk?" And I said, "Yeah, and I want ice in it." They said, "Ice in your milk?!" I said, "I'm seventy-one years old. I can have ice in my milk if I want." So that's my retort when somebody says something with shock: "I'm seventy-one years old. I can have it if I want to."

At my age, I also feel a sense of solitude that is very pleasant. Even though Tracye lived with me, she was away at school in Santa Barbara. She would be home on the weekends, so that sort of prepared me for living alone. Then when she came home, she lived here four years before she got married, but we were always interdependent and independent, you know?

Because of where I live, it's just very quiet and very peaceful here. I just accept that solitude. Also, right now, it's like the wintertime, nesting time. In other places where there's snow and winter, you would hibernate in a way. Even here in California, I feel that natural cycle that the body goes through. I think that's why I got the house painted and then decided if I want this or that, what the rug is going to be like, and all that. Preparing the nest. House beautiful, garden beautiful—although gardening is usually in the summer. But that sense of inner peace. It doesn't mean that things don't anger me or annoy me or bother me or that the car doesn't need new tires, or whatever. But those are everyday necessities. I like living right here where I am. There are parts of L.A. I would not like to live in.

I made a promise to myself that I would stay home November, December, January, February to help Tracye with her baby. Of course, if there's a wonderful opportunity to go someplace—maybe Hawaii in January—I might make an exception. But I just want to take those four months, work in the studio and get caught up on the paperwork and things like that. Try to slow it down a little bit.

My fantasy of aging, my wish for aging, is to see my grandchildren become adults. But you know, I don't know if the numbers are gonna work out. That would place me in my nineties. I come from healthy stock, and I'm a healthy person now. I had a great-aunt who lived to be ninety-four. But, you know, she suffered illness. If I'm gonna live that long, I want to be healthy. I want to have a healthy body and a healthy and creative mind. I don't want to be moanin' or sick or living off of tubes. My fantasy of old age would be to be able to survive here in this environment, in my home, and I think that's part of why I'm fixing it up like I want it. It's not like this is my tomb, but this is where I've spent my life, and I would like to continue to do so.

I have a neighbor—she's Canadian—and when her mother passed, she had her cremated, and she bought a rosebush named "Faith." (I think her mother's name was Faith, too.) She planted it in the garden with her mother's ashes. I told my kids I want to be cremated and I want my ashes in my garden here, because I love it so. So that would be my fantasy.

If I think I would pass on before I could see my kids or my grandkids find their own lives, I would be saddened by that. I don't really dwell on it too much, because I come from a very mixed religious background of Episcopalian, Christian Science, Methodist, and Baptist, depending on where we were living and what we were doing at that time. Through that experience, I have sort of wandered more toward the metaphysical, more toward Unity, nondenominational, and really based my spiritual beliefs on being connected to the God spirit through every living thing. I don't participate in Unity Church now, but when my family was young, my ex-husband and I were Unitarians. I just don't have the patience to sit through it. I love black churches, because I love the music, so I just buy gospel music and listen to it. I just enjoy celebrating the spiritual part of myself every day. Not that I don't lose my temper and then say, "Oh, this is terrible. You're saying mean things about somebody, gossiping, or doing things like that," which is contrary to the truly spiritual.

There has always been a spiritual component to my work. I've just accepted that. But I feel it moving out more into my general life. You know—how I relate to people. And I hope to spread that feeling to my grandchildren. I think about my paternal grandmother. I knew her all through my childhood, even as an adult until my eldest daughter was born. She was never really forceful or anything, but she had a very strong spiritual belief, and she was religious, too. We children would go to prayer meetings with her and so forth. Just how to be true to yourself, how to be true to your race, to your culture. I feel that's important to spread to my grandchildren. They have their parents, and their parents give them everything, but then I think the grandmother has a role in what to give them, too. I want them to feel that they can always come to me, to ask me anything they want, and that I'll be the great calmer. Among my three daughters, two of them have two children, and the youngest one has one. She is just getting started.

Over the years, my work has gone through cycles. I see my work as falling into several main divisions. First, there's this sort of ancestral past, which is totally unknown to me. Except I know that I come from African stock, but I also come from Native American stock and Irish stock. So right now, my work is dealing with those unknown racial cultures, because I don't know what tribe I'm from—from Africa *or* from Native America. I can only guess that because my grandmother is from Louisiana, she was probably Choctaw mixed with African. It's been a challenge to work with that, but I think even in earlier works, I was doing that without the intent of doing it. It was just happening automatically with the fact that I like to integrate different symbols and images from other cultures. The bottom line for me is basically "one people, one world." There are cultural and racial differences, geographical differences, but still we're all from Earth. By that, I mean we're Earthlings, not Martians. So the work has always touched on that. And on the ancestral—the ritual works that have to do with altarlike structures, and so forth.

Second, there was a period in the 1970s when I did political work, social commentary works, with *The Liberation of Aunt Jemima*. I've sort of returned to doing political works. Eventually, that softened and mellowed out into nostalgic work, work with vintage photographs. All along, though, there has been this thread of the mystical, spiritual aspect. Since I'm older, I understand it more, and I can make it more deliberate in the things I combine, and so forth.

I guess the most important thing that I've learned is the aspect of love, and especially love of family. My family comes first. Oh, yeah. Oh, yeah. They come before my work, because work is just stuff, work is just things. I feel that I'm also creating myself as a person, as a woman. I mean, like this purple hair is a palette, you know? I like my clothes and I like my house fixed a certain way. I'm not that much of a cook, but even so, I like to combine colors and textures and tastes. And my garden—it's all creative.

Certainly, I think my lasting contribution would be my daughters and their families, because in turn, they're making their contribution. And while our art is very different, it still comes from the same fountain of making a contribution to add something to someone else's life. It's particularly difficult now with the way the art trend is, where ugly is important. What's cool, what's hip, and what's sometimes mean-spirited, even, is what's trendy. I said to the interviewer yesterday, "The two important aspects of my work are mystery and beauty," which is what life is, too, you know?

The mystery part is, you're not really sure what's going to happen tomorrow or what death is—all those everyday mysteries. That's what I try to encompass in my art, whether it's an installation, the CD-ROM, an assemblage, or a watercolor. They don't all have that quality, but that's my goal in making a major piece of art, and I think that quality of making a contribution to the quality of life has been passed on to my daughters. They do it in different ways with different materials in their own voice, their own creative expression. But that's where I see my heritage continuing, and hopefully with my grandchildren, too, because they're all very creative. They all consider themselves artists—those that can talk and express themselves.

In 1988, Tracye and I went to three venues in Southeast Asia: Malaysia, Taiwan, and the Philippines on an art project. We would see these cute baby clothes, and I said, "I think we're just going to have to buy these baby clothes. Somebody's going to have a baby sometime." Lezley was married. Alison had been married eight years or so. It was like, "Oh, what did I do wrong? They don't want kids!" We came home with all these baby clothes, and then three months later, Alison said, "Oh, we're going to have a baby." I said, "See."

In terms of a romantic relationship now, I don't know. I have a really close friend who lives in Topanga Canyon, and I live here. He's my party buddy. We go to the museums. He's a great dancer, so we have a lot of fun. Sometimes we think it could be a romantic relationship, but our friendship is really more important, you know?

I think one of the things about turning seventy is that you really know that you're set in your ways. Like if I want to take a bath at three in the morning, nobody's gonna say, "You're taking a bath at this hour?" Or if I want to watch TV all night or something. It's like I'm free, you know? I keep saying, "Well, I would like to have somebody around when I'm eighty.

We can go for walks, or something like that." But at this point, there's not anybody like that. I have close friends, and I have dates, and that makes me happy. My life has been so busy that the only thing I'm afraid of is that I might fall in love. I've got too much work to do. But I may mellow out and change my mind about that.

Also, I've always had this aptitude for seeing the bottom line about a person. Sometimes you can be infatuated with someone, and then you say, "Oh, this guy is nuts." Or something else: "There's a weak spot." You spot the holes. We're still friends, but, well, it's just not going to go anywhere.

It's interesting. In my late sixties, I read different things about aging. I read something about Dyan Cannon, the actress who was married to Cary Grant. She said she was playing a role about a woman who aged. She left the studio in her makeup as an old woman, and she was invisible. She was a young woman inside but had the makeup on of an old woman. She wasn't a chickie. Sometimes that's happened to me. I say, "Oh, that's right. I've got gray hair, an older face. I've got wrinkles. So that's what they see."

But I've always been a kid. People say to me, "How old did you say you were?" This is on the telephone. I say, "Right now I'm in my seventies." "But your voice is so young." So I know that I'm really blessed with that, because I notice friends' voices changing. How can your voice change? Sort of crackly. These people are younger than I am. It's partly because I live up all these stairs and my garden goes up the back. I'm not a jock, not athletic or anything, and exercise is a nuisance because I'd rather be making art or gardening. People say, "How can you be seventy years old?" I say, "That's easy, I was born in 1926." I get a lotta compliments.

In my sixties, I said, "Well, it's OK if I've got gray hair." It might have been the time before I had my hair pink, or after, when I was in my grand-mother phase. Now that I'm a grandmother, I can do and say anything I want, because I'm invisible. Gray makes you invisible. In a way, that's not negative. There is a sort of a release to being invisible. Who cares what I do? Who cares what I say? Who cares how I look? I can just do whatever I want.

Except that I *do* like a certain amount of respect, you know? I want my grandkids to respect me. I don't want some young flash-mouth to be sassy or anything. I don't mind when people say, "Yes, ma'am" to me. I say, "Hey, I deserve that respect. I earned that respect."

I think about the difference between my daughters and my great-aunt. My great-aunt passed without ever really finding what her niche was. I think that's true with *most* people now. They don't know where their niche is. What they want. All of a sudden, you're staring at the ceiling in the hospital and you say, "Now wasn't there something I was gonna do?" So I want to do it now.

My advice to other women is to find out who you are and what you really want, and then just do it. If you're a young mother—because that's when my career really started to happen—you can't do it so fast. You just take your time. That's another thing about my independence during this stretch; I don't have to worry about hurrying home and making sure they've got dinner and things like that, because they take care of themselves. But at the same time, with my home, I try to provide a place that they can always return to.

In my work, I speak to a lot of young mothers, either at openings or when I give a workshop, and they say, "Well, if you can do it, I can do it." I say, "That's right." They say, "My kids are messy. They want to get in the paint." And I say, "Well, stop and do it with them. Do some projects with them so they learn how." I think that's one reason my girls all want to work with their kids in the same way, making art. That's what you do. It's OK.

It's a male thing where the man goes to the studio, he works at the studio, but then the little woman is taking care of the kids. Now, there are some husbands, especially later fathers, who bring their kids with them. I hear stories. Like the father will say, "I'm painting this painting, and there's my son over there," who's like a five-year-old, "and he says, 'Why did you put *that* color on?'" The child becomes the critic, you know? But at the same time, the kid is becoming an artist, too.

Women have always had to do that. The kids have always been underfoot, unless you're really wealthy or indifferent to them. Some people sort of abandon their kids or go in another direction, but I always felt very dedicated to my kids, and they were always around when I was making art, and making art with me. There are certain times when you can't have them around or they're in school and you get more done then. But that would be my advice to younger women—live a complete life.

They say, "I want to be an artist. I don't know if I can do it with the kid." I say, "But being a mother is being an artist, too. It's really no different. You have to learn how to do it. It's a very creative kind of thing." Since many women artists are older and are now having children, they realize that you can do it all together.

I would imagine it would be very sad to get toward the end of your life and really have nothing to show for it, either as an offspring or in your work, because you just never found out what your niche is. I think part of my drive as a grandmother is to help my grandkids find out what it is for them. Whether it's art or music or something that's entirely their own that sort of heals them and blesses them and contributes to them and to others.

When my great-aunt died in 1974, I said, "I'm not going out like that. I'm going to do what I want to do. I'm going to take care of my health," not that she neglected her health. "I'm going to eat the right foods, take care of my body and my mind, and I'm always going to have some kind of creative energy and drive keeping me together. I don't want to go staring up at the ceiling in some hospital wondering, 'Where am I?'" I think my art is a real nurturing thing.

One woman who is, I think, absolutely fantastic is Lena Horne, who is now eighty. Her young life was not easy. My life has always been fairly easy. I've had sorrow and heartache and sickness, but I mean she really just keeps reinventing herself. She would be my number one role model.

There isn't any particular time that I prefer to work. I think I'm working on things all the time. I'm thinking about them all the time, because I love to go to the flea market, go shopping for supplies all the time. I select images, and I keep a little sketchbook, and I draw ideas in it. Or I'm read-ing something, and it gives me an idea for a title. It's just like working all the time. Yesterday, I painted a little bit of something before I went to the museum, and I have a whole counter full of mending and sewing and glu-ing and painting and mailing. I consider all of that "the work." Only, some of it goes to the museum, and some of it stays in my house.

I don't really have much of a daily routine. It's not that I'm lazy, but I'm not really a morning person. My days are always changing. I know I need more sleep, but sometimes I get seduced by an old movie, so I'll watch that. Or I'll fall asleep and then wake up in the middle of another one, so I've gotta watch that one. I get up in the morning, open the windows, look out at the gardens, bless the day, bless my body, bless my mind. Have breakfast. Because, during this current period, I have no deadlines. That's usually my schedule—I don't have to be anyplace. I could come down at eleven. You can tell by my storeroom that I haven't accomplished much every day.

But today's a beautiful day, and when you leave, I'm going to get my things together and go over and visit Tracye and the new baby, because her sister Lezley is coming over with her daughters. So I'll be with my family a bit. Then I think Alison's kids are coming to spend the night. They'll come after dinner, but they'll probably have breakfast here. Then I'll check the CD-ROM.

It's just like I look at the day and say, "It's my day today. Whatever you wanna do." When I'm still in bed, I say, "I'll do this and this and this and this." Then when I'm up, I start picking the leaves off the plants, rearrang-ing the flowers . . . ❧

I like being old. It's the best time of my life. I don't want to avoid the term, and I don't want people to avoid it with me. It's OK, it's good; there's nothing wrong with being old and calling it old. The important thing about being seventy is that I define what seventy is by who I am and the way I live. I don't have to conform to what somebody else thinks seventy is or what society says seventy is. We define the age; the age does not define us.

LEAH FRIEDMAN

# Leah Friedman

The Crone's title was related to the word "crown," and she represented the power of the ancient tribal matriarch.

Barbara Walker, *The Crone*

 ## Profile

"CroneLeah@ . . ." read the email address of one of my new classmates in the Ph.D. program at Pacifica Graduate Institute near Santa Barbara, California. Pacifica is the only graduate school in the world that offers a doctorate in mythological studies and depth psychology. As a result, the school draws students from around the globe—Australia, Africa, Germany, Canada—and from as far across the United States as one can go. The courses at Pacifica meet only a few days each month for intensive seminars and instruction. Leah doesn't have to travel quite that far, but going from St. Louis, Missouri, to southern California is not exactly an afternoon jaunt.

When I first met Crone Leah, which is how I now address her, I was touched by her warmth and direct gaze, by her quiet self-assurance. She dresses exactly as one would imagine a crone would dress; long, flowing, vividly colored robes cover a practical and functional single-hued pantsuit. There is always jewelry—earrings, bracelets, necklaces—usually one-of-a-kind, often made by an artist, and always tasteful. Her convenient, breezy hairstyle complements her smiling round face and proves that natural is best, especially when it comes to hair color.

Looking at and knowing Leah make a younger woman hope that she herself will grow up to be a crone. I say *hope,* because not all women do grow up that way. It isn't a matter of being old but of growing older. It's not a question of a life well lived but of an old age well prepared for. I think that's part of the gift of being a crone; the crone makes that last stage in life seem desirable and worth working toward.

What is a *crone?* Why has that word received such malediction over the millennia? And why is there such a thirst among late-twentieth-century women for what she has to offer? In ancient matriarchal, or mother-centered, Goddess-worshiping cultures, the older woman was revered as a powerful elder, as a woman of great wisdom and judgment who functioned as a healer, teacher, and priestess. However, patriarchal religion and society have been ruthless in their opposition to Goddess worship, and the attendant denigration of the crone has resulted in the historic marginalization of older women in human affairs. The crone, or wise old woman, was considered to embody divine wisdom that was thought to grow stronger as she aged.

In the academic environment that I and many others share with Leah, she is revered as a powerful elder, a woman of great wisdom and balance. We are anywhere from five to forty-five years her junior, and she has justifiably been chosen as the class representative.

Leah was born on a farm in rural North Carolina. Her family mainly grew cotton on the land until the boll weevil became rampant in the South and destroyed cotton crops for several years. Her family then turned to tobacco as its main economic base. A younger brother was born deaf when Leah was two. When she was five or six, her mother took the brother on the train to a school for the deaf in St. Louis. Leah wept as she told me, "The sorrow of that separation from my brother has colored my life and my family's life. Not to mention what it did to my brother, a trauma from which he never recovered psychologically."

It had always been a family dream that Leah teach the deaf. She and her brother formed a strong bond during the summers when he was home, and Leah was the person with whom he could most easily communicate. As a college student, Leah was employed by her brother's school for the deaf, and what she saw there was "almost Dickensian." Untrained women acted with "extreme hostility and cruelty toward the children." When Leah tried to point out this mishandling to the school's director, she was told to "mind my own business and not interfere."

Unable to remain in such conditions, Leah left her training at the school and majored in psychology at Washington University in St. Louis. There, she met Norm, a young man who was "brilliant, Jewish, very radical, and outspoken in his point of view." After a row with her Waspy family over her freedom to become involved with Norm, Leah ran away from home to make a life for herself with the man she loved. They were married in 1948, and both finished their undergraduate work a year later at Washington University, where they were the first married couple ever to graduate together. School had always been a primary commitment for Leah, and she was grateful to attend the University of Iowa, again with Norm, and to receive her master's degree in speech pathology and audiology.

After that, it was strictly home economics for Leah, which she loved— raising two daughters, making a beautiful home and garden, loving a husband. All that began to change, however, when Leah turned fifty and her children left the "nest." Her life became her own.

Among her deepest pleasures has been her induction into the world of ritual—so fitting for a crone. She told me of her planned rituals for friends' birthdays and especially of the rite-of-passage observance she conducts for her granddaughters: "We have the most wonderful ceremony. I send out a letter in advance asking members of the family to be prepared to talk about the day the child was born, stories about the child as she was growing up, her qualities, what it's like to be thirteen, our dreams for her future. At the ritual, we all light a candle for her. After we're finished talking about how wonderful she is and have given her all our gifts, which are symbolic of her, the cousins stand up and hold their arms in an arch. The young woman walks through as her symbolic passage from childhood to womanhood and is crowned with flowers. Then each of us offers her a blessing."

Now, how would each of our lives be different, Dear Reader, if we had been given such a jubilant and sacred entry into our own woman-hood? Why is it so unusual when it should be the norm?

It didn't take long before I was asking Leah to help me celebrate my fiftieth birthday this year with a ritual among our fellow students. She replied with abundant generosity and enthusiasm.

I interviewed Leah in May 1998 on the campus of Pacifica Graduate Institute near Santa Barbara, California. Leah was about to turn seventy. She and Norm planned to celebrate their fiftieth wedding anniversary that year by including their family in a special ceremony. During my interview with her, I realized that recognizing and honoring an older woman (an "old" woman, as Leah so pointedly insists) can yield impor-tant and useful information for a younger woman. Leah and I were engaged in our own ritual of sorts—the transmission of wisdom and experience.

The Croning Years

I've lived an entire life since I was fifty. The years from fifty to seventy have been some of the most creative and wonderfully fulfilling years of my life. When I was fifty, my daughters had graduated from college and left home and became more or less established on their own. I felt liber-ated from being a stay-at-home mother. I had always been very much the homemaker. Neither of my daughters are homemakers; they would never think of themselves as homemakers. They don't like to cook. I cooked, I sewed, I gardened. But when they went away, I just knew I had to have a whole new life.

I started learning French. I started doing English-saddle horseback rid-ing and jumping. Norm was terrified I was going to break my bones. One day, the horse I was riding kept balking at a jump, and I finally decided

Norm was right; I thought, "What am I doing?" I also took a class in photography, and that clicked. With that, I started off on my career of fine art black-and-white photography. I had my own darkroom and had many exhibits of my work. Looking back on it now, I realize that was the first big entry for me into the world of the inner life. I didn't know it at the time, but it was extremely significant in my exploration of my inner self.

When I look at some of the photographs, first of all, they explored very strongly my relationship with my mother. I zeroed in on this pretty fast. The photos were still lifes, black and white. I would assemble dried flowers and old photographs and found objects and maybe some textures and other things and arrange them and photograph them. I did some self-portraits, which were included as part of that kind of composition.

One woman saw a series of photographs, a triptych, I did, and she was a Jungian analyst. I didn't know anything about Jungian analysis then. She said, "That's the best representation of 'The Night Sea Journey' [a deep state of depression] I've ever seen." I thought, "'The Night Sea Journey' might be about death, but the photo series was about 'The Dark Night of the Soul.'" Of course, that's what I was going through at the time. There were days when I would stand in the darkroom and watch an image come up in the tray and just sob and sob and sob. Obviously, some of these images resonated so deeply with me, but I didn't know consciously what they were or what was happening.

I began to realize it was bringing up my relationship with my mother, my childhood, everything that I had never before had the means to deal with. There were collages I can remember setting up and photographing, and then I would just look at the image taking shape and get so dizzy I would have to lie down on the floor. It was very profound. I like the word *resonate;* it touched some deep part of me, something I didn't even know was there.

I would say that I was depressed then. I had grown up with a mother who was depressed, and I was depressed, too, but hadn't realized it yet.

About the time I was involved with photography, I took a class called "The Psychology of Gender," which was another huge opening for me.

The instructor introduced the whole concept of women's spirituality and dreamwork through a Jungian approach. I couldn't bear for the class to be over, so I circulated a petition among the women in the group to continue on as a discussion group, which we did.

I was reading a lot of Jungian psychology and going to conferences on spirituality. I just knew something was happening. I wrote a letter to my daughters at that time and said I knew I was "on the beginning of a journey, but I have no idea of where I'm going." Looking back at it now, I realize it was really a journey into old age. It was as if I knew that was coming. I also said, "I know one thing: I'm going to demand more solitude. I'm going to be pulling away. It doesn't mean I don't love you as much, but I know I need this time to be alone. I need time to go inward." It was amazing, when I looked back on that letter once in a while, to see how much I was aware of what was going to happen—without realizing I knew.

Here is a story about my "going inward." One day, one of my daughters was talking about how much she wanted to travel. I said, "You know, that really doesn't interest me anymore. I am concerned now with the 'inner journey.'" She looked alarmed, and said, "Oh, Mom, I hope that doesn't happen to me!" I laughed; it was a good example of the different stages of our lives.

I became deeply involved in ritual work and started planning rituals for people. The first one I did was for a friend of mine on her fiftieth birthday. It was a magical experience. Those women had never been to a ritual. I had never done a ritual. It took a lot of courage, looking back on it. But we really truly entered into another space for that evening and honored her in a very special way. I usually have women talk about another woman who's been important in her life and light a candle in her honor, which we did that night, among other things. Of course, we talked about particular characteristics that are present in that woman that might be helpful to her as she approaches this transition in her life. Then we have each guest talk about what quality of her own has been helpful in her life transitions. So it's a true sharing of women's experiences and stories.

That group evolved into a rather permanent women's ritual group. Every month, we did rituals for several years on various occasions: full moon, solstice, name changing (that is, if we wanted to change our name, what name we would choose for ourselves and what that name would mean to us). We told about a wound we had and wrote a blessing for ourselves—a self-blessing ritual. We did one in which I brought a lot of craft stuff, and we made an object that meant a lot to us and then talked about what that object symbolized. What I would call a "ritual of self-expression." There were many, many kinds of rituals.

After attending many Jungian workshops and other spirituality conferences, I decided I wanted to start Jungian analysis. In St. Louis, there was no one I wanted to see, but in Chicago, where we went regularly, I visited the Jung Institute. The procedure, which I did not know when I first went, was to see an analyst in their referral service for an hour or so, and that analyst would place you with the analyst with whom you would eventually work. They told me who the woman would be who was going to interview me. In the meantime, I listened to one of her tapes, on which she talked about old women and what she had learned from them. I thought, "Yes, this is the woman for me." We interviewed. I loved her. She was from the South, Mississippi; she knew how I grew up. She was perfect for me. Halfway through the interview, she asked me what I was looking for in an analyst. I said, "Someone who has had experience in life, who is as old as I am, and who also has had experience in analysis. I think you're the one." She said, "I'm sorry, this process doesn't allow me to take you as a client." I couldn't believe my ears. No one had told me that before our meeting. I was furious. Finally, the board from the institute consulted among themselves and allowed me to have her as my analyst. I could tell she wanted me as a client, too. We were a good fit. She's still my analyst. I see her in Chicago about once a month, but it was more often in the beginning.

What brought me here to Pacifica? Well, what led me here is that I truly followed my dreams. I'd had a series of dreams about being in a university. In the beginning, Lucy, my analyst, thought—and I agreed with her—that the university that was appearing in my dreams was the University of Iowa, where I had gone to school. When I was in graduate school there, I had been invited by my department to stay for a Ph.D. Norm really wanted to get out of school, to get out in the world; he was tired. So

I agreed to leave. She thought the dreams were a symbol that I was still grieving over not having gone on at that time, but the dreams kept appearing. Finally, one day she said to me, "I think we need to look at these dreams as if they may be calling you to go back to school now." This idea played out, and every time it was near the edge of my mind, I would say, "I'm too old." But that day, for some reason, when I went back to our apartment in Chicago, I sat there and imagined what it would be like if I really did go back to school. This incredible wave of exhilaration washed over me. I was just thrilled. Yes! I knew at that moment it was exactly what I had to do.

Lucy had a client at Pacifica in the depth psychology program, which Lucy recommended to me, but I did go through several catalogues. In the end, this was really the only place I applied to, because it had a perfect combination of depth psychology and mythology. It was just what I wanted. Following my dreams turned out to be the right thing.

I really don't know, at this point, if there is something I want to do with it yet. I came to a point in my photography when I knew it was finished. Whatever I had to do in that particular medium was over. I had to wait a year or two to find out what the next step was, and I waited with patience because I knew at some point it would come to me. It turned out to be going back to school. I feel that something similar will happen when I finish school. Something will present itself, and I will know. I have learned to trust the universe.

I decided just today what I'm going to do for my dissertation. One of the things I've been doing in preparation for my seventieth birthday is to write my life story for my grandchildren. They were so excited when I told them. I've written more concise, more focused pieces already about the pain, the sadness, and the sorrow in my early life. Those were important for me to write, because, for a period, writing served some purpose, like the photography had—my way of working through a lot of depression. I wrote many letters to my mother that I never sent, but it was good. I wrote about some of the experiences in my life.

This quarter, we had to write a paper on Homer's *The Odyssey,* and one of the things that I was struck with was that Odysseus had to tell his own story before he could go back home. I realized that's what I'm do-ing—I'm now telling my own story as preparation for this final stage of my life, my coming home. I was telling my professor, Dennis Slattery, that *The Odyssey* really echoed with me, because of my process of telling my own story. He was very supportive and said, "That would make a great dis-sertation. Tell your story, and develop it around mythological themes." It's already something in me that wants to be expressed, and what a wonderful enrichment it would be to bring in some of these archetypal themes that we've been learning about in class. At the moment, it seems exciting.

One thing about old age is that I really like using the word *old*. I think it's important for us to claim *old* back as an honorable term; we should no longer be embarrassed by it. I have done many cronings for women. In fact, I'm doing a croning for a friend next month. She wanted me to de-lete the word *old* from the letter I sent out to prepare other participants. For instance, "Think about an old woman who has meant a lot in your life." She didn't want me to say that. Or, "Think about what *old* means to you, the fears and the fantasies of being old." She didn't want me to use that word. She wanted me to talk about "unfolding." To me, that's a form of denial. I like being old. It's the best time of my life. I don't want to avoid the term, and I don't want people to avoid it with me. It's OK, it's good; there's nothing wrong with being old and calling it old.

The other important thing about being seventy is that I want to de-fine what seventy is by who I am and the way I live. I don't have to con-form to what somebody else thinks seventy is or what society says seventy is. *We* define the age; the age does not define us.

I'm looking forward to these years. I love being a grandmother. Both my grandmothers died before I was born; I never had that experience of knowing them. So being a grandmother is just an incredibly rich experi-ence for me. Embarking on this exciting part of my journey at this age—what could be bad about it?!

I can't say that I have any specific vision for my later years. I would say that I expect to live into my nineties, so that means I still have quite a few years ahead of me to enjoy the things that I'm learning now. My own mother died at ninety-two, not being very mentally involved. So in that sense, I feel very fortunate that, by doing this challenging work in school, I can keep my mental capacities alive and alert and working. Being with wonderful young people like you and all the rest of the class is also an honor—to be in that mix.

I never healed my relationship with my mother. We did see each other some through the years, but there was never an opportunity to really heal it. In this case, the healing had to take place within me. One of the things I've done about my mother is solitary rituals. I did a good-bye ritual to my mother, right at the time she was dying. Those solitary rituals have been helpful. I had hoped I might do the ritual at her bedside, but I couldn't do it there, so I did it by myself, and that was all right. Those kinds of ceremonies have been helpful to me.

I was telling a Buddhist friend of mine about this interview with you. She said, "Your last twenty years are just like the three stages of life. Your photography was equivalent to your maiden years—playing and doing creative work with enthusiasm and interest. A kind of out-in-the-world stage, both taking and showing your photographs. Then your ritual work I see as the mother phase—very containing, very nurturing, very *womblike.*" (I often think of using that word when we create a sacred space in the circle; it is very much like that.) "Now you're in the crone phase, out there studying material that is deepening and enriching all that has gone before." It is a very apt description. That's why I said that the years between fifty and seventy have truly been a whole new life for me.

I'd like to tell you more about my relationship with my husband. He is and always has been very supportive of me. We've always had a good marriage. He was extremely helpful with the children—an excellent father.

What happened during that middle chunk of our marriage was mostly due to my own withdrawal from the outer world, the intellectual world. Our marriage became much more split. I carried all the emotions, all the family stuff; he carried all of the Apollonian, rational part. My vision of marriage used to be that that's the way it was—each partner carried half of the relationship, and together you made one whole. I used to say, "It's a good marriage, because it's complementary; we each have our strengths. I was very aesthetically oriented and created a beautiful home.

But as I came into my sixties, that really changed. I no longer was satisfied with only carrying half of it. I wanted it all for me, within me. Norm had also been very protective, which I came to resent, because it felt as if I were no longer adequate to really take care of all those things for myself.

So I started a process of getting in touch with my authentic self. If anything, I would say my goal in my analysis has been that search for authenticity, to reclaim that whole part of my life that I had left behind. It included more independence and freedom to do things for myself, by myself. It included much more solitude than I'd ever had, because we had this idea that we had to do everything together. So that changed.

I also started demanding, taking back, what I felt I had given up. We went through a very, very difficult time about six or seven years ago, early in my analysis. I truly turned our lives upside down and all the patterns that we had lived by. I said, "I will not live like this anymore." Though we had been married a very long time, I came to the point where I was willing to risk the relationship in order to develop myself more fully. We went through some hard, dangerous times. Times when we almost separated.

But I remember clearly one year, when we had a family Thanksgiving ritual, I announced to the family that I knew I would stay with Norm, that I wasn't going to leave. I had gotten past the fear that he wouldn't be able to hear my needs, because he finally could understand that not only were these changes liberating for me—they were also liberating for him.

So we found a new way of relating, and we have evolved to a much deeper understanding of ourselves and each other. I think our marriage is better and stronger than it's ever been, but it's had many rocky times. We will have a fiftieth wedding anniversary ritual with our family, and we have been talking a lot about letting the children and grandchildren know that marriage is not just one smooth, happy trail, that you have to continue to work and change, continue to respect the other person's need for growth. In that, we've been fortunate, because we both started out very young, very undeveloped. The fact that we've been able to change and develop and respect the changes in each other over the years is, of course, what has kept us together.

Norm, since his retirement, has written two books. He has always been interested in the philosophy of physics, and when he sold his business about fifteen years ago, he just wanted to study. He read in depth, and it led to a book called *Bridging Science and Spirit,* which had to do with the physics of David Bohm and the Perennial philosophy and how these are related. Norm's second book is *The Hidden Domain,* which is, he feels, the equivalent in physics of Jung's concept of the collective unconscious. In other words, everything that is matter is manifested from a realm that he calls the "hidden domain" or what David Bohm calls the "implicate order." It's fascinating stuff! He's working on a third book now.

Norm is very rational and very interested in science, but he has evolved a tremendous interest and respect for the spiritual side of life. We belong to a group that meets at the Salk Institute two or three times a year to talk about consciousness. The group at the Salk is divided between scientists and some of us who are not scientists but are very interested in it. It's fascinating to watch that macrocosm which is a microcosm in our marriage. We've had to learn how to listen to each other. Norm speaks a language that's strange to me. When I speak, I feel I speak in terms of wholeness—soul language. Sometimes I've felt he doesn't understand that you don't use analytical tools with that kind of material. It's not to be treated that way. One does not appreciate the beauty of a flower by ripping off its petals! So this is something we're learning more and more about each other.

The same polarity also exists in this group. At the most recent get-together, a woman had had a most incredible experience in India, a magical experience. I was very afraid that Norm would question her rationally about it, which I felt would have destroyed the true awesomeness of what she had experienced. So we had a lot of conversations around that and had a hard time that weekend, because it was painful for us to look at these differences. But it also helped clarify for us the two modes of thinking—how we handle them, how to learn to listen to and respect each other. I think we will be able to bring back to the group a deeper understanding of that. It was very interesting to me to see that dynamic. It extends to society at large. It applies on many levels and within me. I have my own analytical, skeptical, "Oh, are you kidding?" sort of voice in me, as well. That was an important lesson, and something we'll continue to work on in our marriage—respecting those two different ways of looking at life.

To be a crone is an honor. One of the most fulfilling, satisfying evenings of my life was my croning when I was sixty-five. That's around the age I would call cronehood. As our life expectancy extends, it just gets pushed back further. Fifty-six is the youngest age traditionally for croning. I have done cronings for women at fifty-six, but I think it's a bit young for to-day's women. They're not quite there yet. I think sixty-five, seventy, might be even more appropriate. Fifty to sixty-five or seventy is just an entirely different range and lifestyle.

We are building up to the crone years, which are about coming into maturity and this whole business of being willing to look at the possibility of death and the end of your life span. I think cronehood is a deeper acceptance of death. Knowing that it's part of life, just the way it is, and it's all right. There's also the feeling that, "Yes, I've done all these wonderful things." I feel that if I were to die tomorrow, I've lived a very full life, and I would not regret it. That would be fine. That's part of the richness that comes with old age—that sense of serenity and acceptance about life and what it brings you.

∽

In a poem she wrote titled "I Know," Leah condensed her forty years into ten lyrical stanzas.

I Know

I know life on a farm in the South—
Walking barefoot through freshly turned earth, riding a
    mule-drawn wagon,

drawing water from a well, picking cotton, barning tobacco,
    killing hogs,
eating hot biscuits cooked in a wood-burning stove.
I know being born in a house built by my grandfather.

I know the sorrow of separation—
having my three-year-old deaf baby brother snatched away,
taken a thousand miles from home, left among strangers,
screaming in anger, frustration, and terror.
I know seeing his soul slashed, seared, and forever scarred.

I know the turmoil and confusion of adolescence—
incipient anorexia and burgeoning sexuality accompanied by
    guilt, fear, and shame;
being the apple of my Father's eye, but
appearing to my Mother as an evil and threatening Eve.
I know yearning, and isolation, and not-belonging.

I know being eighteen years old—
falling in love with a young man in every way the *stranger:*
Jewish, atheist, radical, intellectual;
being imprisoned in my own home, and running away.
I know taking a train across the country to an uncertain and
    unknowable future.

I know the hunger for knowledge and the energy of determined
    feminism—
working as a maid to support myself as I continued my studies,
refusing to be the graciously submissive wife,
insisting on equal partnership.
I know receiving my Bachelor's and Master's degrees alongside
    my husband.

I know motherhood and homemaking—
giving birth to two daughters, holding them and suckling them,

sewing frilly dresses with long sashes, making wedding dresses,
frying chicken and mashing potatoes, and baking banana bread.
I know trying to be a different kind of mother.

I know the deep dark pit of depression—
desiring only death, detecting no hope, seeing no light,
feeling utterly worthless;
also crawling out of the pit into the freshness of life, grasping
    joy and hope.
I know the welcome wellspring of worthiness.

I know being fifty years old—
beginning a newly liberated life, surprised to find an artist within;
smelling darkroom chemistry, the dizziness of watching
    powerful images
reveal themselves in the developing tray.
I know seeing the reflections of my soul hang on gallery walls.

I know being married to one man for fifty years—
learning about love and loyalty and compassion and friendship,
experiencing passionate lovemaking, and stormy arguments;
having happy times, and sad times, and times when I thought
    we would never make it.
I know the quiet pleasure that comes with shared memories.

I know being old, being a Crone—
entering my eighth decade on this earth, a time of satisfying
    reflection,
of heartfelt gratitude, of beginning yet another life as student,
of developing wisdom and humility and examining the great
    mysteries.
I know walking the many turns that make up the labyrinth of my life.

LEAH FRIEDMAN ❧

The Author

Cathleen Rountree is a writer, visual artist and photographer, cultural mythologist, lecturer, and educator. She is the author of six books, including the highly acclaimed decade series on women and aging: *On Women Turning 40: Coming into Our Fullness*; *On Women Turning 50: Celebrating Midlife Discoveries*, and *On Women Turning 60: Embracing the Age of Fulfillment*. She is currently writing a book about the confluence and interrelationship between film and psychology. She lives in northern California and teaches at the University of California, Santa Cruz.

DATE DUE